D1351564

EXCELLENCE IN ACTION

A PORTRAIT OF THE GUARDS

EXCELLENCE IN ACTION

A PORTRAIT OF THE GUARDS

With a Preface by
Her Majesty The Queen

General Editor
Rupert Uloth

THIRD MILLENNIUM
PUBLISHING, LONDON

EXCELLENCE IN ACTION: A PORTRAIT OF THE GUARDS

Copyright © 2008
Third Millennium Publishing Limited

First published in 2008 by
Third Millennium Publishing Limited,
a subsidiary of Third Millennium Information Limited

2–5 Benjamin Street
London
United Kingdom
EC1M 5QL
www.tmiltd.com

ISBN: 978 1 903942 68 0

British Library Cataloguing in Publication Data

A CIP catalogue record for this book is available
from the British Library.

All rights reserved

No part of this publication may be reproduced or
transmitted in any form or by any means, electronic
or mechanical, including photocopying, recording
or any information storage or retrieval system,
without permission in writing from the publisher

Designed by Matthew Wilson and Susan Pugsley
Production by Bonnie Murray
Printed by Butler and Tanner Ltd, Frome, England

CONTENTS

For many, the Household Division is immediately associated with the precision and colour of State Ceremonial, performing an important role which draws from and reflects upon the distinctive characteristics of this country. While that role is of itself important, it derives from a military tradition which, as vividly portrayed in this book, has seen the regiments of the Household Division take part in almost every operation undertaken by the Army throughout its history. Indeed, this volume is published following a year during which each regiment of the Household Division has deployed on active service abroad.

'Excellence in Action' is the standard applied by the Household Division whether to operations, training or ceremonial duties. As Colonel-in-Chief of the seven regiments of the Household Division, I am therefore pleased to acknowledge this tribute to its former and current soldiers and, especially, to those who have perished or been wounded in the service of our nation.

Elizabeth R

INTRODUCTION

Major General W.G. Cubitt CBE
Major General commanding the Household Division

It is very likely that readers of this book will have seen, for real or in pictures, the legendary soldiers of the Household Division who guard Horse Guards, Buckingham Palace, St James's Palace, Windsor Castle and Her Majesty's Tower of London, as well as taking part in most State ceremonies. They are recognised around the world and stamp a hallmark of excellence on the nation, and particularly its Armed Forces.

However, the Guards are not just for ceremonies. The two regiments of Household Cavalry and the five regiments of Foot Guards combine their privileged position as the Sovereign's personal troops with a fully combatant role as armoured reconnaissance troops and infantry soldiers. They have a long tradition of excellence in action going back to the 17th Century, having taken part in all the major campaigns of the British Army, started the Special Air Service, provided one of the first battalions of the Parachute Regiment and a squadron of the Long Range Desert Group, provided entire divisions in both World Wars, fought in Aden, Borneo and the Falkland Islands, countered terrorism in Northern Ireland over 38 years, helped to establish peace in Bosnia and maintain it in the Former Yugoslav Republic of Macedonia, led the way into central Kosovo, and fought in Iraq, Afghanistan and elsewhere. This continues today: all the six regiments have been on active service in Iraq, Afghanistan, Bosnia or Kosovo during 2007.

The Guards have always been famed, on active service overseas and at home, for selfless adherence to the highest professional standards, smartness, precision, gallantry and loyalty, even under the most dangerous and trying of circumstances. Even today, Guards regiments maintain a certain formality in their way of doing things that has been lost elsewhere. There is also glamour and an elite status that attaches to this unique organisation which combines fully operational military capability with Royal Duties. These characteristics are as important today as yesterday in giving Guardsmen a fierce pride in a reputation that must not be tarnished and in demonstrating to the world the loyalty of the British Army to the Crown.

Not everyone who would like to is able to achieve or maintain the standards of the Guards. However those who can are fortunate indeed to belong to a close-knit organisation, based on seven individual regiments with a common bond as Guardsmen – *Septem Juncta in Uno* – from initial training through to their final resting place, through service in the active regiments to membership of the network of Guards associations around the country and overseas – 'Once a Guardsman, always a Guardsman'. All are conscious of the unique privilege it is to be part of something recognised as truly first class the world over.

A recent development is the association of The London Regiment of the Territorial Army with the Guards. This new relationship has been cemented immediately with the deployment of a company of the Londons, comprising Territorial Army soldiers and regular Guardsmen, with the Grenadier Guards in combat in Afghanistan in 2007.

I hope that readers who have not served in the Household Division will find this book interesting in that it gives a glimpse into a unique part of the British Army as well as telling a representative story of the Army's activities and highlighting its core values – selfless commitment, courage, discipline, integrity, loyalty and respect for others – through the prism of one of its oldest, most famous, smartest, and most active, components.

I hope also that serving or former Household Cavalrymen and Guardsmen will recognise in this book some of their own service and the ethos of which they are justly proud and which makes being a Guardsman, of whatever variety, more than a mere label.

Active service comes at a price and the Household Division has suffered its share of losses throughout its history. This book is dedicated to those Household Cavalrymen and Guardsmen who have died in the service of their country, to those who have been bereaved by such losses, and to those who have been wounded physically or mentally.

Excellence in Action is a superb encapsulation of everything the Guards stand for.

EDITOR'S NOTE

Rupert Uloth, General Editor

This book is a snapshot of the Household Division as it is now. The Guards are a modern, highly motivated, well-ordered group of men who undertake enormous challenges in testing conditions. Traditions evolved through their various histories play a large part in forming their character and one of the most outstanding qualities is the ability to adapt to present day conditions, as these pages demonstrate.

In the last few years each of the regiments has been involved in an intensity and tempo of operations not seen since the Second World War, which is why the time seems right to reflect their extraordinary commitment and achievements.

It has been my privilege to meet so many members of this amazing organisation in preparation for this book. It has given me a unique insight into how the different regiments work, their very different characters and how their unifying ethos shines through.

Whether I was having lunch with the Coldstream Guards officers in their Windsor Barracks; talking to Troopers of the Household Cavalry in the dusty environs of Iraq's main port at Umm Qasar; discussing discipline with the Regimental Sergeant Major of the Irish Guards at Basra Airport; waving off members of the Welsh Guards as they set off across Europe on their bicycles from their base in Bosnia or talking to Grenadiers who had just returned from Afghanistan, I was always aware of the strong links that bind these different regiments together.

The sense of history is powerful. Every soldier and officer knows that he has much to live up to. Paintings, silver, photographs and uniforms are all reminders of great events in their past such as Waterloo, the Crimea, and the Seven Years War. The blue, red, blue flash worn on combat clothing indicates membership of a club where the best is expected. They are proud to be part of the Household Division and their regular ceremonial commitments constantly remind them of their close connection with the Sovereign.

Unmistakably British, unfailingly professional and unbelievably effective, they have done much to make us proud.

I would like to thank Julian Platt, chairman of Third Millennium for commissioning me to produce this book and all his staff including Christopher Fagg, Matthew Wilson and Neil Burkey for their good humoured professionalism throughout. Sebastian Roberts, who was the Major General Commanding the Household Division at the time, made the project happen and his enthusiastic support was amply maintained by his successor, Bill Cubitt. The project would have floundered at the first ditch without the representatives of each regiment who gave many hours of invaluable time to ensure accuracy and sense. In particular Grant Baker, Hugh Boscawen, Tom Bonas, Robin Bullock-Webster, Henry Hanning, Julian Lawrie and Paddy Tabor. The chairman of the editorial committee, Oliver Lindsay, has been especially lavish in his support, encouragement and enthusiasm and displayed a Guardsman-like grip and determination when it was needed.

As well as the many contributors who produced articles and anecdotes mention should also be made of the Brigade Major, Colonel Toby Gray, who opened many doors and of the Staff Captain, Alex James, who never complained about strange requests. Photographer Julian Andrews was a genial travelling companion as well as a first rate practitioner of his art. I thank my wife, Louisa, and family for sharing and tolerating the highs and lows of putting a book together and I am very grateful to my editor at Country Life magazine, Mark Hedges, and other colleagues for their understanding and support.

But most of all I would like to thank all the officers and men of the Household Division who have demonstrated at every turn why this is such a worthwhile publication. I have enjoyed meeting old friends and making new ones of all ranks during my researches. This book is dedicated to the memory of all their comrades who have given their lives in the service of their regiments and country and to all those who still live with the consequences of injuries suffered on operations.

FROM RESTORATION TO
THE 21ST CENTURY

THE GUARDS: 1642–2008

This Timeline is a selective, not an exhaustive survey of seven regiments over 365 years. Battle Honours borne on the Colours, Standards and Drums are in bold type as are regiments' names when in a noteworthy context.

1642–51
The English Civil Wars (also fought in Scotland and Ireland)

The **Scots Guards** originated from a 1,500-strong regiment raised by the Marquess of Argyll to act as King Charles I's bodyguard while he campaigned in Ireland, although in the event he never went to that country.

1656
While the future King Charles II was in exile in Bruges in Flanders, a new regiment, the Royal Regiment of Guards, the forerunners of the **Grenadier Guards**, was formed under Lord Wentworth.

1660
Restoration of the Monarchy. Charles II greeted by General George Monck at Dover (May). Parliament passes Act disbanding the Cromwellian New Model Army.

1661
Creation of the standing British Army. Charles II signed a Royal Warrant for what has become known as 'the birth certificate of the British Army' on 26 January. Monck's Regiment (1,440 strong) enters royal service as the Lord General's Regiment of Foot Guards soon known as the **Coldstream Guards (14 February)**. **Scots Guards** reformed as a regiment of six companies (1662).

1650
Monck's Regiment of Foot formed by Oliver Cromwell, later becoming the **Coldstream Guards** after the town on the Scottish border from which Monck and his troops began the 1660 march to London which led to the Restoration.

1659
Eighty loyal gentlemen led by Lord Gerrard of Brandon formed themselves into the King's Life Guard at the court of the exiled King Charles II in Bruges.

1660
The **Life Guards** founded between March 1660 and April 1661 as four Troops of Horse Guards each of about 160 men. The Troops' soldiers were all 'private gentlemen', some of whom had served in General Monck's Life Guard, and officers were the courtiers who had provided Charles II with a mounted bodyguard during his exile.

The **Royal Horse Guards** trace their origins to the New Model Army in 1650 but, at the Restoration in 1660, were re-officered with royalists under the Earl of Oxford, and renamed the Royal Regiment of Horse, later the Royal Horse Guards – (the 500 cavalrymen popularly known as **The Blues** from the colour of uniform they had worn under the Commonwealth and continued to wear from 1661). Charles II commissioned Colonel John Russell to raise His Majesty's Foot Regiment of Guards (1,200 men) on 23 November. The new unit was amalgamated with Wentworth's in 1665 as the First Regiment of Foot Guards. Irish Regiment of Foot Guards raised in Dublin follow James II into exile in France 1691.

1661–2
The **Royal Dragoons** (1st Dragoons), initially known as the Tangier Horse, raised 100-strong by King Charles II to form part of the garrison at Tangier in Morocco, which had been acquired on his marriage to Catherine of Braganza as part of her dowry. They became known as **The Royals. Tangier** (1662–80) later became the first British Army Battle Honour, for **The Royals**, **First Guards** and the **Coldstream**.

Above: Lieutenant and Lieutenant Colonel Randolph Egerton MP, the King's Troop of Horse Guards, by Jan Wyck, c.1672.

Above: King Charles II being led into London by The Life Guards prior to his coronation on 22 April 1661.

1664 Detachment of **Coldstream Guards** on sea service at capture of New Amsterdam (New York) from the Dutch.

Detachment of Foot Guards sent to restore order in the colony of Virginia.

1676–8 Three Troops of Horse **Grenadier Guards** (213 enlisted soldiers serving as mounted infantry) join **The Life Guards** and **The Blues. First, Coldstream and Scots Guards** form four foot grenadier companies each, that is soldiers trained to throw grenades.

1686 Scottish Regiment of Foot Guards (13 companies since 1666) brought on to the establishment of the English Army from that of Scotland.

1690 Battle of the Boyne. King William took a force that included **The Life Guards, The Blues** and **The Royals** (first two from Flanders) to Ireland to oppose the Jacobite Rebellion there. On 1 July he decisively defeated James II.

1695

1666 Soldiers from the King's Life Guard and the Foot Guards earn considerable praise for their assistance in fighting the Great Fire of London and in keeping order.

1685 Battle of Sedgemoor. **The Life Guards, The Blues, The Royals** and all the Foot Guards regiments were involved in suppressing the West Country rebellion by the Duke of Monmouth.

1689–97 The Nine Years War. King William III sent a force to Flanders under the command of the Earl of Marlborough. First occasion on which all five existing Guards regiments were on active service together against the French.

1695 Siege of **Namur**, Low Countries. The **Foot Guards** provided the assault troops and also gained their second battle honour (not awarded until 1910). Preceded by their grenadier companies, the two Guards brigades advanced across open country against the concentrated fire of the French defenders. On reaching the palisades they thrust their flintlocks through, fired one volley, and then stormed the defences. A Marshal of France was captured. The Guards brigades were commanded by Lord Cutts and afterwards he was appointed a 'Brigadier of the Guards', the first time this honour had been conferred.

Left: King William III and his army at the Siege of Namur, 1695, by Jan Wyck, c.1700. The King and his officers to the right, with columns of British and Dutch troops advancing on the town during the Nine Years War.

Excellence in Action

Right: Brigadier and Lieutenant Richard Gifford, 4th Troop of Horse Guards, c.1727.

Above: Lieutenant-General John Manners, Marquis of Granby, c.1763, by Sir Joshua Reynolds. The Marquis of Granby is shown here in his uniform as Master-General of the Ordnance, leaning on a 13-inch land service mortar.

1704
War of the Spanish Succession 1702–13. Victory at **Blenheim** (1702). The **First Guards** were the only Household troops to gain this Battle Honour. The same applies to **Ramillies** (1704) but the **Coldstream Guards** joined them in 1708 to form a Guards Brigade for Marlborough's two other great victories over the French at **Oudenarde** (1708) and **Malplaquet** (1709).

1707
Act of Union. Scottish elements of the Household troops were brought south.

1739
War of Jenkins' Ear (with Spain). 120 corporals and privates of Foot Guards made sergeants in six new Marine regiments.

1750
Horse Guards building re-designed by William Kent. It was occupied by the Guards and the Secretary at War and his staff.

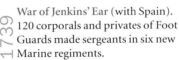

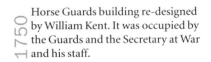

1702

1702–13
Defeat in Spain. A composite Guards Battalion (200 **First Guards** and 400 **Coldstream Guards**) was sent to reinforce **Gibraltar** after it was captured in 1704. The battalion helped repel several attacks. However, in 1707 it was part of the entire British force compelled to surrender at the Battle of Almanza. The disaster was repeated in 1710 when another British force at Brihuega was besieged and finally surrendered with The Royal Dragoons and 1st Battalion the Scottish Regiment of Foot Guards among its number.

1712
In February the 2nd Battalion of the Scottish Regiment of Foot Guards was ordered from Edinburgh to London. The Regiment did not do duty in its native land again until 1911. It was officially given the title of Third Regiment of Foot Guards.

1742–8
War of the Austrian Succession. When Britain sent an expeditionary force to the Continent in 1742 it included a **Household Cavalry** Brigade, created for the first time, with **The Life Guards**, **The Blues**, and **The Royals**, but also a Guards Brigade (1st Battalions of all three Regiments of Foot Guards). The Battle of **Dettingen** (27 June 1743) was the last occasion on which a King of England, King George II, personally led his army into action. The **Household Cavalry Brigade** (Earl of Crawford) made several charges against the French Foot Guards and finally drove the enemy back against the river. During one charge by **The Life Guards**, Lord Crawford's trumpeter urged his comrades on with the notes of *Britons Strike Home*. Life Guards trumpeters still play a fanfare version today. The King was in the thick of the fighting and escorted by the Gold Stick and 36 men from **The Life Guards**. Two years later the **Foot Guards Brigade** won glory but not victory against their French equivalents at Fontenoy in Flanders.

1756–63
The Seven Years War. **The Blues** formed part of a Cavalry Brigade under Major General the Marquis of Granby, who had just become their Colonel. They were the only Guards present at the Battle of Minden on 1 August 1759, when six British line infantry battalions attacked and drove back 40 French battalions, supported by 60 squadrons of cavalry. **The Blues** and **The Royals** distinguished themselves at the Battle of **Warburg** on 31 July 1760. Granby lost his hat and wig during one charge and, because he was hatless and wigless when he later saluted Prince Ferdinand, **The Blues** have retained the custom of saluting their officers, even when bare headed, a custom unique in the Army today. Foot Guards battalions under Major Julius Caesar later campaigned in Germany in 1761–3.

The American War of Independence.

The force that set sail for America in 1776 included a composite **Guards Brigade** of 1,100 drawn from all three regiments. Almost immediately they helped capture New York. The Guards Brigade fought throughout the campaign, and was involved in most of the engagements of 1776–7, followed by two years of garrison duty in New York, before it was sent south to join Lieutenant General Lord Cornwallis in the Carolinas. At the Battle of Guildford Court House (15 March 1781) his tiny army, including 482 Guards, beat twice their number of Americans, but their 600-mile march ended in surrender at Yorktown, the last major battle of the War.

1776–83

The Four Horse Guards Troops and the Horse Grenadiers reformed as the 1st Life Guards and 2nd Life Guards, each of 320 men.

1788

French Revolutionary and Napoleonic Wars 1793–1815

In 1793 the **Foot Guards** formed six 'light [infantry] companies' from the 2nd Battalion in each Regiment. They wore a form of shako with a green plume, and became the Left Flank companies, while the grenadier company continued to hold the right flank. The Foot Guards were hurriedly formed into a **Guards Brigade** (1st Battalion of each regiment, with a fourth, or Flank Battalion formed from the grenadier and later the light companies). These 2,500 men sailed for Holland in February 1793 and

1793–1800

were the first British troops to engage the armies of Revolutionary France on the Continent. At **Lincelles** (18 August) near Lille these first three battalions totalling 1,100 under Major General Gerard Lake (First Guards) stormed a hilltop village incurring 181 casualties, taking it from 5,000 French who lost 670 men and their 12 guns. **The Blues and The Royals** excelled in cavalry charges at **Beaumont** and **Willems** the following spring but the allied Flanders campaign ended in winter retreat and failure (May 1795) as did a brief First Guards return to Holland in late 1799.

1800

1780 The Gordon Riots. After agitation against a pro-Catholic Bill caused riots in London by a crowd of up to 50,000 people, a Guards Brigade of 4 battalions camped in St James's Park. Guards were mounted on key points, while detachments patrolled the streets. The Life Guards guarded Parliament throughout and had to charge the crowd in Parliament Square. The week-long June riots were eventually put down once troops were given permission to open fire, and 285 rioters were killed. From then on the Foot Guards were called upon to provide a nightly picquet to guard the Bank of England, a duty which continued until 1973.

1793 Present officers' mess built at St James's Palace for the officers of the Household troops on guard duty there and at Horse Guards. Hyde Park Barracks built for whichever regiment of **The Life Guards** was responsible for carrying out policing duties in London.

Right: 'The return of the Grenadier to his wife and family', c.1798, depicting a Coldstream Guardsman of the grenadier company.

Above: The Battle of Alexandria, 21 March 1801. Oil on canvas after Philippe Jacques de Loutherbourg.

Above: Lieutenant General Sir John Moore, KB dressed in Lieutenant General's coatee.

The Egypt Campaign. Bonaparte had conquered Egypt in 1798 and from June 1800 Lieutenant General Sir Ralph Abercromby assembled 16,000 troops to expel the French. One of his five brigades was formed by the Guards under command of the one-armed Major General Lord Ludlow (1st Battalion **Coldstream Guards** and 3rd Battalion **Scots Guards**). On 8 March 1801 they made a textbook and much rehearsed assault landing at Aboukir Bay in their boats under fire. The Guards repelled a French cavalry charge in the surf. On 21 March the army defeated a fierce French night attack at the Battle of Alexandria, Third Guards taking 186 casualties. After a siege, Alexandria fell on 2 September, with the surrender of 10,500 French veterans. In December Ludlow's Guards Brigade sailed for home after a triumphant campaign.

1801

2nd Guards Brigade took part in a daring and highly successful expedition. **Copenhagen** was captured and the Danish fleet removed just ahead of Napoleon, who had had a similar idea.

1807

1801

1804

New cavalry barracks for 496 soldiers were completed at Windsor and occupied by **The Blues** who were much favoured by King George III. He spent most of his time at Windsor Castle, and had his own Troop, frequently turning up for parades wearing the uniform of a Captain in the Regiment. He formed the Regiment's first Band, and personally presented them with a pair of solid silver kettle-drums still used today.

1808–14

The Peninsular War. As Lieutenant General Sir John Moore watched the 15,000 survivors of his ragged and dispirited army plod down the slope towards **Corunna** on 11 January 1809 he made comments since revered by the Guards (recorded by the Army historian Sir John Fortescue):
'A brigade caught the General's eye at a distance, for they were marching like soldiers. "Those must be the Guards," he said, and presently the two battalions of the **First Guards**, each of them still 800 strong, strode by in column of sections, with drums beating, the drum major twirling his staff at their head and the men keeping step as if in their own barrack yard …The senior regiment of the British infantry had set an example to the whole army.'

The Battle of Talavera, 28 July 1809. The 2nd Guards Brigade, as part of 1st Division, was in the British centre, and after a severe artillery bombardment, they were attacked by at least 15,000 French infantry.

The British held their fire until the enemy were only 50 yards away, and then halted them with a volley. Before the French could recover, the whole division charged, and drove them back. The two Guards battalions each lost some 300 men of about 1,000. It became a Battle Honour for both the **Coldstream** and the **Third Guards**, and a special medal was struck for issue to 'meritorious officers'.

At **Barrosa**, 5 March 1811, outside Cadiz the 2nd Battalions of each Foot Guards Regiment, after 15 hours' marching, attacked uphill against fresh infantry and cavalry twice their number and drove them from a strong position. It was costly with the Guards losing one man in three in a battle that only lasted for an hour and a half. The sortie commander Lieutenant General Sir Thomas Graham later received a letter from the NCOs and private soldiers thanking him for 'the noble manner in which you prepared us…which made us forget the fatigues of 18 hours under arms

when the word was given for battle'. Barrosa was a worthy Battle Honour for which a gold medal was awarded.

By 1812 five Foot Guards Battalions were serving in the Peninsula and Wellington formed them into two Guards Brigades. A Household Brigade of Cavalry, consisting of both **The Life Guards** and **The Blues**, joined them, commanded by Colonel Sir Robert Hill of **The Blues**. The brigade came under the cavalry commander in Spain, Lieutenant General Sir Stapleton Cotton, later Lord Combermere, the name eventually given to the **Household Cavalry** Barracks at Windsor. It was the first time that Wellington found the **Household Cavalry** under his command, although **The Royals** had already charged to effect for him at **Fuentes D'Onor** (5 May 1811).

Above: The Sortie from Bayonne. Coloured aquatint by T. Sutherland after W. Heath, 1815.

1809

1st Guards Brigade (2,860 strong) was part of a big expedition to try and capture Antwerp but the attack stalled as 'Walcheren' miasmic swamp fever decimated the force and, from September, the expedition was evacuated home

1815

Waterloo Campaign. Wellington's army contained a **Household Cavalry** Brigade (Major General Lord Edward Somerset), part of the allied cavalry under Lieutenant General Lord Uxbridge, which consisted of **1st Life Guards**, **2nd Life Guards**, **Royal Horse Guards** (**The Blues**) and 1st King's Dragoon Guards. **The Royals** were also present, in the Union Brigade. The **Foot Guards** provided 1st and 2nd Guards Brigades as the 4,000-strong 1st Division commanded by Major General Sir George Cooke (First Guards), the first such all-Guards infantry division. The action is covered later in the book

1820

The **Blues** were elevated to the status of **Household Cavalry** by King George IV.

Cato Street Conspiracy. A platoon from 2nd Battalion **Coldstream Guards** captured nine out of the ten conspirators planning to assassinate the Cabinet at dinner in 44 Grosvenor Square. The ten conspirators were then taken to the Tower of London by **The Life Guards**, the last occasion on which the **Household Cavalry** were to carry out this duty.

1828

After the French army was defeated at Vittoria, it retreated across the mountains into France. Wellington could not pursue until he had captured the coastal fortress of San Sebastian, which stood in his way. The siege was successful but took from July to September 1813 and resulted in heavy casualties, particularly in the Guards Battalions, whose volunteer assault party of 200 suffered no fewer than 160 casualties. San Sebastian finally stormed, Wellington thrust into France and both **1st** and **2nd Guards Brigades** joined in a series of bold river-crossing operations, over the Bidassoa, the Nivelle, the **Nive**, and the Adour; 2nd Guards Brigade distinguished itself on this last complex pontoon-bridge operation when six companies of Third Guards and two of **Coldstream Guards** crossed the river before dark, and held a precarious bridgehead all night, supported by Congreve rocket fire.

1813–4

Antwerp. A composite 3rd Guards Brigade from all three Regiments joined another attempted expedition against Antwerp. Again disaster struck due to an unsuccessful night storming attempt (8/9 March) on the fortress of Bergen-op-Zoom, which ended in the death or capture of two thirds of the 1,000 Guardsmen involved.

Napoleon abdicated for the first time (5 April).

The French commander of Bayonne refused to believe news of Napoleon's abdication and made a last, desperate sortie against the British, with 6,000 men at 3 am on 14 April. He was met mainly by 1st and 2nd Guards Brigades and after five hours fierce, confused fighting in the dark, the French were repulsed. The last action of the war had been fought, each side losing over 800 men. The Guards suffered 508 casualties. Afterwards, they set up their own military cemetery at Bayonne, which still exists today.

1816–54

The Long Peace. For the Foot Guards this continued until the Crimea and for the **Household Cavalry** it lasted 67 years.

1826–8

1st Battalions **Grenadier** and **Scots Guards** served in a 5,000-strong expedition to Portugal to deter a feared Spanish invasion and support constitutional rule. King William IV renamed Third Guards the Scots Fusilier Guards.

Left: Waterloo Medal 1815 awarded to Thomas Bird, 1st (or Royal) Dragoons.

Above: The Battle of Inkerman, 5 November 1854.

Crimean War. Queen Victoria forbade her **Household Cavalry** to leave the country but a Guards Brigade set sail in March 1854. Battle of the **Alma** (20 September 1854). The Colour Party of the **Scots Fusilier Guards** was almost surrounded but stood firm until the battalion could rally round it. Afterwards the Queen's Colour was found to have 12 bullet holes.

The Royals took part in the successful Heavy Cavalry Brigade charge at **Balaclava**.

At the Battle of **Inkerman** the Russians heavily attacked positions held by 1st Guards Brigade. The succession of attacks was repulsed but the Guards lost 600 All Ranks out of 1,300. It was the last time any Regimental and Queen's Colours of the Guards were taken into battle.

1834 Wellington Barracks completed. Home Secretary commended the Guards for fire-fighting efforts at the Houses of Parliament.

1854–6 At the Battle of **Inkerman** the Russians heavily attacked positions held by 1st Guards Brigade. The succession of attacks was repulsed but the Guards lost 600 All Ranks out of 1,300. It was the last time any Regimental and Queen's Colours of the Guards were taken into battle.

1862–5 1st Battalion **Grenadier Guards** and 2nd Battalion **Scots Fusilier Guards** sent to Canada to protect the frontier during the American Civil War. They saw no fighting.

1865–70 New barracks were completed at Chelsea (sold in 2007) and at Shorncliffe in Kent. Both the Cavalry and Infantry barracks at Windsor were rebuilt, and the Foot Guards quarters at St John's Wood, Portman Street, and in Dublin were given up.

1834

1838–42 2nd Battalions **Grenadier** and **Coldstream Guards** served in Canada helping quell a French-speaking revolt.

1856 Appointment authorized of a Major General commanding the Brigade of Guards (all Regiments of Foot Guards). He set up his headquarters in the Horse Guards building.

The Household Brigade Cricket Club was given permission to adopt the Royal racing colours of blue, red, blue for its tie. It is now the 'Brigade' tie, worn by all ranks, and the colours have been adopted as those of the **Household Division**.

1862 An official Guards journal, today called *The Guards Magazine*, was started.

1870 The Major General became responsible for the Home District (now London District), as well as commanding the Brigade of Guards.

Above: A group of survivors of the cavalry charge at Balaclava on 25 October 1854, taken on the 33rd Anniversary Dinner in 1887.

1877 Training organisation expanded by moving the Guards Depot from Warley in Essex to Caterham in Surrey where it was to remain until 1960.

1882 Egyptian War. Queen Victoria was persuaded to permit a composite **Household Cavalry** regiment made up of three squadrons, one from each regiment (1st and 2nd Life Guards and Royal Horse Guards) to deploy to Egypt. Its 470 men made the famous moonlight charge at Kassassin. The **Guards Brigade** was commanded by the Duke of Connaught, son of Queen Victoria. Their first action was the Battle of **Tel-el-Kebir** where the rebel Egyptian Army was routed.

1882 The Guards took on a site at Pirbright near Woking in Surrey as a training and musketry area.

1884–5 First Sudan War (attempted Relief of Khartoum). All three regiments of **Household Cavalry** and **The Royals** contributed 150 soldiers to the Heavy Camel Regiment (Colonel the Honourable Reginald Talbot, 1st Life Guards). The Foot Guards served in the 400-strong Guards and Royal Marines Camel Regiment (Colonel the Honourable Evelyn Boscawen, **Coldstream Guards**). The Camel Regiments had all now abandoned scarlet and blue for a khaki uniform, although Queen Victoria was unenthusiastic about her troops wearing 'a sort of *café-au-lait* shade'. On 28 January 1885 the desert expedition came within sight of Khartoum, only to learn that it had fallen two days before and General Gordon was dead.

1898 The Battle of Omdurman. Kitchener defeated Mahdi outside Khartoum. 1st Battalion Grenadier Guards take part.

1899

1880 Hyde Park Barracks were rebuilt and the first occupants were **The Blues**, who gave an Opening Ball, attended by the Prince and Princess of Wales, which cost every officer £70.

1885 Suakin. Another Guards Brigade defeated a Mahdist army near the Red Sea. A New South Wales battalion was attached to the Brigade, the first time that Australian troops had fought as part of the British Army outside their own country.

1899–1902 Second Boer or South African War. When the small British garrisons in Kimberley, Mafeking and Ladysmith were besieged by the Boers, reinforcements were hurried out including two Guards formations. A **Household Cavalry** Composite Regiment joined 2nd Cavalry Division, while **1st Guards Brigade** was also mobilised, and joined 1st Division commanded by Lord Methuen (Scots Guards). Battles of Belmont and Modder River. The **Household Cavalry** Composite Regiment was part of the force that relieved **Kimberley**. When the Boers moved on to their guerrilla warfare phase, more troops were sent out including two Guards battalions as part of 16th Brigade. Overall, seven Guards units served in the war. The **Household Cavalry** returned home in November 1900 and the **Foot Guards** formed two Guards Mounted Infantry Companies.

The **Coldstream** and **Scots Guards** were both directed to raise a 3rd Battalion.

Below: The Moonlight Charge at Kassassin by the Household Cavalry, 28 August 1882.

Excellence in Action

Right: 1st Life Guards, forming a Sovereign's Escort, 1905.

1900

The **Irish Guards** formed 1 April by order of Queen Victoria 'to commemorate the bravery shown by the Irish Regiments during the operations in South Africa'.

1902

The **Irish Guards** acquired a Regimental mascot, the only one officially approved within the **Household Division**. He was an Irish wolfhound, given the name Brian Boru, after the famous warrior King of Ireland, who died in 1014.

1906

Household Cavalry Privates were renamed Troopers. When campaign medals were being issued for the South African War, King Edward VII noticed, when distributing them to the **Household Cavalry** that those for the men were inscribed with the rank of Private. This rank had held some significance in the seventeenth and eighteenth centuries, when members of **The Life Guards** were in fact 'Private Gentlemen' and were addressed as Mr. The rank was now applied throughout the Army, and the King considered that his personal troops should again have a distinctive title. He therefore decreed that men of the **Household Cavalry** should be called 'Troopers'.

First World War. All the Guards elements in France and Flanders were involved in the opening British Expeditionary Force (BEF) battles of manoeuvre (**Retreat from Mons, the Marne** and **Aisne**). Trench warfare at the First Battle of **Ypres**, north-west Belgium prevented a German breakthrough to the Channel Ports, but by 12 November the 1st and 4th Guards Brigades were reduced to about 2,470 All Ranks out of about 8,500 All Ranks in August. The regiments of **Household Cavalry** initially fought as a 350-strong Composite Regiment but, with the expansion of the army, were later to field two complete cavalry regiments. At various times they acted as cavalry, infantry, cyclists, artillerymen and machine gunners.

1914

The Royals retained their horses from 1914–8 and fought at **Ypres, Loos**, Hohenzollern Redoubt and against the **Hindenburg Line**.

1900

1901

Queen Alexandra sent a personal gift of Shamrock to the **Irish Guards**, a tradition maintained ever since.

1905–6

When the new Liberal government came to power, its army cuts demanded disbandment of two Guards battalions; 3rd Battalion **Scots Guards** was disbanded the next year but 3rd Battalion **Coldstream Guards** was saved at the last moment by a call for the battalion as reinforcements in Egypt and survived for another 50 years.

1913

While watching summer manoeuvres, King George V noticed that the **Household Cavalry**, wearing khaki for the first time in peacetime, had no badges for their new khaki caps. He offered his own Royal Cypher as the design, which was adopted.

1915

Formation of the **Welsh Guards** on 26 February by order of King George V. First King's Guard mounted 1 March.

Formation of the **Guards Division** on 18 April. Created by Lord Kitchener in great secrecy, the Guards Division (1st, 2nd and 3rd Guards Brigades, each of four battalions of Foot Guards together with the usual Divisional Troops including a Pioneer Battalion, formed from 4th Battalion **Coldstream Guards**, and a Cyclist Company, manned by the **Household Cavalry** who also provided a Divisional Cavalry Squadron). The divisional sign and then adopted for the whole formation was the 'Eye'.

Battle of Loos (September–October). A grim battle that resulted in the **Welsh Guards** taking Hill 70 but casualties were so heavy that the whole division was then withdrawn.

Left: The Coldstream Guards Changing the Guard at St James's, c.1905.

The Battle of the Somme
(July–November)

Ginchy-Lesboeufs. The Guards Division was not committed until mid-September when ten tanks were allotted to it. For the only time in their history three **Coldstream Guards** battalions advanced together in line. Behind them, in the second wave, were both battalions of **Irish Guards**, also in action together for the first time. Steadily, the leading troops pressed forward but the divisions on both their flanks failed to keep pace. The tanks had not arrived on time and did little to help. Eventually the third objective was captured but the survivors were now totally unsupported, no reinforcements were available and they were forced to pull back and dig in. The cost to the division was 4,964 casualties in eight days, and the Prince of Wales's Company of the **Welsh Guards** was led back by a Lance Corporal.

Also in September 1916 the **Household Cavalry** formed an infantry battalion called the **Household Battalion** (Lieutenant Colonel Wyndham Portal of 1st Life Guards) which suffered 438 fatalities until disbanded in February 1918.

1916

On 21 March 1918 the Germans launched what Churchill described as 'without exception the greatest onslaught in the history of the world'. On a front of 54 miles, 64 German divisions advanced against 32 British divisions. The Allies were forced to withdraw over a wide front, and on 11 April Haig issued his dramatic Order of the Day: 'To all ranks of the British Army in France. With our backs to the wall and believing in the justice of our cause, each one of us must fight to the end.' At this crucial moment, the newly formed 1,800-strong **4th Guards Brigade** dug in to hold positions at the village of Vieux Berquin, near **Hazebrouck** road/railway junction, at all costs, for at that moment it was almost the only fighting formation between the Germans and the Channel coast. For two days, the Guards held on against overwhelming odds. It was the end of the brigade (1,283 casualties) but the Germans did not break through.

1918

Between March and May 1918 both Regiments of **Life Guards** gave up their horses and reformed as 1st and 2nd Guards Machine Gun Battalions. **The Blues** formed the 3rd Guards Machine Gun Battalion, reverting to their former identities and roles shortly after the Armistice.

Hindenburg Line. On 27 September 1918 the **Guards Division** had its final challenge, when it was ordered, as part of the BEF attack on the Hindenburg Line, to cross the Canal du Nord. All three brigades took part, and every objective was gained with 728 prisoners, 18 guns, 12 mortars and 143 machine guns for the loss of just over 1,000 casualties. The last success was the capture of Mauberge on 9 November and then at 1100 hours on 11 November, came the Armistice.

The private soldiers of the Brigade of Guards were given the title of 'Guardsmen' for their war service by the King on 22 November.

1919

1917 Third Battle of Ypres (Passchendaele) (July–October). The **Guards Division** took part in the successful initial attack on 31 July 1917 and advanced two and half miles on a front of some 1,500 yards, capturing 632 German prisoners, a major achievement. However, the rain fell for the next four days and rendered the whole battlefield impassable. During this offensive the Guards Division advanced 6,000 yards capturing 1,180 Germans (excluding wounded able to walk) as well as 4 guns, 31 machine guns and 9 mortars but at a cost of 303 officers and 7,898 other ranks.

Battle of **Cambrai** (November-December) 2nd Guards Brigade was given six hours notice to capture Bourlon Wood over unfamiliar ground against unknown enemy defences. Unknown to the planners the Germans had been preparing their own attack for the same day (27 November) and had ample reserves to hand. The 2nd Guards Brigade gained its objectives and fighting continued all day against seven German battalions, with positions being won and lost several times over. By day's end, 3rd Battalion **Grenadier Guards** and 1st Battalion **Coldstream Guards** had lost every officer and most non-commissioned officers, while 2nd Battalion **Irish Guards** had lost 320 All Ranks out of 400. Three days later the Germans launched a powerful counter-offensive but the Guards Division, resting after the earlier fighting, happened to be in their path. It had no artillery support, but 1st Guards Brigade checked the three-mile German advance, recapturing the village of Gouzeaucourt; the tank-assisted 3rd Guards Brigade regained Quentin Ridge with about 100 British guns lost earlier. Four hundred German prisoners were also taken.

1919 Victory March of the **Household Cavalry** and the Guards Division (22,000 strong) through City of London to Buckingham Palace on 22 March.

Above: Grenadiers climbing a steep path to their forward positions in Italy.

The **Irish Guards** sailed for Constantinople to join the international force stationed there to keep the Dardanelles open. When the situation became more tense 2nd Battalion **Grenadier Guards** and 3rd Battalion **Coldstream Guards** went out to reinforce them and formed 1st Guards Brigade but returned home in October 1923 after the new Turkish Republic was recognised.

1922–3

The two regiments of Life Guards were amalgamated to form **The Life Guards** (1st & 2nd) simplified to **The Life Guards** (1928).

1927–9

2nd Battalions **Coldstream Guards** and **Scots Guards** sent to Shanghai and Hong Kong to protect British interests during the Chinese Civil War.

1939–45

Second World War. The **Life Guards** and the **Royal Horse Guards** were reformed into 1st and 2nd **Household Cavalry** Regiments (1 HCR and 2 HCR).

Home Front. A detachment of **Household Cavalry** armoured cars was detailed to escort King George VI when he travelled in potentially dangerous areas.

The **Coldstream Guards** Holding Battalion provided a company to guard the Prime Minister at his country base at Chequers, Buckinghamshire, from September 1940 to July 1943 and the Coats Mission, which protected the Royal Family until January 1943. The **Grenadier Guards** provided the Windsor Castle Defence Company.

1926

1926

Guards Battalions played a key role in keeping food supplies moving in London during the General Strike.

1937–8

3rd Battalion **Coldstream Guards** and 1st Battalion **Irish Guards** sent from Egypt to Palestine to keep the peace between the Arabs and the Jews.

The British Expeditionary Force (BEF) deployed again to France from September 1939, under General Lord Gort VC (Grenadier Guards), including **1st** and **7th Guards Brigades**.

24th Guards Brigade (including 1st Battalions **Scots Guards** and **Irish Guards**) sent to Norway in April 1940.

On 21 May 1940 the **20th Guards Brigade** was ordered to move to France the same afternoon and within 36 hours was facing the German 2nd Panzer Division on the outskirts of **Boulogne** where 2nd Battalions of the **Irish** and **Welsh Guards** made a determined stand.

The BEF was evacuated at **Dunkirk**, the Guards played a crucial role in holding the perimeter, 2nd Battalion **Coldstream Guards** providing the final rearguard.

North Africa 1940–3. The 3rd Battalion **Coldstream Guards** were the only Guards Regiment involved when 'Wavell's Thirty Thousand' captured 133,000 Italian prisoners in the Western Desert. With the motorised 2nd Battalion **Scots Guards** the Coldstreamers formed what became **201st Guards Brigade** fighting Rommel's Afrika Korps from 'Knightsbridge' Box' and Rigel Ridge for 17 days in May–June 1942.

1 HCR was part of a truck-based force that relieved Habbaniya in Iraq, occupied **Baghdad** and then captured the **Palmyra** oasis just ahead of the Vichy French. In September 1941, having crossed the desert for the third time, the regiment occupied Tehran, just ahead of Britain's new allies, the Russians. As an armoured car regiment, 1 HCR fought the Battle of **El Alamein** (October–November 1942) under General Montgomery, as did **The Royals**.

Above: Winston Churchill inspecting Guard of Honour, Scots Guards, Potsdam Conference, 1945.

G (Foot Guards) Patrol of the Long Range Desert Group set up in December 1940 initially with 40 volunteers in 12 vehicles.

The Special Air Service (SAS) was formed in July 1941 in Egypt by the **Scots Guards** officer Second Lieutenant David Stirling with an initial 66 all ranks, including officers and NCOs from the Foot Guards who like Stirling had earlier volunteered for the Commandos. **Guards Armoured Division** formed in May 1941. When first assembled it consisted of **2 HCR** (Reconnaissance Regiment), 5th Guards Armoured Brigade and 6th Guards Armoured Brigade (which left the division in October 1942). The divisional sign was a modified version of the 'Eye' used by the Guards Division in 1915–9. The new version was designed by the artist Rex Whistler, then serving in 2nd Battalion **Welsh Guards**.

Longstop Hill. On 22 December 1942, 2nd Battalion **Coldstream Guards** were invloved in an intense battle for three days to capture Longstop, in order to open the way for the British 6th Armoured Division to break out and capture Tunis.

By March 1943, there were nine Guards Battalions in three Guards Brigades (1st, 24th and 201st) fighting in North Africa. The Deputy Allied Supreme Commander was General Sir Harold Alexander (Irish Guards) and under him, Lieutenant General Oliver Leese (Coldstream Guards).

The Irish Guards Group captured the start line for Operation MARKET GARDEN and led the advance; the Grenadier Group took the Nijmegen Bridge (20 September). The Division fought on the German border and in Namur in December 1944; in the Reichswald battles in February 1945, and in the breakout across the Rhine from March, ending the campaign near Cuxhaven. 6th Guards Tank Brigade (4th Grenadiers, 4th Coldstream and 3rd Scots (Churchill tanks) seized the hill at Caumont (30 July) and fought alongside the Division in the Bocage; the Brigade fought on the Maas in October-November 1944, in the Reichswald, before advancing on Münster (March–April 1945) and ending the war near Kiel, on the Baltic.

Surrender of the southernmost Italian island of Lampedusa taken by a 95-man company of 2nd Battalion **Coldstream Guards**.

1961

Monte Camino, 7–14 November 1943. 6th Battalion **Grenadier Guards** and F Company **Scots Guards** were joined by the **Coldstream Guards** took over for the next three days, and on the 14th, the mountain was evacuated completely. It was finally captured three weeks later as a result of a Corps attack including 201st Guards Brigade.

Italy 1943–5. 201st Guards Brigade landed at **Salerno** near Naples on 9 September amid heavy fighting, the first Guards units to set foot on mainland Europe since Dunkirk.

The Guards Armoured Division, comprising 2nd (Armoured) Grenadiers, 1st Coldstream and 2nd Irish Guards (Sherman tanks); 2nd Welsh Guards (armoured reconnaissance); 1st Grenadiers, 5th Coldstream, X Company Scots, and 1st Welsh Guards (infantry) landed in Normandy in June 1944. They fought South of Caen (Operation GOODWOOD) and in the Bocage towards Vire (July-August) before leading the breakout across the Seine in September, in Regimental Groupings. 2nd Welsh Guards won the race to Brussels (3 September).

Medjez Plain battle honour including Djebel Bou Aoukaz 27–8 April 1943 or 'The Bou'. 24th Guards Brigade (5th Battalion **Grenadier Guards**, 1st Battalion **Irish Guards** and 1st Battalion **Scots Guards**).

All three Guards Brigades were present when both Tunis and Bizerta were captured and all Axis forces in North Africa surrendered by 16 May.

1945-65 **Farewell to Empire.** 1st Guards Brigade served in Palestine (1945–8); 2nd Guards Brigade in Malaya (1948–51, the Emergency continued to 1960); and the Household Cavalry and Guards Battalions served variously in Cyprus 1955–9; Suez 1956; Kenya 1959–62; Bahrain and Kuwait 1961; 1st Battalion **Grenadier Guards** in British Southern Cameroons Southern Cameroon 1961; British Guiana 1962 and Mauritius 1965.

Right: Members of the 2nd Battalion Gordon Highlanders supported by tanks of the Guards Brigade during the capture of Kleve, 11 Feb 1945.

Left: A bearer party of the Queen's Company 1st Battalion Grenadier Guards carry the union jack-draped coffin of Sir Winston Churchill up the steps of St Paul's Cathedral.

The Life Guards and The Blues and Royals form a 'union' consisting of the Household Cavalry Regiment and Household Cavalry Mounted Regiment.

Three Foot Guards 2nd Battalions disbanded.

1st Bn Coldstream Guards served in Bosnia in UNPROFOR.

NATO intervention in Bosnia, Household Cavalry Regiment and 1st Bn Grenadier Guards deploy.

1964–7 Insurgency in Aden. 1st and 2nd Battalions **Coldstream Guards** and then 1st Battalions **Irish** and **Welsh Guards** served in the Radfan and Aden State, South Arabia.

1967 The name Household Brigade changed to the **Household Division**.

B Squadron of **The Life Guards** and the Guards Parachute Company helped quell race riots in Hong Kong.

1982 The Falklands War. Both the 2nd Battalion of the **Scots Guards** and the 1st Battalion of the **Welsh Guards** – as well as an armoured recce troop and **The Blues and Royals** – were committed and served in 5th Infantry Brigade.

1993–5

1964

1965 Sir Winston Churchill's Funeral (2nd Battalion **Grenadier Guards** bearer party). **G Squadron** of the **Special Air Service** created, consisting of officers and Guardsmen of the Household Brigade.

1969 Northern Ireland Troubles began: a Squadron of **The Life Guards**, together with 2nd Battalion **Grenadier Guards** were among the first reinforcements. Numerous tours of duty followed.

1969 The Royal Horse Guards (The Blues) and the **Royal Dragoons (1st Dragoons)** amalgamated to create **The Blues and Royals** on 29 March.

1990–1 The Gulf War. **The Life Guards** deployed to the Gulf on Operation GRANBY. One Challenger tank squadron took part in the 100-hour ground assault into Iraq.

Because of the confused build-up to the War by February 1991 some 500 **Grenadiers** were dispersed among 14 different units. 1st Battalions **Coldstream** and **Scots Guards**, the **Scots Guards** Band and other Guardsmen served in Op Granby.

1997 Diana, Princess of Wales's funeral (**Welsh Guards** bearer party).

Right: Pristina, 13 June 1999. After months of conflict, ethnic Albanians slowly emerge to greet Four Company, Irish Guards.

Left: 1st Battalion Coldstream Guards in the First Gulf War, February 1991.

1999 Kosovo. The **Irish Guards** Battle Group (including D Squadron Household Cavalry Regiment) were the first NATO troops to reach the capital, Pristina, where they were rapturously welcomed.

2002 **Irish Guardsmen** form the bearer party for Queen Elizabeth the Queen Mother's funeral.

2004 The **Welsh Guards** and 1st Battalion **Scots Guards** deployed to Basra in Iraq (Al Amarah).

The **Coldstream Guards** deployed to Iraq on Operation TELIC 6 and lost two soldiers to roadside bombs.

2006 **Welsh Guards** operational tour to Bosnia to disarm the local population.

2008

2001– War in Afghanistan D Sqn **Household Cavalry** with 3 Para June–October.

Below: Household Cavalry, Afghanistan, troop protection for bridge building, early in the morning.

2003– Invasion and occupation of Iraq (Operation TELIC). A troop from D Squadron Household Cavalry Regiment was involved in a 'friendly fire' incident from American aircraft. Trooper Christopher Finney RHG/D was awarded the George Cross for his actions. **Irish Guards** Battle Group in Operation TELIC 1 lost two soldiers killed in action and won three MCs during the British capture of Basra 6–7 April.

2005 1st Battalion **Grenadier Guards** operational tour in Bosnia included disarming the civilian population to counter organised crime. It then became part of EUFOR, the first British regiment to serve under the European banner.

2007 D Squadron **Household Cavalry Regiment** posted to Helmand Province, Afghanistan with their Scimitar tracked vehicles.

The 1st Bn **Grenadier Guards** posted to Helmand Province in Afghanistan.

1st Bn **Coldstream Guards** deployed to Helmand Province, with a company of 1st Bn **Scots Guards**, who also had companies deployed in Iraq and the Falkland Islands.

The 1st Bn **Irish Guards** and B Squadron Household Cavalry Regiment (a brigade reconnaissance force) posted to Basra in Iraq on Operation TELIC 10.

The 1st Bn **Welsh Guards** ended the British military presence in Bosnia on 24 March.

The Queen opened the new **Household Cavalry Museum** in June on Horse Guards marked by a historical pageant.

THE CRIMEAN WAR, SOUTH RUSSIA 1854–6

Colonel Oliver Lindsay

By 1 March 1854 three Guards Battalions, thirsting for military glory and filled with excitement, had left England en route for the Crimea to fight the Russians. The war arose from a dispute between Russia and Turkey. Neither the British nor French wanted the ambitious Tsar Nicholas I to gain a southern capital or new harbours in the Black Sea at the expense of the declining Ottoman Turkish Empire. 'A sense of uneasiness prevailed' wrote Captain (later General Sir George) Higginson, (Adjutant, 3rd Battalion Grenadier Guards). 'To meet the dangers of war, there was no improvement in our weapons, no increase of artillery, no accumulation of stores. Our fighting force was practically incapable of undertaking any service out of Great Britain beyond the maintenance of the Indian reliefs and Colonial garrisons.' Higginson might have added that there was virtually no land transport, no reserves nor any adequate medical service.

On the other hand, 9,000 men of all arms had started training together at Chobham, Surrey – the first gathering of troops since the peace of 1815. All those chosen for the Crimea had at least seven years service and were 'worthy representatives in physique and bearing'. The outcome would depend, as usual, on the fighting quality of the British troops.

On 20 September the first of the momentous Crimean battles took place on the heights beyond the River Alma to the north of the Anglo-French objective – the Russian naval base at Sevastopol. The Guards Brigade consisted of 3rd Battalion Grenadier Guards and 1st Battalions Coldstream and Scots Fusilier Guards. Each battalion had been reduced by sickness, largely cholera, from 1,000 to about 800 men. The Guards and the kilted Highland Brigade were on the left rear, commanded by the inexperienced Duke of Cambridge, Queen Victoria's cousin. To their front, the Light [Infantry] Division with great gallantry reached the heights but suffered heavily from dug-in Russian cannon before being forced back by immense Russian columns.

Having crossed the River Alma, the three Guards Commanding Officers ordered their leading files to halt to enable the men at the rear to close up. Such was the crisis, however, that the Scots Fusilier Guards were ordered to advance upon the Russians' Great Redoubt immediately to support the hard-pressed Light Division. 'The Battalion was tremendously shaken by the Russian fire, especially from grape shot and canister which came in a regular hurricane', wrote Lieutenant Robert Lindsay. 'The left wing suffered severely. The Russians, seeing the prospect of victory, sprang out of their earthworks and rushed forward to capture our Colours.' The

GRENADIER GUARDS - 1854

Left: The 3rd Battalion Grenadier Guards departing for the Crimea, February 1854.

Below left: The Battle of the Alma, 20 September 1854. The 7th Royal Fusiliers and the Coldstream Guards attack Russian-held heights.

Duke of Cambridge later wrote to Lindsay's father: 'I watched your son with the Queen's Colour. I thought him gone; the Colour fell and he disappeared under it. But he raised it again and waved it over his head.'

With their flanks undefended and confusion caused by an order 'Fusiliers, retire', the Battalion halted, unaware that the order was probably intended for the 7th Fusiliers nearby. At this critical moment the Grenadier and Coldstream Battalions overtook the Scots Fusilier Guards 'advancing in perfect order', firing as they went. Even so, Lindsay believed that he was the first to gain the earthworks, 'planting the Standard on the Russian Redoubt'. By now his Colour was 'shot through in a dozen places and the Colour staff was cut in two'. Two of the six-man Colour Party had been killed.

The Russians were faced with a new threat. The French advance, close to the sea, helped by fire from the combined Allied fleets, had reached the high ground largely unopposed. The Highlanders and the British artillery were particularly effective. 'The Russian columns suddenly turned and fled. Bounding over the parapet our Grenadiers flung themselves on the remaining Russians', wrote Higginson. It was a glorious victory but the Guards Brigade had lost 41 dead and 345 wounded of whom many subsequently died.

Lord Raglan (Colonel of The Blues and formerly Grenadier Guards) commanding the British Army found his French colleagues strongly opposed to an immediate attack upon Sevastopol's north side. They decided therefore to transfer all their forces by an easterly flank march to the south, thereby hoping to make use of the harbour at Balaclava which was on the peninsula's southern shore. This they did.

In more open country near Balaclava the Cavalry Division, consisting of the Heavy and Light Brigades, had the opportunity to participate in the fighting. (Queen Victoria had earlier made it plain that she did not wish her Household Calvary to go to the Crimea.) The Royal Dragoons had sailed on 26 September but had run into an appalling storm in the Black Sea. 'The whole of the stabling broke adrift and the horses were dashed from one side to the other', wrote Sergeant Major Cruse to his wife. The Commanding Officer reported that 'on that fearful night the Regiment lost more horses than at Waterloo. Total loss 150.' Fortunately he mounted his second squadron when the Light Brigade sent them 75 horses.

On 25 October the Russians captured the redoubts held by the Turks on the Causeway Heights, almost two miles north of Balaclava, and then turned south. They were held off by the 93rd Highlanders, dubbed 'the thin red line', which hardly suffered a casualty.

The Royals participated in the Heavy Cavalry Brigade's 20-minute long charge, careering into the Cossacks' right flank, breaking their lines. The Royals and Scots Greys then witnessed the Light Brigade's epic charge and 41 per cent loss in men before being sent to cover the Light Brigade's withdrawal. Both the Royals and Greys received heavy casualties 'A more terrible fire was never heard … the shot and shell and bullets came down on us like hail.'

Below: Tableau of Lieutenants Lindsay and Thistlethwayte with the Colours of the Scots Guards. They fought valiantly and managed to stop the Colours being captured by the Russian forces. For this act of heroism two of the three men were awarded the Victoria Cross.

Below left: Major-General (later Lieutenant-General Sir) Charles Ashe Windham, Coldstream Guards, standing in front of the Redan, Sebastopol, c.1855.

On 16 October many battalions besieging Sevastopol had formed a small body of sharpshooters, each consisting of an NCO and nine men: 'Good shots, volunteers preferred.' Private William Stanlake (Coldstream Guards) quickly distinguished himself by crawling within six yards of a Russian sentry, preventing him from raising the alarm and thereby enabling 'others to pounce on the picket and bear their knapsacks and arms back to camp'.

On the 26th the Russians made a powerful reconnaissance in force towards the left flank of the Guards Brigade. Captain Gerald Goodlake, another Coldstreamer, commanded all 30 of the Guards sharpshooters. He deployed his men with such success that 38 Russians were killed and three taken prisoner. 'Most exciting,' he wrote. 'I and a sergeant were nearly caught in a cave but we made a bolt for it and got off with a bullet through my coat and he got shot in the arm.' The Guards sharpshooters roamed beyond the 1st Division's boundaries killing Russians wherever possible.

By early November 1854, the strength of the three Guards Battalions besieging Sevastopol had dropped from almost 3,000 to 1,360 since leaving England some eight months previously. 'It was my duty to parade the reliefs for the outposts in the trenches between three and four in the morning, and the sight of our gaunt Grenadiers, dimly illuminated by the light of the lantern, filled me with much admiration as foreboding. Not a man faltered, although in many cases their feet protruded from their worn-out boots, and the ragged trouser was tied around the ankles with string, while hollowed cheeks told a story of suffering and endurance,' recorded Captain Higginson, the Battalion's Adjutant.

The night of 4 November was miserably cold; sleety rain fell incessantly. The 'off duty' soldiers huddled together as closely as possible in their tents.

Little did they know that General Soimonov was planning to break out of Sevastopol marching south-east with 19,000 men and 38 guns, while General Paulov with 21,000 and 96 guns was approaching the Allies from the undefended ground in the north east. As soon as the junction was affected, General Dannenberg was to attack the right of the Allies, rolling them up in a southerly direction. In the meanwhile Prince Peter Gorchakov in the south east was to pin down the French Corps. The Russians were then to sweep the Allies invaders into the sea.

The troops available to meet their extraordinary challenge consisted of the British 2nd Division, 3,000 strong with 12 guns, and the Guards Brigade – the only men Lord Raglan could spare for the defence of his extremely vulnerable eastern flank.

At 2 am on the 5th the most forward sentries heard the tolling of Sevastopol's church bells. The faint sounds of distant chanting arose in the thick air. 'It was Sunday morning and the Russians were singing Matins. There's nothing in it. All is well', the sentries believed.

Shortly before dawn Major Prince Edward of Saxe-Weimar was in the process of relieving his Grenadier Company with another one when he became aware of the approaching Russians. He advanced against their flank in skirmish order and opened such a heavy fire that the Russians gave ground.

General Soimonov sent forward an overwhelming 12 battalions to attack Home Ridge where they were initially repelled by troops of the 2nd Division. Soimonov himself was shot dead by British sharpshooters. More columns of Russians then advanced.

The Duke of Cambridge brought up 3rd Battalion Grenadiers and 1st Battalion Scots Fusilier Guards, leaving only the Coldstream to support

The Coldstream were then brought forward, being received with cheers by the Grenadiers and Scots Fusilier Guards on their left. 'Thus, a black thread of about 1,300 Guardsmen was drawn across the ridge ... the vital ground was thinly edged by the *Tria Juncta in Uno* [Three Joined in One] ranged two deep with The Duke of Cambridge in command', recorded the Coldstream history.

Around the Sandbag Battery, the bodies of the dead and dying soon strewed the ground like slaughtered animals, in some places three deep. The only Colours carried that day were those of 3rd Battalion Grenadier Guards. Passed from hand to hand, regardless of rank, they were the rallying point. More than once from the lips of a Guardsman came the shout, 'Hold up the Colours!', fearing, no doubt, that in the mist and smoke they might lose sight or touch of these honoured emblems, which they were determined to preserve, or die in their defence. Fortunately, the Russian columns were sternly repulsed and faded from the field when the French reinforcements arrived.

The Crimean winter now closed in: a terrible storm lashed the Crimean coast sinking 21 Allied ships. As the snow, frost and icy winds swept over the inadequate tents, cholera, dysentery and scurvy killed many: Lord Raglan himself was to succumb to the strain of operations in June 1855. Fortunately general conditions improved during 1855, although the deadly siege of Sevastopol dragged on until 8 September when the Russians abandoned the southern half of the city, following the French capture of the key strongpoint within the city walls. Both sides claimed victory; six months later the peace treaty was signed in Paris.

The war ushered in welcome changes – field hospitals, the electric telegraph, the Enfield rifle and the use of railways to move wounded and supplies. Training was made more realistic.

The French had 96,000 dead, the British 23,000, the Russians an estimated 450,000. The Guards had 425 killed and 972 wounded while 1,793 had died of sickness. They had won 13 Victoria Crosses among whom were Russell and Percy of the Grenadiers, Stanlake and Goodlake of the Coldstream and Lindsay of the Scots Fusilier Guards. All 13 VCs were presented by Queen Victoria.

In July 1856 the Queen addressed the three Battalions at Aldershot and 'quite broke down and burst into tears when she talked of the fellows that were not there to receive her thanks'. Her Majesty took a very deep personal interest in all those who had served in the Crimea.

Nevertheless 1,000 men of the Guards Brigade were quickly discharged without pension or gratuity. 'Many of those good fellows were soon wandering penniless and without employment throughout the country', recorded Higginson. It was a sorry ending to a campaign in which the Guards had won such distinction at Alma and Inkerman.

The Household Division today can be proud of the great endeavours of their Regiments involved in the titanic struggle in the Crimea almost 150 years ago.

the picquets overlooking the valley to the east and to deter the Russian cavalry beyond.

The Battle of Inkerman which followed was fought in a fog which made cohesion and control very difficult for both sides. It was the day for regimental officers and their men fighting independently, rather than for grand manoeuvres by the High Command. It was one of the hardest and most gruelling battles the three Regiments have ever fought.

Desperate fighting, dominated by the bayonets of the Grenadiers and Scots Fusilier Guards, centred round the taking and retaking of the cannon-less Sandbag Battery. At one point Lieutenant Sir Charles Russell jumped into the Battery waving his revolver shouting 'Come on my lads, who will follow me?' His men did so, advancing with a second Grenadier officer, Captain the Honourable Henry Percy. Beyond the Battery in the mist most of them were cut off having charged too far. Nearly surrounded and without ammunition they were in extreme danger. Fortunately Percy, although wounded, extracted 50 men from different regiments, leading them back to safety where ammunition was obtained and they could resume the onslaught.

TREASURES AND ARTEFACTS

There are two museums dedicated to the regiments of the Household Division. The Guards Museum was opened in 1988 in Wellington Barracks off Birdcage Walk near Buckingham Palace and it covers the history of the five regiments of Foot Guards. The new Household Cavalry museum was opened in June 2007 by Her Majesty the Queen on Horse Guards. The entrance is a few paces from where the Queen's Life Guard changes each day, and allows visitors to see the horses in their stables and the men preparing for their duties.

Over the years the regiments of the Household Division have amassed substantial collections of military items many of which have never been displayed. Pictures and regimental silver will usually find a home in the Officers' Mess or the Warrant Officers' and Non-Commissioned Officers' mess but there are many other treasures that would otherwise be consigned to a store room.

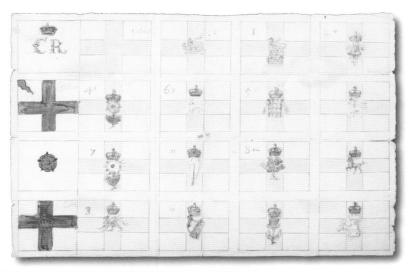

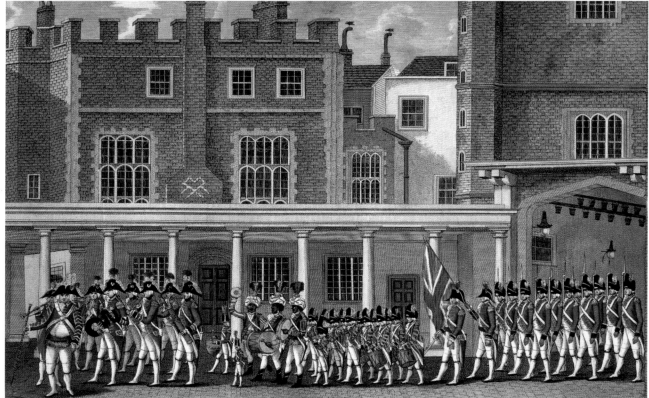

Above: The original watercolour designed for Charles II. On being shown the designs, Charles II didn't like the original CR cipher and amended that design in his own hand to become a reversed C.

Left: Guard mount at St James's Palace, 1770s. Although drummers were often recruited as young as eight years old they were dressed largely in the same way as the Grenadier company and exaggerated the great height of the Grenadiers who would have been the tallest men in the regiment. In addition to their musical skills they were also the administrators of punishment with the cat o' nine tails.

In the Guards Museum the collection of weapons, paintings, uniforms and memorabilia includes personal items, not only of the Dukes of Marlborough and Wellington, but also of the equally heroic men who served them. There are the tattered colours carried at Waterloo, bloodstained uniforms worn in the Crimea, together with superb collections of regimental silver by masters such as Paul Storr and Benjamin Smith. There is also a wonderful display of the Orders and Decorations of the two Dukes of Cambridge designed by the world's greatest craftsmen at the time. In the Household Cavalry Museum, the exhibition includes silver kettle drums, presented to The Blues by George III and Boer War medals awarded to a horse.

Left: The Duke of York vase. This centrepiece was made as a presentation piece for the Duke of York, made famous by the rhyme of the Grand Old Duke of York. When he left the Coldstream Guards he was promoted from the Coldstream to the Grenadiers as Colonel and this was given to him by the officers of the Regiment. It was made by one of the great smiths of the time, a Benjamin Smith. On the Duke of York's death in 1827 he was reputed to have owed 3 million pounds sterling, and it was sold. It was bought by the Cambridge family. The Duchess of Cambridge decided that it was not quite large enough and had a second plinth made.

Left: Thomas Needham coat. This is a Third Guards coat, which predates the regulation for the spacing of buttons. The silver gilt buttons are made on a horn backing. Each coat would have been made individually and embroidered to the size of the man.

Right: Sergeant J. Skinner was a member of the King's Company of the First Guards who was awarded a medal for distinguished conduct for despiking 12 French guns in Fort Batz at the entrance to the River Scheldt, 1809. The army did not award medals for bravery at that time and they were generally provided at the expense of the commanding officers or senior officers who felt such an award was justified. There is a sad end to this story, after Skinner was promoted to recruiting sergeant. He altered a cheque from £5 to £15 and was flogged and reduced to the ranks.

Above: Known as the Honorary Distinctions and often referred to as the battle honours of the regiment, they are a representation of the State Colour of the Scots Guards, which is only carried when members of the Royal Family or visiting heads of state are on parade. It has the collar of the order of the thistle, surrounding the badge of the thistle; the royal crown, Egypt and the Sphinx, representing the battle against Napoleon in 1801; and going as far as 1885, when the colour was presented by Queen Victoria, and therefore later battle honours do not appear on this particular Colour.

Above: Cast of the skull of Corporal John Shaw, of the 2nd Life Guards. Shaw achieved fame for his heroic actions at the Battle of Waterloo. His body was buried on the battlefield, but his skull was recovered and returned.

Left: Gold Stick, inscribed with the Royal cipher of King William IV, carried by Earl Cathcart, Colonel of the 2nd Life Guards 1797 to 1843. The most senior officers of the Household Cavalry have been responsible for the personal safety of the Monarch at all times. This privileged position is symbolised by the carrying of a gold-headed staff by the Colonels of The Life Guards and The Blues and Royals. These officers are referred to as the Gold Stick and take turns to attend on The Queen – though now only on ceremonial occasions.

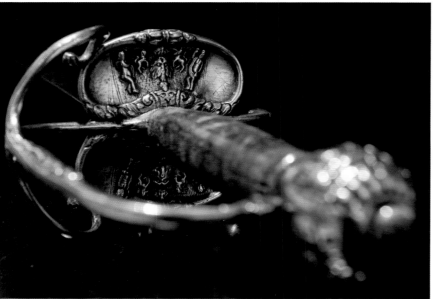

Left: Private Gentleman's Sword 1660 to 1688, The Life Guards. On his return from exile, Charles II created a new bodyguard made up of 500 'private gentlemen' who all paid for the privilege of guarding the King. This sword was used for both active service and ceremonial occasions. The relief design on the hand-guard shows a key moment during the English Civil Wars, with a representation of the oak tree in which Charles sheltered after the Battle of Worcester, with an angel protecting him from the searching Parliamentarians who are depicted with devils' tails.

Above: Artificial leg of Lord Uxbridge (1st Marquis of Anglesey). Lord Uxbridge commanded the cavalry at Waterloo and was badly wounded towards the end of the battle. He was beside Wellington when he was struck by a grape shot on the right knee, which shattered the joint. 'By God sir', he is supposed to have said to Wellington, 'I have lost my leg.' 'By God, sir, so you have,' Wellington is alleged to have replied, reflecting his intense dislike of the man who had eloped with his sister-in-law. Later that same night his leg was amputated above the knee yet he made a remarkable and complete recovery. He commissioned a limb maker to design an artificial leg that was articulated at the joints, which became known as the Anglesey Leg and was patented.

Left: When the First World War started Guards officers in their traditional way were not dressed quite like anybody else and the khaki caps of their service dress had elaborate gold lace peaks. Early on they lost so many officers in a short space of time, it became obvious that snipers were picking them up simply because of their caps. One commanding officer, not wishing to send his officers into battle without head dress, ordered all his officers to wear their caps back to front.

Right: The Irish Guards are the only regiment in the Household Division to have a mascot. The first one was Brian Boru (named after one of the Kings of Ireland). This picture was taken outside the Tower of London where they were stationed at the time. He was handled by a boy drummer and the drum major was responsible for them both. Below is a ceremonial collar worn by the mascots.

Left: Queen's South Africa Medal of 'Freddy' of the 2nd Life Guards, 1903. Freddy was the only horse to return to England from the Boer War in 1900. He took part in every action in which the Regiment was engaged and covered 1,780 miles. Freddy became the lead horse in the Household Cavalry Musical Ride and was introduced to Queen Alexandra at the Royal Tournament. She asked why he had no campaign medal, and immediately demanded that he be awarded one.

Far Left: Military Cross 2006, awarded to Corporal of Horse Michael John Flynn of The Blues and Royals. During an ambush in Afghanistan, Flynn came to the aid of a vehicle that had been destroyed. In his attempt to identify survivors, his own vehicle was disabled and he co-ordinated the withdrawal of his men to safety under heavy enemy fire. He then helped a fellow crewman from a second burning armoured vehicle. Throughout the incident Flynn showed exceptional courage in the face of overwhelming enemy fire.

Left: The Zetland Trophy, 1874. When Lord Zetland left The Blues in 1874, he failed to give the customary leaving present to the officers' mess. When he was asked about this omission, the wealthy Zetland casually remarked, 'Oh, buy a piece of silver and put it on my bill'. The officers took him at his word and duly commissioned an enormous table centrepiece. It took four men to lift it and it cost the then astronomical sum of £1,000. The base of the trophy has four mounted horseman with a central column depicting The Blues at the Battle of Waterloo. A figure of Mars, the god of war, stands on top holding a spear and shield.

The Editor and publishers wish to express their thanks to The Guards Museum and The Household Cavalry Museum for information and assistance provided in this section.

THE GUARDS CHAPEL

The Royal Military Chapel, Wellington Barracks, more usually known as the Guards Chapel is the spiritual home of the Household Division. When the first chapel was opened in 1838 it was a plain rectangular building with a double tier of galleries on three sides to enable as many Guardsmen as possible to attend Divine Service. Over the years the Chapel's decoration became increasingly elaborate.

On Sunday 18 June 1944 the Chapel was hit by a German V1 flying bomb at 11.10am during Morning Service. No fewer than 121 worshippers and Musicians, including the officiating Chaplain, were killed. Another 141 were seriously injured. The cross and six candlesticks on the altar remained standing and the candles continued to burn throughout the incident. They are all still used for Sunday services.

The Apse, with its splendid mosaics, also survived the bombing, as did the font. After the war, a hut was erected within the ruined walls. Services resumed on Christmas Day 1945. In 1956 the Household Brigade War Memorial Cloister, designed by H.S. Goodhart-Rendel, was built between Birdcage Walk and the Chapel. It houses the regimental Rolls of Honour and leads to the Household Brigade Cenotaph.

Bottom left: The 'Mareth Cross': the memorial to the fallen of 6th Battalion Grenadier Guards at the Battle of Mareth, Tunisia, 14–15 March 1943.

In 1963 the new Chapel, designed by the architect Bruce George with a capacity of more than 400, was completed. It incorporates the Apse from the previous building and the War Memorial Cloister.

The mosaics in the Apse show, from left to right, Christ on the way to the Crucifixion and the Deposition of Christ from the Cross. Above these mosaics appears the story of Easter. The Risen Christ stands in front of the Empty Tomb, flanked by Angels holding symbols of the Passion. On the left appear Mary and the women on the way to the Tomb. On the right St John the Divine and St Peter are making the same journey.

On the south side of the Chapel there are six small chapels, one for the two regiments of Household Cavalry and one each for the five regiments of Foot Guards. The regimental badges and battle honours are worked into the stonework. The Chapel contains Standards of the Household Cavalry and Colours of the Foot Guards, the earliest of which date from 1770.

In the south-west corner of the Chapel are memorials to those who died in 1982 in the Falklands Islands War and the Irish Republican Army attack on The Queen's Life Guard. The west walls of the Chapel bear the names of all whose memorials were destroyed when the chapel was bombed in 1944.

Every Sunday there is a service at 11 am, at which the choir of the Guards Chapel and one of the Bands of the Household Division perform. The Chapel also hosts a variety of other events such as weddings and memorial services for past and present members of the Household Division.

REGIMENTS OF THE GUARDS

HOUSEHOLD CAVALRY

Household Cavalry Actions and Heroes

Actions

The Battle of Sedgemoor, 6 July 1685
(Monmouth's Rebellion against King James II)

The Battle of Sedgemoor was fought in the foggy morning of Monday 6 July 1685 on the low lying and wet ground immediately east of the town of Bridgwater in Somerset. The 36-year-old James Scott, Duke of Monmouth, the illegitimate son of King Charles II and formerly Captain of the King's or 1st Troop of Life Guards, had landed in Dorset from Europe with 82 men and four small cannon and was trying to claim the throne for himself and the Protestant cause from the Roman Catholic King James II, Charles II's younger brother and the legitimate holder of the throne. Monmouth's force was ill-prepared and he did not receive the popular support that he had expected.

After his landing Monmouth marched around the West Country thrusting for Bristol and Wiltshire trying to attract support, but after three weeks was trapped by James II's royal army outside Bridgwater. Monmouth's gamble of a surprise night attack, a plan which could have worked had it been conducted with well-trained troops, failed. His 3,600-man force was destroyed and he had to flee. He was captured, and beheaded nine days later in the Tower of London.

The last pitched battle on English soil was not one of the more demanding or exciting engagements in which the regiments which now form the Household Cavalry took part, nor as an action fought against fellow-countrymen at home can it ever be a Battle Honour. However, it is very significant for their history as it is the first time that all the regiments that today comprise The Household Cavalry – The Life Guards, The Blues and The Royals – fought together (750 strong) as well as the first three battalions of Foot Guards. More significantly, it was also the first battle in which the new British Army created at the Restoration in 1660 had fought as an entity and proved that well trained and equipped troops, loyal to the Sovereign, would ensure victory over untrained volunteers.

Royalist casualties at Sedgemoor were very light, although the rebels suffered severely and many of those who escaped death on the battlefield were subsequently executed during the 'Bloody Assizes'. Whereas before

Above: James Duke of Monmouth. Coloured mezzotint by W. Baillie, after Netcher and Wyke, 1774.

Right: Marquis of Granby relieving a sick soldier. Oil on canvas by Edward Penny, c.1765.

Household Cavalry

The Life Guards and The Blues and Royals form two composite regiments: The Household Cavalry Regiment, which is in the Armoured Reconnaissance role based at Windsor, Berkshire, and The Household Cavalry Mounted Regiment which is based in Knightsbridge to fulfil the ceremonial role.

The Life Guards

Colonel of the Regiment: General the Lord Guthrie of Craigiebank GCB LVO OBE

Formed: March 1660

Role Today: Armoured Reconnaissance and Mounted Ceremonial

Battle Honours: Combined Battle Honours of 1st Life Guards and 2nd Life Guards, with the following emblazoned: Dettingen, Peninsula, Waterloo, Tel-el-Kebir, Egypt 1882, Relief of Kimberley, Paardeberg, South Africa 1899–1900 **The Great War:** Mons, Le Cateau, Retreat from Mons, Marne 1914, Aisne 1914, Messines 1914, Armentieres 1914, Ypres 1914, '15, '17, Somme 1916, '18, Albert 1916, Arras 1917, '18, Scarpe 1917, '18, Broodseinde, Poelcapelle, Passchendaele, Bapaume 1918, Hindenburg Line, Epehy, St Quentin Canal, Beaurevoir, Cambrai 1918, Selle, France and Flanders 1914–18 **The Second World War:** Mont Pincon, Souleuvre, Noireau Crossing, Amiens 1944, Brussels, Neerpelt, Nederrijn, Nijmegen, Lingen, Bentheim, North-West Europe 1944–5, Baghdad 1941, Iraq 1941, Palmyra, Syria 1941, El Alamein, North Africa 1942–3, Arezzo, Advance to Florence,

Gothic Line, Italy 1944 **Post Second World War:** Wadi al Batin, Gulf 1991, Al Basrah, Iraq 2003

Notes: 1. The Regiment maintained the fiction of separate regiments until 1928, receiving in 1927 two separate sets of Standards with different (but almost identical) Battle Honours emblazoned.

2. The revised combined list issued May 1933, omitting from emblazonment 'Passchendaele' and 'St Quentin Canal' of the 1st Life Guards.

3. The 1991 and 2003 Honours were awarded jointly to The Life Guards and The Blues and Royals, for services of the Household Cavalry Regiment.

Marches: Quick – *Millanollo*
Slow – *Life Guards Slow March*
Trot Past – *Keel Row*

Traditional Nickname: The Tins

Motto: *Honi Soit Qui Mal y Pense* (Shame on He Who Evil Thinks)

Allied Regiment: The President's Bodyguard of Pakistan

Email Address: homehq@householdcavalry.co.uk

The Blues And Royals
(Royal Horse Guards and 1st Dragoons)

Colonel of the Regiment: HRH The Princess Royal KG, KT, GCVO, QSO

Formed: 29 March 1969 by an amalgamation of the Royal Horse Guards (formed 26 January 1661) and the Royal Dragoons (formed 6 September 1661)

Battle Honours: Tangier 1662–80, Dettingen, Warburg, Beaumont, Willems, Fuentes d'Onor, Peninsula, Waterloo, Balaclava, Sevastopol, Egypt, Tel-el-Kebir, Relief of Kimberley, Paardeberg, Relief of Ladysmith, South Africa 1899–1902 **The Great War:** Mons, Le Cateau, Retreat from Mons, Marne 1914, Aisne 1914, Messines 1914, Armentieres 1914, Ypres 1914, '15–'17, Langemarck 1914 Gheluvelt, Nonne Bosschen, St Julien, Frezenberg, Loos, Arras 1917, Scarpe 1917, Somme 1918 St Quentin, Avre, Broodseinde, Poelcapelle, Passchendaele, Amiens, Hindenburg Line, Beaurevoir, Cambrai 1918, Sambre, Pursuit to Mons, France and Flanders 1914–18 **The Second World War:** Mont Pincon, Souleuvre, Noireau Crossing, Amiens 1944, Brussels, Neerpelt, Nederrijn, Veghel, Nijmegen, Rhine, North-West Europe 1944–5, Baghdad 1941, Iraq 1941, Palmyra, Syria 1941, Msus, Gazala, Knightsbridge, Defence of Alamein Line, El Alamein, El Agheila, Advance on Tripoli, North Africa 1941–3, Sicily 1943, Arezzo, Advance to Florence, Gothic Line, Italy 1943–4 **Post Second World War:** Falkland Islands 1982, Iraq 2003

Marches: Quick – *Quick March of The Blues and Royals*
Slow – *Slow March of The Blues and Royals*
Trot Past – *Keel Row*

Motto: *Honi Soit Qui Mal y Pense*

Allied Regiments: The Royal Canadian Dragoons, The Governor General's Horse Guards

Email Address: homehq@householdcavalry.co.uk

Recent Operations and Highlights

2002 – Household Cavalry Regiment: C Squadron relieved A Squadron in Bosnia. Several officers took part in the vigil for the Lying-in-State for Queen Elizabeth The Queen Mother in April. Regiment manned fire stations in London during a strike.
Household Cavalry Mounted Regiment: Street liners and marching party for the funeral of Queen Elizabeth The Queen Mother in April. Captain's Escort in Edinburgh for the Opening of the General Assembly of the Church of Scotland. 242 horses on parade for Queen's Golden Jubilee in June. Regiment won the Inter-Regimental polo in July.

2003 – HCR: D Squadron took part in the invasion of Iraq, with 16 Air Assault Brigade, taking three fatal casualties. The Queen presented new Standards in May. A Squadron deployed to Bosnia. Exercises with Marine Commando Brigade. Exchanges with the French Army.
HCMR: provided a Double Standard Escort for the visit of President Putin of Russia in June and another Escort for the visit of President Bush of the United States in November.

2004 – HCR: A and B Squadrons deployed to Basra in Iraq as part of 1st Mechanised Brigade. Varied role which involved IED incidents, counter-attacking to rescue a patrol of the Argyll and Sutherland Highlander, mentoring Iraqi Border Police and combating hijackers on the Kuwaiti border. Several Household

Cavalry soldiers took part in a round-the-world sailing trip run by the Household Division.
HCMR: A Captain's Escort deployed to Paris to take part in the Centenary celebrations of the Entente Cordiale on the Champs Elysées.

2005 – HCR: spent four months in Canada acting as enemy for exercising battle groups at the British Army Training Unit Suffield (BATUS) in Alberta. The Regiment converted one of its reconnaissance squadrons to a command and support squadron including a surveillance troop, forward air controllers cell (TACP), a specialist liaison team and an NBS troop. The rest of the year was taken up in exercising with 19 Light Brigade, 1st Mechanised Brigade and 16 Air Assault Brigade.
HCMR: provided two officers to the successful Army Cresta team. Help was given to the Regiment's sister ship, *HMS Westminster* for her re-dedication parade in Portsmouth. A tent pegging team was sent to the USA in May. A Captain's Escort accompanied The Queen along the Mall for the 60th Anniversary of the end of the Second World War. The BBC screened an 8-part series, *The Queen's Cavalry*. The Regiment took part in the State Visit of the President of the People's Republic of China in November.

2006 – HCR: D Squadron deployed to Afghanistan with 16 Air Assault Brigade for five months as the first armoured reconnaissance troops to go there. Two fatal casualties were sustained; one Conspicu-

ous Gallantry Cross (Lance Corporal of Horse A.G. Radford) and three Military Crosses (Captain P.J. Williams and Staff Corporals S.K. Fry and M.J. Flynn CGC) were awarded for gallantry.
HCMR: The Household Cavalry Musical Ride performed in Stuttgart and Vienna.

2007– HCR: In May, A and B Squadrons departed for Iraq. In October, RHQ, C Squadron and much of Headquarters Squadron deployed to Helmand Province in Afghanistan as part of 52 Brigade. In November, the Household Cavalry Regiment Battle Group had nine sub-units (squadrons and companies) under command for a major operation around Musah Qa'leh. During the deployment, the Battle Group had at least one member of every Regiment of the Household Division under command.
HCMR: Household Cavalry Pageant on Horse Guards Parade to mark the opening of the newly completed Household Cavalry Museum by The Queen. On 20 July, a small ceremony marked the 25th Anniversary of the IRA bombing in Hyde Park which killed four members of The Blues and Royals' Queen's Life Guard in 1982. Sovereign's Escort for the State Visit of the King of Saudi Arabia in October.

2008 – HCR: RHQ, C Squadron and much of Headquarters Squadron continued in Afghanistan till April. In that month D Squadron departed Afghanistan as part of 16 Air Assault Brigade.

Corporal of Horse Byron Gibson, The Life Guards

On being a Gunnery Instructor

I was down at the main Royal Armoured Corps School for Gunnery at Lulworth for two years. I was taking courses for everything from the basic course for a trooper all the way up to Squadron Leader on CVR(T), Challenger 2, and guided weapons.

A young trooper learns about laying the weapons system, using the optics, the sights and the controls and firing it at the target. Then as he progresses through his career and becomes a vehicle commander, he learns more about the weapon handling, touching the weapon, making sure it is loaded correctly, getting over any problems that the weapons system has, allowing the gunner to then fire it and supervises the gunner. So it is a progression with experience through the gunnery systems that are on the vehicles.

On the CVR(T)s we have got 30mm Rarden Cannon, L37 7.62mm machine gun and the smoke grenades which are classed as a weapons system. Out here in Iraq we have been using predominantly L7 machine guns which are mounted on to the vehicles.

A basic gunnery course covers cleaning the gun, servicing and maintaining the weapons system on the vehicles and the application of fire.

Within the vehicles you have the various sights including the thermal imaging sights, which have laser range finding incorporated. When I joined up there was a lot more on the user to estimate ranges to targets and relate that to a point on your monocular sight, whereas nowadays the computer is doing it all for you. You raise a target, it tells you the range and gives you a cross on the screen so you don't even have to calculate where you have to aim. It's all done for you and it's just a case of laying that cross onto the target and hopefully firing and getting a first round strike.

To build skills we use simulators. Every regiment holds a simulator and for a gunner to qualify he needs so many hours on that. That is finalised by a range package which is the first time that he is even going to fire the weapons system for real, and hopefully by that time, the only thing new to the whole aspect of firing is the gun going BANG!

Ten years ago using your thumbs and looking at the screen was very difficult, but nowadays, for the Playstation generation, it seems like second nature. To them it's just a new game.

On What Makes A Good Gunner

A good gunner is somebody that can identify and have the confidence to know that he has seen a target. He needs to be happy that where he is laying a gun is going to give the results that he wants. Because it is a strange area to be, inside a tank when it is firing; because there is a lot going on, the gun's firing, the radios are squawking in your ear, the driver is shouting, the commander is shouting and all that confusion in your head; it's got to be somebody that can switch off from that, concentrate on his sight, see the target and then fire. And that is what makes him stand out.

Left: A trooper in the Household Cavalry inspects his vehicle, whilst on the ranges.

Below: A trooper in The Blues and Royals stands by his horse's head ready for inspection before going out on the morning exercise, known as watering order, from Hyde Park Barracks.

What is remarkable about Granby's action is that his control was so effective that he was able to charge, regroup and then charge again to ensure the destruction of the enemy, pursuing them about 10 miles. After the humiliation of the British cavalry failing to charge at Minden in 1759, Warburg was a huge triumph. Although this battle did not finish the war in Germany, it contributed significantly to the eventual French defeat.

Sedgemoor the regiments of the Household Cavalry had operated mostly as individual Troops of horse and in a policing role, from 1685 onwards they were to be involved in nearly every major campaign fought by the British Army.

The Battle of Warburg 31 July 1760 (Seven Years War, Germany)
Both The Blues and The Royals were present at Warburg fought in north Germany on 31 July 1760. This action took place in the Seven Years War, when the British and their German allies were trying to expel the French from northern Germany and to defend Hanover, then ruled by King George II as its Elector. Warburg was important because it was a textbook cavalry action in which Lieutenant General The Marquis of Granby, the allied cavalry commander, exercised impeccable control over an arm which was renowned for being unruly.

The 25,000 French had become separated and their commander, the Chevalier de Muy, had established poor positions north and west of the town of Warburg on a ridge. Granby, realising the French mistake, grouped the 8,000 British cavalry and horse artillery and advanced quickly during the stiflingly hot morning of 31 July. By 1pm, just as the mist was clearing, he positioned his force parallel to the French with six regiments in his first line and with The Blues in the centre. He launched a series of three charges against the French which routed them with casualties totalling 8,000. At the same time another allied force, which included The Royals, attacked from the north.

The Battle Of Waterloo 18 June 1815 (Napoleonic Wars, Belgium)
Waterloo, fought on Sunday 18 June 1815, was the bloodiest action in which the Household Cavalry has ever taken part. All the regiments that today comprise the Household Cavalry were present. The Life Guards and The Blues were in the Household Brigade and The Royals in the Union Brigade. It was their charge, over the Mont St Jean Ridge, against the massed might of General Count d'Erlon's I Corps and which represented Napoleon's main effort, which effectively saved the day for Wellington. The seven regiments, which had been kept in the dead ground behind the ridge and could not see what was happening to their front, advanced on the trumpet call and smashed into d'Erlon's 16,000 infantry and their associated 800 Cuirassiers, the *corps d'élite* of the French cavalry. They defeated them in bloody hand-to-hand fighting and then charged on to the 80 French cannon massed in the Grand Battery a mile beyond.

This was their undoing. Had they managed to regroup after their first attack, they would have been available as a reserve for Wellington thereafter, but many were cut down as they trudged back on exhausted horses from the Grand Battery. Enough, however, got back to form a partial reserve and they were to make further charges during the afternoon. It was their action against d'Erlon's corps which enabled Wellington to hold Napoleon and then eventually with the promised aid of Field Marshal Gerhard von Blücher's Prussians defeat him by eight o'clock on that bloody Sunday evening.

Right: A member of a Household
Cavalry support troop preparing
demolition charges.

*Right: A member of a Household
Cavalry support troop preparing
demolition charges.*

*Below: The decisive charge of The
Life Guards at Waterloo, 1815.*

*Above: A dismounted patrol
in Basra talks to a local.*

*Left: A trooper of The Life
Guards removes his Jack
Boot after coming off
parade.*

The First Battle of Ypres 20 0ctober–21 November 1914
(First World War, Belgium)

At the start of the First World War the Household Cavalry first deployed
a Composite Regiment consisting of a squadron from each of 1st and 2nd
Life Guards and The Blues. As the war intensified, all three regiments
served in Flanders. The Composite Regiment took part in the advance to
and then the retreat from Mons, but by the end of October 1914, 1st and
2nd Life Guards and The Blues formed the dismounted 7th Cavalry
Brigade deployed just to the east of Ypres, trying to defend the town and
the approach to the Channel Ports, from the Germans.

On the night of 30 October the regiments, about 1,500 strong, were
dug in in a rough semi-circle when they were attacked by six fresh
German divisions supported by four Jaeger regiments supported by 260
artillery guns. The trenches at this stage in the war were not the
sophisticated defences of later years, and they only had time to prepare a
rough series of shell scrapes. For a nightmarish 48 hours the cavalrymen
fought hand-to-hand with many being killed with bayonets or being
buried alive in the trenches from shell fire. In the words of Field Marshal
Lord Haig 'the trenches were soon blown in and at 8am after 1¼ hours
bombardment the whole of the 39th German Infantry Division and four
battalions of Jaegers attacked their shattered positions. The time had
come to slip away and orders were issued for retirement to a second line,
but the greater part of two squadrons of The Life Guards on the left, and
The Royal Horse Guards machine guns could not get away and were cut
off and died to a man except for a few wounded prisoners.'

Further south, the Composite Regiment, at Wytschaete near
Messines, was also attacked, and within 24 hours the 350-strong regiment
could only muster 30 men of The 1st Life Guards' squadron, three from
The 2nd Life Guards and 30 Blues. Although the casualties were not quite
as bad as at Waterloo, it was one of the bloodiest actions in which the
Household Cavalry has participated but, together with The Royals
fighting at nearby Hollebeke, they had helped stop the German advance
and save the Channel Ports.

Contemporary Operations, Iraq And Afghanistan, 1990-1, 2003–8

The Household Cavalry was first deployed to the Middle East in 1940, and
took part in operations in Palestine, Syria, Iraq and Iran from 1940-42.
The 1st Household Cavalry Regiment were part of the force that took
Baghdad in 1941. In 1991 a Squadron of The Life Guards was part of the
allied force which liberated Kuwait; D Squadron The Blues and Royals
deployed in 2003 as part of the Joint American and British force that
invaded Iraq and overthrew Saddam Hussein's regime. During that
operation D Squadron defeated the 6th Iraqi Armoured Division,
although in doing so lost 10 per cent of its men and a quarter of its vehicles,
some, regrettably to an accidental strike by American aircraft. During that
short campaign D Squadron soldiers were awarded a George Cross, a
Distinguished Service Order, a Conspicuous Gallantry Cross and a
Military Cross. In 2006 that same squadron deployed with the first British
troops into Helmand in Afghanistan where they were involved in some of
the fiercest fighting against the Taliban. During this five months, three of

commander of the British cavalry. A rich and influential man, who was heir to the Duke of Rutland, Granby was also one of the few contemporary British commanders who were genuinely concerned for their soldiers' welfare. He lent money to those being discharged so that they could start pubs, which is why there are so many named after him today (20 in London alone as of 1987), and throughout his life maintained contact with those who had fought with him. He was also a brave and competent tactician, whose control of the cavalry was exceptional and which allowed him to rout the French at Warburg (see page 43). He famously lost his hat and wig in the charge and after the battle was forced to salute Prince Ferdinand of Brunswick bald headed. From that day on soldiers of The Blues (and now The Blues and Royals) have been the only ones in the British Army to salute without headdress. Granby, who rose to be Commander-in-Chief (1766–70), is important for the history of the Household Cavalry because he set the style for how the heavy cavalry, and the British Army in general, would develop and would show that, when properly led, they were unbeatable. In 1990 his name was given to the operation codename for the British deployment to the First Gulf War.

Corporal John Shaw, 2nd Life Guards (1789–1815)

Corporal John Shaw became a national hero for his exploits at Waterloo. A very well-built man, over 6 feet 3 inches tall and weighing 15 stone, he was 'The model of the whole British Army in himself – I'd give a £50 note to be such a figure of a man', according to Charles Dickens in his 1852 novel *Bleak House*. Already famous as a successful boxing prize-fighter, and in contention for the National Championship, Shaw's main interest was the 2nd Life Guards with whom he fought in the Peninsula and at Waterloo.

It was his feats at Waterloo that earned him such renown. He had been sent foraging that morning and had returned only just in time to have a tot of rum and take his position in the left hand squadron of the 2nd Life Guards, in other words on the extreme left of the Household Brigade. His first victim was a Cuirassier whose face he sliced off 'as if it had been an apple'. He then dispatched a further nine men, getting round the problem of his sword being shorter than his opponents by smacking at their faces with the hilt. His problem was, as with many of his comrades, he did not stop having defeated the Cuirassiers but continued to the Grand Battery. That is where he was killed. He had allegedly killed another ten Frenchman by this point, one of whose decapitated heads remained balanced on his knapsack, when his sword broke and he was back to using the hilt as a club; thereafter he used his helmet as a flail and is reputed to have finally succumbed to wounds caused by a drummer boy firing a pistol at him from a ditch. His dead body was found well to the rear of the French positions after the battle. He became very much the epitome of the heroism and self-sacrifice that the Household Cavalry had shown that day.

Above: Abu Klea, Sudan: The death of Colonel Burnaby, 17 January 1885.

their number were killed and a further Conspicuous Gallantry Cross and three Military Crosses were awarded to Household Cavalrymen.

Heroes

General John Manners, Marquis Of Granby (1721–70)

Granby was the Colonel of The Royal Horse Guards (The Blues) and enjoyed the unusual distinction of also commanding them on active service in Germany during the Seven Years War when he was the

Regiment in the desert action against the Mahdi's forces at Abu Klea on 17 January 1885, where 1,250 British formed a square and withstood repeated assaults by 11,500 Mahdists. Burnaby was cut down trying to close a gap in the square. He was one of the first to fall, speared through the neck. Corporal Mackintosh of The Blues rushed out to save his Commanding Officer, driving his bayonet into the back of Burnaby's assailant, but he was overwhelmed and quickly cut down as well.

Burnaby's death had a huge impact on the Army in which he was well known and very well regarded, although more so by the soldiers than by the officers. 'Oh! Sir; here is the bravest man in England dying and no-one to help him' said a young private who was one of the first to reach him when the square was finally secure. Burnaby was not necessarily a great soldier but what he did was re-establish the fighting reputation of the Household Cavalry after a time of ceremonial stagnation between Waterloo and their deployments to the Sudan, and it was very much his example which set the pattern for the future exploits of the regiments in the later years of the nineteenth century.

Second Lieutenant John Dunville VC, 1st Royal Dragoons (1896–1917)

John Dunville is the only Household Cavalryman (in terms of the 1969 amalgamation) to date to have been awarded the Victoria Cross. A Northern Irishman, he had joined The Royal Dragoons (after fighting in another cavalry regiment at Loos) in York in 1916 and found himself with the regiment in the trenches between Épehy and Vendhuile in May 1917. It was imperative here for them to try to dominate No-Man's Land and deny the initiative to the Germans. One way of doing this was to raid the enemy trenches and one such raid was ordered for 25 June. Dunville, as a new Second Lieutenant, was in the party. He led his men on a compass bearing over an extremely difficult piece of country straight to the German wire. The British barrage ended early when the raiding party was still 850 yards from its objective. Despite this, Dunville ran forward directly the barrage lifted and helped the Sappers put their Bangalore 'torpedos' under the wire to blow it up. Then he was the first through the gap and was wounded by German rifle fire, but used his own body to shield the Royal Engineers as they continued with their work, 'calling to them in a cheeriest way' that he was hit. By the time the Engineers had finally finished, all surprise was gone and the only option was to withdraw, which they did dragging the badly wounded Dunville with them.

He died in hospital next day. In a letter to his family a fellow officer wrote: 'I hardly dare to offer any words of sympathy. It seems so cold and formal. To me his death is a tremendous blow. He joined the same day at York as I did and many are the days hunting and cheery evenings we had together. Of course in the regiment he was a general favourite from the day of his arrival and I don't think there was a dry eye yesterday when the Last Post was sounded at his graveside. It must be a great comfort to you to know that he died as he did, the whole regiment admiring his pluck and mourning his loss.'

Colonel Frederick Gustavus Burnaby, Royal Horse Guards (1842–85)

Of all the interesting men who have served in the Household Cavalry, Colonel Fred Burnaby must rank among the most eccentric. He was a giant of a man, 6 feet 4 inches tall and weighing over 20 stone. He was extraordinarily strong and a great adventurer/writer and during his early career made a 2,000-mile ride to Khiva, deep in central Asia, went campaigning in Bulgaria, got caught up in the Carlist revolt in Spain, crossed the Channel in a balloon and was the *Times* correspondent in Sudan where he went on anti-slavery expeditions and became a firm admirer and friend of Major General Charles Gordon. He was commanding The Blues during General Sir Garnet Wolseley's campaign to relieve General Gordon in Khartoum in 1884–5. Although he was prevented specifically by the War Office from deploying, he took sick leave out of England to join Wolseley's army and the men of his regiment who were riding camels down the Nile. He was with the Heavy Camel

Trooper Christopher Finney GC, The Blues and Royals (born 1985)

'On 28 March 2003, D Squadron Household Cavalry Regiment were probing forward along the Shatt-Al-Arab waterway, north of Basra in Iraq, some 30 kilometres ahead of the main force of 16th Air Assault Brigade. In exposed desert, their mission was to find and interdict the numerically vastly superior, and better equipped, Iraqi 6th Armoured Division.

Trooper Finney, a young armoured vehicle driver with less than a year's service, was driving the leading Scimitar vehicle of his troop, which had been at the forefront of action against enemy armour for several hours. In the early afternoon the two leading vehicles paused beside a levee to allow the troop leader to assess fully the situation in front. Without warning they were engaged by a pair of American Coalition Forces ground-attack aircraft. Both vehicles were hit and caught fire and ammunition began exploding inside the turrets. Trooper Finney managed to get out of his driving position and was on the way towards cover when he noticed that his vehicle's gunner was trapped in the turret. He then climbed onto the fiercely burning vehicle, at the same time placing himself at risk from enemy fire, as well as fire from the aircraft should they return. Despite the smoke and flames and exploding ammunition, he managed to haul out the injured gunner, get him off the vehicle, and move him to a safer position not far away, where he bandaged his wounds.

The troop officer, in the other Scimitar, had been wounded and there were no senior ranks to take control. Despite his relative inexperience, the shock of the attack and the all-too-obvious risk to himself, Finney recognised the need to inform his headquarters of the situation. He therefore broke cover, returned to his vehicle, which was still burning, and calmly and concisely sent a lucid situation report by radio. He then returned to the injured gunner and began helping him towards a Spartan vehicle of the Royal Engineers which had moved forward to assist.

At this point Finney noticed that both the aircraft were lining up for a second attack. Notwithstanding the impending danger he continued to help his injured comrade towards the safety of the Spartan vehicle. Both aircraft fired their cannon and Finney was wounded in the lower back and legs and the gunner in the head. Despite his wounds, Finney succeeded in getting the gunner to the waiting Spartan. Then, seeing that the driver of the second Scimitar was still in the burning vehicle, Finney determined to rescue him as well. Despite his wounds and the continuing danger from exploding ammunition he valiantly attempted to climb up onto the vehicle but was beaten back by the combination of heat, smoke and exploding ammunition. He collapsed exhausted a short distance from the vehicle and was recovered by the crew of the Royal Engineers' Spartan.

During these attacks and their horrifying aftermath, Trooper Finney displayed clear-headed courage and devotion to his comrades which was out of all proportion to his age and experience. Acting with complete disregard for his own safety even when wounded, his bravery was of the highest order throughout.

The George Cross (GC) is the highest award that can be bestowed for gallantry in the face of the enemy.'

Extracted from The London Gazette

LIFE ON THE FRONT LINE: The Household Cavalry Regiment, 2007

By Lieutenant Colonel Edward Smyth-Osborne

In the twilight of the false dawn on 7th December 2007, the Household Cavalry battle group moved into blocking positions astride the Musá Qul'eh Wadi, just south of the infamous Taliban held town, as part of the continued coalition forces incremental build of pressure on the enemy within, and to frustrate their key avenue of escape. The battle group consisted of a broad sweep of capabilities: C Squadron Household Cavalry Regiment (HCR) in their light armour; Scots Guards Right Flank Company in their Warriors; the Commando Recce Force in their articulated Vikings; B Squadron King's Royal Hussars in their MASTIFF troop carriers; and Afghans with their mentors from the 2nd Battalion The Yorkshire Regiment, all battle hardened by months of operations in southern Helmand. The block inserted according to plan and further succeeded in drawing Taliban attention from the point of 'break in' by 1st Battalion/508th from the US 82nd Airborne and the 3rd Brigade of the Afghan Army, and remained in place until the town fell. Thereafter the battle group, released from its enabling tasks, pushed east, conducting a series of combined arms-clearance operations against Taliban-held positions.

For the HCR this operation marked the middle of 18 months of continuous operations for the regiment, with Squadrons deploying from Combermere Barracks in Windsor, both east and west of Persia, in a variety of reconnaissance-based roles. Following a year of intensive and varied training across the country and as far as Belize, both A and B Squadrons deployed to Iraq in May 2007 with 1 Mechanized Brigade.

A Squadron deployed in a classic Formation Reconnaissance task in the harsh desert summer of the Maysan Province along the Iranian border (normally the home of the Bedouin and Marsh Arabs), initially operating in CVR(T) and heavily armed Landrovers before converting to a more conventional role as part of the ongoing counter-insurgency operation. Meanwhile B Squadron, as the Brigade Reconnaissance Force, worked direct to the Brigade HQ conducting a variety of surveillance tasks within the urban confines of Basra city, both Squadrons relishing the diversity and complexity of conducting reconnaissance tasks in such an operationally challenging environment.

Meanwhile, in September, C Squadron and the HCR battle group HQ deployed to Afghanistan as part of the newly formed 52 Infantry Brigade to the Helmand Province of southern Afghanistan, as part of the international effort to bring security and regeneration to an area destabilised by decades of fighting and more recently victim of the brutal grip of the Taliban. The HCR battle group, which included B Company 1st Battalion The Royal Gurkha Rifles first deployed to Garmsir, blocking Taliban routes originating from the deep south and the Pakistan border, along the Helmand River and the adjacent Western and Red deserts. Two months later the reconfigured battle group swapped the dust and heat of the desert for the snow-capped foothills of the Hindu Kush and deployed north as part of Operation MAR KARADAD, resulting in the successful re-capture of Musá Qul'eh. From then on the HCR battle group, often referred to as the Helmand Nomads, with five Infantry Companies, two Armoured Squadrons, Afghan Scouts and the Brigade Reconnaissance Force under command, took control of the north, some 2,000km² surrounding and including Now Zad and Musá Qul'eh. In April 2008, D Squadron, an intrinsic part of 16 Air Assault Brigade who were involved in hard fighting in Helmand two years before, returned for the second time to replace C Squadron, to an operation which has tangibly matured, with a more secure Helmand and a safer population, but with plenty of work still to do.

Under 52 Brigade, three elements of the Household Division – the Household Cavalry Regiment, the Coldstream Guards, and Right Flank Scots Guards – have been fortunate enough to be able to fight together in one battle group, all sharing a natural affinity and common ethos, demonstrated by a bond that has been remarked on by the remainder of the Brigade. Many of the other units serving alongside have only over seen the ceremonial pomp and circumstance of the Household Division in London or on television. Now, having served alongside regiments of the division, they are only too aware of the professional approach and high standards that we demand and enjoy. Elements of the Division have been heavily committed in both Iraq and Afghanistan and have firmly proved that, in stark contrast, we can excel on the parade square and battlefield alike.

At Formation Reconnaissance squadron level, operating in Afghanistan and indeed Iraq presents a number of challenges. The squadrons operate at range, often deployed in the desert for up to six weeks at a time, enhanced by a plethora of assets including light guns and close air support, searching, finding and closing with the enemy, whilst being sustained by steadfast ground logistic support, via helicopters or parachute. The soldiers face not just a wily and dangerous enemy but also some of the most wild and demanding environments, with severe climates and extreme terrain, compensated to some degree by breathtaking vistas – often not appreciated when under indirect fire or repairing damaged vehicles!

The performance of the Household Cavalry has been exceptional; all ranks have risen to the challenges, Troopers, Non Commissioned Officers and Officers alike. The increased tempo of operational deployments has been met head on, with the Regiment successfully stepping up to the mark in providing Brigade-level reconnaissance in both of the Army's theatres of operation. What impresses most is the ability of the Squadrons, particularly relatively new troopers, to adapt and conquer the challenges that they face aplenty. Although provided with lengthy and comprehensive training for operations, troopers recently fresh from ceremonial duties in London have swiftly adjusted to the battlefield, handling the persistent pressures with calm maturity, gritty determination and good humour that belie their years. The comparisons between the parade ground and combat are initially difficult to square, but self-evidently the responsibilities and demands placed on our young soldiers in Knightsbridge, the requirement to care and manage for both horse and equipment, the ceremonial perfection and discipline demanded on parade, and the consequent pride in duty and loyalty to troop, squadron and regiment is as relevant on Horse Guards as it is in the Green Zone or wadis of Afghanistan or Iraq. Young and older soldiers alike, operating for weeks on end, reassuring the local population, maintaining vehicles and equipment in extreme conditions, constantly seeking the enemy and remaining calm and firm in the face of Rocket Propelled Grenade ambush or mortar or rocket attack, and yet measured and deadly in response, have proved to be the corner stone of the Household Cavalry, and many of these attributes are forged, in part, at the Mounted Regiment.

By October 2008 all Squadrons of the Household Cavalry Regiment will be back together again in Windsor, safely returned to their families – the hidden strength of the Regiment. For most it will be a welcome chance to recover and relax, before preparing and training for the next deployment to Afghanistan. For some however, it won't be long before they are dusting off their equipment and refining drills, before launching once again into the public glare, but this time with the relative security of the 'Cav Black', back in the saddle and back on parade.

GRENADIER GUARDS

Grenadier Guards Actions and Heroes

Actions

The Storming of The Schellenberg 2 July 1704
(War of The Spanish Succession, Germany)

King Louis XIV was attempting to increase the power of France by putting his grandson on the Spanish throne and it fell to the Duke of Marlborough to lead Britain in the Grand Alliance with the Netherlands and the Holy Roman Empire against France and Bavaria. Marlborough became Colonel of the First Guards in 1704, the year in which he leapt into the public consciousness in the first of a series of spectacularly successful battles.

After a legendary 250-mile march from the Low Countries to Bavaria on the Danube, Marlborough came up against the Schellenberg hill fort above the Danube fortress of Donauwörth on 2 July, well defended by 13,500 Bavarians and French with 16 guns. The Duke decided to attack immediately even though his 25,000 troops and a few field guns had just completed a 16-hour forced march. They had to attack uphill, crossing a series of ditches before storming the breastworks, all the while receiving direct cannon fire. The spearhead that was inevitably in the most dangerous position, and thus known as the Forlorn Hope, was found by the Grenadier Company of the First Guards.

As well as his musket, every soldier carried a fascine (a bundle of sticks) to assist in crossing the ditches. Consequently he was unable to use his musket during the advance, which began just before 6 pm. Despite heavy casualties being inflicted by the enemy batteries, the lines moved steadily forward. A short distance from the breastworks heavy musketry fire tore gaps in the advancing infantry and the confident Bavarians sortied out to counter-attack. The First Guards had lost all their senior officers and about half their strength. The Grenadier Company which had been 82 men now emerged with only 23. Incredibly they reformed, faced the counter-attack and drove the Bavarians back to their trenches. For over an hour there was desperate hand-to-hand fighting on the parapets but the First Guards could not quite overwhelm the defenders.

It was only once Marlborough had launched two further assaults that the combined efforts of the allies prevailed. Unable to escape across the river when a bridge collapsed, half of the Bavarian army was destroyed.

The First Guards Grenadier Company was commanded by Colonel Lord Mordaunt and, incredibly, he was one of the survivors who escaped

Above: Grenadiers lead the assault on Schellenberg – only a quarter of them emerged. Watercolour by Reginald Wymer, c.1910.

Opposite: A private in the Grenadier Company of the 1st Foot Guards, from a tapestry in Blenheim Palace.

Left: A Grenadier Guardsman in ceremonial dress carrying an SA80 rifle. Even when on ceremonial duty, the Foot Guards always parade with the issue personal weapon of the day.

Grenadier Guards

Colonel of the Regiment: Field Marshal HRH The Prince Philip, Duke of Edinburgh KG, KT, OM, GBE, AC, QSO

Formed: June 1656

Role Today: Light role infantry battalion, with Nijmegen Company on Public Duties.

Battle Honours: Tangier 1680, Namur 1695, Gibraltar 1704–5, Blenheim, Ramillies, Oudenarde, Malplaquet, Dettingen, Lincelles, Egmont-op-Zee, Corunna, Barrosa, Nive, Peninsula, Waterloo, Alma, Inkerman, Sevastopol, Tel-el-Kebir, Egypt 1882, Suakin 1885, Khartoum, Modder River, South Africa 1899–1902 **The Great War:** Retreat from Mons, Marne 1914, Aisne 1914, Ypres 1914–17 Langemarck 1914, Gheluvelt, Nonne Bosschen, Neuve Chapelle Aubers, Festubert 1915, Loos, Somme 1916, '18, Ginchy, Flers-Courcellete, Morval, Pilckem, Menin Road, Poelcappelle, Passchendaele, Cambrai 1917, '18, St Quentin, Bapaume 1918, Arras 1918, Lys, Hazebrouck, Albert 1918, Scarpe 1918, Hindenburg Line, Havrincourt, Canal du Nord, Selle, Sambre, France and Flanders 1914–18 **The Second World War:** Dyle, Dunkirk 1940, North Africa 1942–3, Mareth, Medjez Plain, Salerno, Volturno Crossing, Monte Camino, Anzio, Cagny, Mont Pincon, Gothic Line, Nijmegen, Battaglia, Reichswald, Rhine, Italy 1943–5, North-West Europe 1940, 44–5; **Post Second World War:** Gulf 1991, Wadi Al Batin

Uniform: The senior regiment of Foot Guards, the Grenadiers have the following identifying features: a flaming grenade on the buttons, the buttons evenly spaced on the tunic, braid on the collar, a white plume on the left side of the bearskin and a red cap band on the forage cap. The grouping of buttons on the tunic is a common way to distinguish between the regiments of Foot Guards. Grenadier Guards' buttons are equally spaced and embossed with the Royal Cypher. Today Grenadier Guardsmen wear a cap badge of a 'grenade fired proper'.

Recruiting Areas: Birmingham, Bristol, Coventry, Derby, Grimsby, Manchester, Northampton, Nottingham, Oxford, Stoke-on-Trent and Wolverhampton.

Marches: Quick- *The British Grenadiers, The Grenadiers March*
Slow – *Scipio*, from the eponymous opera by Handel. He composed the march for the First Guards, presenting it to the regiment before he added it to the score of the opera.
The Duke of York's March

The Sovereign's Company: The tallest men are normally chosen for the Sovereign's Company though the height standard has varied over the years depending on the demands and successes of recruiting. Since 1908 the average height has varied between 6ft 1in and 6ft 4in, the lowest being in 1980 and 1986 and the highest in the Tercentenary year of 1956.

Allied Regiments: The Canadian Grenadier Guards, 1st Battalion The Royal Australian Regiment

Website address: www.grenade.org.uk

Recent Operations and Highlights

2001 – Northern Ireland – based in Belfast during the riot season and Holy Cross School episode.

2002 – Six -week exercise on Canadian plains training for conventional war with live ammunition and artillery.

2002 – Number 4 Guard on The Queen's Birthday Parade

2003 – Firefighting teams around East of London (6 hours of training), saw action at numerous car and building fires. Breathing Apparatus Response Teams (specialised teams with 4 weeks training) dealt with more complicated incidents.

2003 – Heathrow airport terrorist incident. Whole battalion deployed around airport and Windsor Great Park on 11 February in order to provide a sizeable armed presence on the ground.

2004 – The Queen's Company deployed as Spearhead Lead Element to Kosovo within 24 hours, in order to restore order around Pristina following inter-communal rioting.

2004/2005 – Bosnia – Banja Luka Metal Factory. Battalion saw transition from the NATO Stablisation Force to EUFOR (first EU force) on a six-month tour.

2005 – Ceremonial, Queen's Birthday Parade – Number 3 Guard.

2006 – Battalion move from Victoria Barracks, Windsor to Lille Barracks, Aldershot.

2006 – Rear Operations battle group, Shaibah Logistic Base. Four month tour. Patrolling Basra, southern Basra and Baghdad.

2006/7 – Recovered from Iraq, and went through shortest tour interval and deployed to Afghanistan.

2007 – Camp Shorabak, Observation, Mentoring and Liaison Teams. Mentoring both in barracks and on the ground fighting the Taliban throughout Helmand Province. A Grenadier was located in every outstation in Helmand Province. Five killed in action and 33 severely wounded.

2008 – Two Companies in rotation expected to deploy to Falkland Islands.

2008 – Battalion move to Wellington Barracks, London.

with three bullet holes through his clothing, while another officer, Colonel Richard Munden, had five through his hat. This rapid conquest of a Danube fortress and crossing place was of great psychological significance, the more so as it was rapidly followed by the Battle of Blenheim.

The Battle of Blenheim 13 August 1704
(War of The Spanish Succession, Germany)
Six weeks after the Schellenberg, The First Guards was held in reserve under Marlborough's personal control but on this occasion he launched the unit in the open with four battalions of the line against the Blenheim village position strongly defended by French troops. Twice they assaulted with great gallantry and, while unable to penetrate the defences, accomplished what was required of them by containing the French infantry in Blenheim village, preparing the way for the cavalry which broke through and inflicted a crushing defeat on the Franco-Bavarian army.

Admittedly the number of allied casualties, 12,000, was very high but the enemy lost 34,000 plus 60 guns and 300 Colours and Standards.

The battle put paid to the myth that Louis XIV's French were invincible, secured Imperial Vienna from them and knocked Bavaria out of the war. The First Guards were the only Household Troops to gain this Battle Honour.

The Waterloo Campaign 16 June–3 July 1815
(Napoleonic Wars, Belgium/France)

This battle won for the First Guards the name Grenadier (from 29 July 1815), the only title earned by a British regiment as a direct result of its performance in battle.

There were two brigades of Foot Guards. The 2nd Battalion (commanded by Colonel Sir Henry Askew) and the 3rd Battalion (commanded by Colonel the Honourable William Stuart) of the First Guards, formed 1st Guards Brigade under Major General Sir Peregrine Maitland.

Maitland, Major General Sir George Cooke (commanding the 1st all-Guards Division) and Lieutenant General Sir Henry Clinton, commanding 2nd Division were all officers of the First Guards. All Guards battalions were initially over 1,000 strong. On the first day the Guards marched 26 miles in 13 hours from their initial position to the west through a blisteringly hot June day. It was not a terribly auspicious start. Ensign Joseph St John wrote: 'By the time that we got three miles out of the town [Brussels] I began to feel ashamed of the Guards. Half the men were so tipsy that they kept tumbling into ditches, but really it was so ridiculous I could not help laughing.'

They reached the strategic crossroads at Quatre Bras at 5 pm on 16 June where the French had already gained possession of the vital feature of Bossu Wood. Both First Guards battalions were flung straight into the battle driving the French out with heavy losses and restoring the line at the cost of 548 killed and wounded.

Left: The Roll Call, a depiction of the
Battle of Inkerman by Elizabeth
Thompson, Lady Butler.

Below: John Churchill, 1st Duke of Marlborough, Captain-General
of the English forces and Master-General of the Ordnance, c.1702.
Oil on canvas, attributed to Michael Dahl.

Two days later, at Waterloo, the two First Guards light companies, under command of Lieutenant Colonel Lord Saltoun, held the walled garden and the orchard at Hougoumont Farm. These 200 men threw the French out of the orchard several times but were horribly mauled by an artillery piece at close range. The few survivors were eventually relieved and rejoined their own battalions on the ridge.

Hougoumont was held at a cost of over 600 Guards and allied casualties while the increasingly desperate French lost 8,000 men in their vain assaults.

In the main part of the battle the French cavalry attacked after the failure of their infantry. Wellington ordered the troops to take cover behind the reverse slope. Marshal Ney took this to be a withdrawal and ordered an attack by 5,000 cavalry. The First Guards and other infantry battalions formed 'square' and Wellington took his place in the square of the 2nd Battalion.

The French horsemen charged five times for over an hour but were beaten off. Then two fresh infantry battalions of the 3rd Chasseurs closely followed by the 4th Chasseurs assaulted two exhausted battalions of the First Guards. Wellington waited calmly until the enemy were only 40 yards away before announcing 'Now Maitland, now's your time.' The repulse of Napoleon's Imperial Guard marked the end of a European era. Only 15 days later Paris surrendered to Wellington and Blücher's victorious armies.

Grenadier Heroes
John Churchill, Prince of Mindelheim (Bavaria) and
1st Duke of Marlborough, KG (1650–1722)

John Churchill, Duke of Marlborough was without doubt the greatest soldier to have served in the ranks of the First Guards. He became Ensign (junior officer) of the King's Company in the First Guards in

1667 and served as a volunteer in Tangier the following year. In 1685 he played a significant part in suppressing the Monmouth rebellion, two battalions of the First Guards coming under his command. King James II made him a Lieutenant General, and still aged only 35, he had virtual command of the Army. However, it was only three years later that he transferred his allegiance to Prince William of Orange, shortly to relieve James of his throne in the 'Glorious Revolution'. Created Earl of Marlborough, Churchill fought successfully for King William III in Ireland. As Queen Anne's Captain General between 1702 and 1711 the Duke directed ten successful allied campaigns against Louis XIV winning 30 sieges (Lille being the most famous) and a series of celebrated pitched battles against the French including Blenheim 1704, Ramillies 1706, Oudenarde 1708 and Malplaquet 1709. He was Colonel of the First Guards from 1704 until his death.

'Corporal John' was an opportunist, often cunning and devious and, though generally admired, was unstinting in pursuit of wealth, honours and status. But to his men he was a god. 'He never fought a battle he did not win, nor besieged a town he did not take', wrote one early biographer. The Duke was almost recklessly brave and was nearly killed on more than one occasion. He was energetic and tireless, a fine tactician and strategist, skilled diplomat and a first-class administrator. His military judgement was flawless.

General Sir George Higginson GCB, GCVO (1826–1927)

George Higginson was a towering figure in Victorian times and beyond, living to the tremendous age of 101 and being known as the 'Father of the Guards'. He joined the Regiment in 1845, to be greeted by the Quartermaster, who had been his father's colour sergeant at Corunna.

Being both able and industrious, Higginson was soon Adjutant. For several years he virtually ran the 3rd Battalion, his commanding officers dropping in now and then to pursue their hobby. In the Crimea he was present at every major action and played a notable part in saving the Colours at Inkerman. He was immortalised as the mounted figure in Lady Butler's famous 1874 painting *The Roll Call*. He served the rest of the campaign as a brigade major and adapted himself well to the grim winter conditions, keeping his feet warm on an 18-pounder shot heated on the fire. His mother at home proved equally practical. He sent her his bearskin cap, peppered with Russian bullet holes, expecting her to display it reverently in a glass case. She sliced off the end and turned it into a muff!

He commanded 2nd Battalion Grenadier Guards from 1870 to 1877 and progressed to senior commands at Horse Guards and the Tower of London. On his centenary the Regiment marched through his home town of Marlow-on-Thames and the General visited the 1st Battalion at Windsor. There, the youngest drummer presented him with a basket of roses. 'Take them away boy', growled the old warrior with a curl to his lip, 'and give them to your girlfriend.'

Field Marshal John Vereker, Viscount Gort VC GCB, CBE, DSO and 2 Bars, MVO, MC (1886–1946)

Lord Gort achieved the astonishing count of five decorations for gallantry. Only 32 when he took command of a battalion, he was promoted from Brigadier to full General in the space of three years in the 1930s and appointed Chief of the Imperial General Staff (head of the Army). He led the British Expeditionary Force to France in 1939, and in May 1940 took the crucial decision, against the express wishes of the British War Cabinet and the French high command, to withdraw to Dunkirk, thereby saving the greater part of his force.

During the Great War, after a frustrating time at General Headquarters, Gort was given command of the 4th Grenadiers in April 1917 and led them with great distinction in the offensive battles of Third Ypres and Cambrai, being wounded on each occasion. In 1918 he took over the 1st Battalion to face the Ludendorff offensive and then to turn the tables in the final 'Hundred Days' advance of the war. Showing leadership and bravery of the highest order, he led the attack on the Premy Ridge, by the Canal du Nord in September 1918, fearlessly disregarding German fire. Though twice wounded, he forced himself on and would not be

Above: General Lord Gort VC saluting the sentry outside the War Office the day after his return from the 'Flaming Hell' of Flanders and Dunkirk, June 1940.

Below: Training in Belize in 2007.

evacuated until the success signals had gone up. 'The sight of this dauntless man, with his square figure, clipped moustache, fair windswept hair, cap tilted over his left ear and blood soaked bandages, leaping into action, stirred our hearts and impelled us to efforts we thought were beyond our powers.' He was awarded the Victoria Cross.

He commanded the Regiment from 1930 to 1932 and only five years later he was appointed Chief of the Imperial General Staff by Leslie Hore-Belisha, the reforming Secretary of State for War.

Although Gort's decision to withdraw to Dunkirk damaged his own prospects, he preserved an army that helped deter Hitler from invading and then one able to fight against Germany in North Africa and Italy before returning to Normandy four years later to finish the job. Back in England Lord Gort became Inspector General to the Forces before being appointed in succession: Governor of Gibraltar, Governor of Malta during the last few months of its heroic siege, High Commissioner for Palestine and Transjordan. Tragically, Gort died young of cancer. His Chief Secretary in Palestine gave this verdict: 'He was the finest man I ever served. Like Gideon, he was a mighty man of valour.'

General the Lord Jeffreys KCB, KCVO, CMG (1878–1960)

George Jeffreys, descended from the brother of the notorious 17th-century judge, was known as 'Ma', after a lady of that name who kept a house of ill-repute in Kensington in the 1890s. Perhaps she was more disciplinary than motherly, for certainly he was, and sometimes 'Ma' was taken for 'Martinet'.

Jeffreys joined the Regiment in 1898 and served at Omdurman and in South Africa. In 1914 he was commanding the Guards Depot when sent to be second in command of the 2nd Battalion, which he led for much of the Retreat from Mons, the Battles of the Marne and the Aisne. He took over command in 1915 and remained on the Western Front for the rest of the war, except for a period in 1916 when recovering from severe wounds. By 1918 he was a Major General, commanding the 19th Division.

He was General Officer Commanding London District at the time of the 1926 General Strike and later GOC-in-C Southern Command in India. On retirement he became MP for Petersfield in Surrey. In 1952 he was created a Baron and appointed Colonel of the Regiment, the first outside the Royal Family since The Duke of Wellington.

Lieutenant Colonel Fred Turner OBE, DCM (1898–1968)

George Frederick Godwin Turner enlisted in November 1915. In the last few weeks of 1918, just before the war drew to a close, he won the Distinguished Conduct Medal during the Battle of the Canal du Nord. As a corporal of the 2nd Battalion he maintained communications between his battalion and company headquarters under conditions of the utmost difficulty and danger.

A champion shot and water polo player, he was a Company Sergeant Major within five years and in 1934 became Regimental Sergeant Major of the Guards Depot, quickly moving onto the same post in the 3rd Battalion, and in 1939, becoming its Quartermaster.

Here he would instruct the young officers that 'no gentleman consents to serve beyond the range of a medium [5.5in-calibre] gun'. He saw his battalion through the exhausting and desperate days of the Dunkirk campaign. Over 21 miles of the retreat he was said to have fired 21 shots and accounted for 21 enemy. He went on to serve in the headquarters of British First Army in North Africa, where in May 1943 he celebrated victory there with the three Grenadier battalions in theatre. Moving on to the Second Army Turner was promoted to Lieutenant Colonel. As well as the MBE advanced to OBE in 1944, he was awarded the Croix de Guerre with Gilt Star.

He ended a life of exceptional service as a Military Knight of Windsor. His funeral in St George's Chapel drew one of the greatest gatherings of Grenadiers ever remembered.

Lance Corporal Harry Nicholls VC (1915–75)

Harry Nicholls of the 3rd Battalion Grenadier Guards won the first Victoria Cross of the Second World War to go to a non-commissioned officer or soldier.

A Nottingham man and one of a family of 13, Nicholls enlisted in 1936 and soon distinguished himself as a boxer, becoming both the British Army and Imperial Services heavyweight champion.

On 21 May 1940, the Battalion was dug in along the west bank of the River Escaut (Scheldt) in Belgium. Lance Corporal Nicholls was commanding a ten-man section in the right-forward platoon of his company when ordered to counter-attack a surprise German river assault crossing mounted in great strength. At the very start of the advance he was wounded in the arm by shrapnel, but continued to lead his section forward. As the company came over a small ridge, the enemy opened heavy machine-gun fire at short range.

Realising the danger to his company, Nicholls immediately seized a Bren gun and dashed forward, firing from the hip. He succeeded in silencing the machine gun, and then two others, in spite of being severely wounded. He then went up on to a higher piece of ground and engaged the German infantry massed behind, causing many casualties, continuing to fire until he had no ammunition left. He was wounded at least four times in all but (as was later discovered) had forced the enemy to recross the river.

Lance Corporal Nicholls was reported to have been killed in action and in August 1940 his widow received his Victoria Cross from King George VI. It was not until many months later that he was discovered alive and in a prisoner-of-war camp. He was repatriated in May 1945, returned to Nottingham to a hero's welcome and was himself presented with his Victoria Cross by the King.

It is believed that this is the only time a Victoria Cross has been presented twice.

Guardsman Nicholas Wintel, Grenadier Guards

Drummer

I used to play drum kits and I joined up because I thought the life would benefit me and I liked the idea of the machine-gun platoon which is the war role for Drummers. When I joined we had six side drummers and then about seven or eight people that played the flute. We play for the Queen's Guard. When our Battalion comes on we normally march them from the Palace and then we go to St James's.

In Afghanistan we were mainly doing fire support. We also did a few ambushes in case it got a bit hairy. I was there eight weeks and we got contacted by the Taliban about 27 times. It was quite lively. In one incident we were assaulting a compound and Guardsman Harrison was in front of me. He was lying on the other side of the door, I couldn't reach him, so we all started pumping grenades over the top of this hill. He was getting shrapnel in the back of his legs. A bullet must have ricocheted off his head and then bounced out of his helmet. He lost his right eye and the side of his face.

Times have changed. I spoke to an old Drummer who was in during the 1970s and he comes up to help us out with a few things and he goes 'I wouldn't like to be doing what you are doing, because we never used to do the machine guns'.

I would like to be Drum Major one day but apparently I'm too short. You have to be over 6ft to be a Drum Major. Anyone in the Queen's Company has to be over 6ft 1 in.

Captain Robert Nairac GC (1948–77)

Robert Laurence Nairac joined the Regiment from Oxford University and Sandhurst in 1973. In a short four years he undertook four tours of duty in Northern Ireland, where he proved to have conspicuous abilities. In his fourth tour he was a liaison officer at the headquarters of 3rd Infantry Brigade, working on surveillance operations.

On the night of 14/15 May 1977 he was abducted from a village in South Armagh by at least seven men. Despite fierce resistance, he was overpowered and taken over the border into the Republic of Ireland where he was subjected to a succession of exceptionally savage assaults in an attempt to extract information that would have put other lives and future operations at serious risk. These efforts to break his will failed entirely. Weakened as he was in strength – though not in spirit – by the brutality, he made repeated and spirited attempts to escape, but on each occasion was eventually overpowered by the weight of the numbers against him.

After several hours in the hands of his captors, Captain Nairac was callously murdered by a gunman of the Provisional Irish Republican Army, who had been summoned to the scene. His assassin subsequently said, 'he never told us anything'.

Six terrorists were later convicted and jailed for his kidnap and murder, but his body was never found. Nairac was awarded, posthumously, the only George Cross ever to go to a Grenadier.

Left: Captain Robert Nairac GC.

Above: Guardsmen Harrison and Bangham in Kajaki, Afghanistan, 2007.

LIFE ON THE FRONT LINE: 1st Battalion Grenadier Guards, 2007

Lieutenant Colonel Carew Hatherley

The 1st Battalion Grenadier Guards arrived in Afghanistan in March 2007, only six months after returning from a tour in Iraq. Although deployed as a battle group, with the full Grenadier headquarters, we did not operate together but were spread the length and breadth of Helmand Province. The Grenadier main effort was to train and mentor the entire 3rd Brigade of the Afghan National Army, an infantry brigade just under 3,000 strong. Based on The Queen's, Number Two and Inkerman Companies along with Headquarters Company, just over 200 Grenadiers embedded themselves in March and did not leave the side of their Afghans until the end of the tour late in September. From the very first day we deployed into the Afghan camp thirty minutes drive away from the main British Camp Bastion. This method of teaming up with specific Afghan battalions from the very first day was based on the successful model used by the SAS in the Oman though, as with everything else in life, the best or right way of doing things is normally the hardest – in this case it was no different. Mentoring took place at every level: from myself at brigade command level to guardsmen at section and sometimes platoon level. Wherever the Afghans went, and whatever they did, we were by their side. At times it was nothing short of ferocious: close range, full-on warfighting, with no quarter given by either side.

We decided early on to try to deploy the entire battalion on the tour and because the mentoring job required mainly officers and seniors we were able to reform Number Three Company, which had gone to the wall in 1993. Initially deployed to Garmsir in the southern area of operations, they conducted company level operations very much on their own, with only the gunners to back them up with fire support if they got into really heavy fire fights or

the Taliban tried assaulting their position. They lived in the most austere conditions, made contact with the Taliban on average about four times a day and (as with the rest of the Grenadier battle group) gave them a bloody nose on every occasion.

Our Reconnaissance Platoon, bumped up in numbers by some of our snipers, mortarmen and anti-tankers, made up well over two-thirds of the Brigade Reconnaissance Force (BRF). This formed the eyes and ears of Task Force Helmand, also operating under the toughest and most arduous conditions and carrying out their missions with bravery and discipline – and modesty at the quality of information they were providing. At times they were used as an offensive grouping, which they seem to have thoroughly enjoyed. Secretive at all times, even with other Grenadiers, they became prime targets for merciless ribbing about what they where actually up to when they left camp on missions.

Forty more of the Battalion deployed as part of Somme Company, The London Regiment, by chance the Territorial Regiment to which the Foot Guards are now affiliated. We embedded one of our best Company Sergeant Majors with them long before they started mobilisation and incorporated them in all Battalion training events. As a result they reached a higher standard than is normal for the TA and, besides simply manning sangars in Camp Bastion, were often used to protect firebases in the Helmand Valley and sometimes as platoons within regular companies on offensive operations, seeing some quite ferocious engagements with the Taliban. Other individual Grenadiers filled various posts with the Camp Bastion organisation, from clerks to unit stores accountants. Two Grenadier rifle sections and two mortar teams back-filled the Royal Anglian battle group. All set the highest example.

The risks to be encountered in Afghanistan were serious. Five Grenadiers were killed and many more injured. Those who say that the young men who join our proud regiment belong to the Playstation generation could not be more wrong. Every Grenadier who came to Afghanistan was put in harm's way, often in the most austere and testing circumstances. The fortitude, good humour and sheer guts shown by the youngest of them was

amazing, though not unexpected. They know, as all past Grenadiers do also, that they belong to something unique. The kit and equipment may now be more complex, but the manner in which Grenadiers go about their business has not changed – and thank goodness for it.

Guardsmen David Atherton, Simon Davison, Neil Downes, Daryl Hickey and Daniel Probyn died in different circumstances but were all taking the fight to the Taliban. Thirty-two Grenadiers were wounded in action, with injuries ranging from limbs being amputated, to loss of hearing or eyesight, to gunshot and fragmentation wounds. Of those, four were officers, eleven guardsmen, four corporals and thirteen members of the Sergeants' Mess. Forty-five more of the battle group sustained injuries and sickness when out of contact with the enemy, including broken bones, dislocations, scorpion stings, dengue fever and malaria. A number returned home on compassionate grounds, following our traditional attention to the importance of families. Those injured will require our fullest support.

The stories of dramatic fighting with the Taliban were accompanied by those of individual acts of heroism: the Grenadier who pinched the end of a bleeding artery with one hand and drove his badly injured comrade to safety with the other; the Grenadier who dashed out into the middle of an ambush area to drag to safety another soldier critically injured and unable to move; the Grenadier who prodded a safe lane through a minefield with his bayonet (after one vehicle had already been destroyed) so that a casualty could be evacuated safely by helicopter; the Grenadier who fought alongside and urged on his Afghans to victory against a stiffly contested Taliban stronghold despite being knocked off his feet twice in one hour; the Grenadier sniper with 38 confirmed kills. Some will be recognised in the Operational Honours and Awards list. Many others will not – there are never enough awards to go round – but their contribution to the success of this tour is none the less impressive.

The Battalion is re-invigorated by its experiences in Afghanistan. The Regiment can hold its head high. We achieved much in Afghanistan. Helmand is a better place for the ordinary Afghan, but more than that we proved the 1st Grenadiers to be every bit as good as (if not better than) the best of British infantry battalions. Past and present of all ranks can be rightly proud of their heritage, for it is the efforts of those throughout our recent history, and not just those serving now, that have set the foundations for what the Battalion achieved. In the face of extreme danger every soldier of the Battalion held his ground and prosecuted the defeat of the Taliban wherever and however he was asked to do it. In time-honoured fashion Grenadiers fought shoulder to shoulder and set the highest standards for both the Afghan National Army and other British units to emulate.

The war is by no means over: the Battalion expects to return to Afghanistan in 2009.

COLDSTREAM GUARDS

Coldstream Guards Actions and Heroes

Actions

The Battle of Dunbar 3 September 1650 (Scotland)

In June 1650 Charles II landed in Scotland and was proclaimed King, and the Commonwealth government in England found itself threatened by a Scots invasion. The then Captain General Oliver Cromwell was recalled from Ireland and ordered north with 3,500 cavalry and 7,500 infantrymen, mostly New Model Army veterans: he took the experienced George Monck with him as a supernumerary Colonel. On 11 July Monck was given a regiment formed from five companies apiece of Sir Arthur Hazelrigg's and Colonel George Fenwick's Regiments.

General David Leslie, the veteran Scots commander, occupied strong positions around Edinburgh and waited for Cromwell to attack; the latter established a base at the port of Dunbar and sent forces to reconnoitre Leslie's positions. Following skirmishes in poor weather and rough terrain, Cromwell, up to 5,000 of whose men were suffering from sickness, withdrew towards Dunbar, hoping to entice the Scots into a battle. Leslie was persuaded to follow by a council of war, however, and occupied Doon (or Doun) Hill, three miles south of Dunbar, cutting Cromwell's land supply route to Berwick-on-Tweed and England. On 2 September the Scots moved troops into lower, less broken ground, probably facing the road south, their left protected by the Brox (now Brock) Burn, a swollen stream, and their backs to Doon Hill. The deployment threatened the New Model Army – but the move onto lower ground exposed the Scots to attack by Cromwell's cavalry.

Cromwell and Major General John Lambert thought that the Scots, despite their 2:1 advantage, had over-extended and weakened their line (now nearly two miles long). They held a council of war, which initiated a night outflanking movement and a dawn attack against the Scots' right flank. The night was wet and windy, muffling sounds of movement: at 4 am on 3 September Lambert with six regiments of horse and Monck with three regiments of foot surprised the Scots right wing. Leslie's men recovered and fought back bravely. Cromwell then emerged from an outflanking movement and, with local superiority in numbers rolled up the Scots cavalry on the right, precipitating a collapse in the centre. Many Scotsmen on Doon Hill slipped away as their countrymen were cut down by the New Model Army.

Above inset: Dunbar Medal. The Coldstream Guards are the only unamalgamated regiment to have fought on that occasion and to be in possession of one of these medals.

Left: Cromwell defeats the Scots at the Battle of Dunbar, 3 September 1650. From Smith's History of the Rebellion, *c.1750.*

Left: Before going on guard at Windsor Castle, members of the Coldstream Guards rehearse the guard mount at Victoria Barracks.

Coldstream Guards

Colonel of the Regiment: General Sir Michael Rose KCB, CBE, DSO, QGM DL

Formed: 13 August 1650

Role Today: Light role infantry battalion, with Number 7 Company on Public Duties.

Battle Honours: Tangier 1680, Namur 1695, Gibraltar 1704–5, Oudenarde, Malplaquet, Dettingen, Lincelles, Egypt [the Sphinx surmounted by 'Egypt'], Talavera, Barrosa, Fuentes d'Onor, Salamanca, Nive, Peninsula, Waterloo, Alma, Inkerman, Sevastopol, Tel-el-Kebir, Egypt 1882, Suakin 1885, Modder River, South Africa 1899–1902 **The Great War:** Mons, Retreat from Mons, Marne 1914, Aisne 1914, Ypres 1914, '17, Langemarck 1914, Gheluvelt, Nonne Bosschen, Givenchy 1914, Neuve Chapelle, Aubers, Festubert 1915, Loos, Mount Sorrel, Somme 1916, '18, Flers-Courcelette, Morval, Pilckem, Menin Road, Poelcappelle, Passchendaele, Cambrai 1917, '18, St Quentin, Bapaume 1918, Arras 1918, Lys, Hazebrouck, Albert 1918, Scarpe 1918, Drocourt-Quéant, Hindenburg Line, Havrincourt, Canal du Nord, Selle, Sambre, France and Flanders 1914–18 **The Second World War:** Dyle, Defence of Escaut, Dunkirk 1940, Cagny, Mont Pincon, Quarry Hill, Estry, Heppen, Nederrijn, Venraij, Meijel, Roer, Rhineland, Reichswald, Cleve, Goch, Moyland, Hochwald, Rhine, Lingen, Uelzen, North-West Europe 1940, 44–5, Egyptian Frontier 1940, Sidi Barrani, Halfaya 1941, Tobruk 1941, 1942, Msus, Knightsbridge, Defence of Alamein Line, Medenine, Mareth, Longstop Hill 1942, Sbiba, Steamroller Farm, Tunis, Hammam Lif, North Africa 1940–3, Salerno, Battipaglia, Cappezano, Volturno Crossing, Monte Camino, Calabritto, Garigliano Crossing, Monte Ornito, Monte Piccolo, Capture of Perugia, Arezzo, Advance to Florence, Monte Domini, Catarelto Ridge, Argenta Gap, Italy 1943–5; **Post Second World War:** Gulf 1991

Uniform: Garter Star on the buttons, buttons grouped in two on the front of the tunic, the Garter Star again on the collar, a red plume on the right of the bearskin cap and a white cap band on their forage caps.

Special Day: St George's Day, 23 April

Recruiting Areas: Northumberland, Yorkshire, East Anglia, Sussex, Cornwall, as well as in Coldstream itself.

Marches: Quick *Milanollo*
Slow *Figaro* (Mozart)

Traditional Nickname: Lilywhites

Motto: *Nulli Secundus* (Second to None) (and *Honi Soit Qui Mal y Pense*, Shame on Those Who Evil Think, on the Garter Star)

Allied Regiments: Governor General's Foot Guards (Canada), 2nd Battalion The Royal Australian Regiment

Website: www.army.mod.uk/coldstreamguards

Recent Operations and Highlights

2003 – The Battalion left Londonderry, Northern Ireland at Easter where it was part of 8th Infantry Brigade, and moved to Lille Barracks, Aldershot. There it became part of 12th Mechanized Brigade and spent the remainder of the year starting the Bowman combat radio trials and going through mechanised conversion for the Saxon, a wheeled armoured personnel carrier since replaced by Bulldog.

2004 – The majority of the year was spent carrying out Bowman radio trials.

2005 – This year was spent in preparation for and carrying out an operational tour in Iraq on Operation TELIC 6. Number 1 Company went to Al Amarah with the 1st Battalion Staffordshire Regiment battle group. Numbers 2 and 3 Companies and A Company 1st Staffords went to Basra, and formed the Coldstream Guards battle group based in the Shatt al-Arab Hotel. The tour lasted from April to October. Sadly, Guardsman Wakefield and Sergeant Hickey were killed by roadside bombs.

2006 – The Battalion moved to Windsor and became part of London District, performing ceremonial duties, including Queen's Guards, Windsor Castle Guards and any other ceremonial duties. Several individuals were away on Operation HERRICK in Afghanistan as part of the Operational Mentoring and Liaison Teams. These included Lance Sergeants Swift and Conibear both of whom did particularly well on what was a very challenging tour. Captain Guy Lock, commander of the Guards Parachute Platoon, received a serious shrapnel wound from a grenade on this tour.

2007 – Towards the end of 2006 the Battalion was warned that it would become part of the 52nd Brigade for a tour in Afghanistan. The Battalion deployed in October.

They are currently a light role battalion, equipped with all the usual infantry weapons and now fully digitized with Bowman Carriers.

Cromwell rallied his men; a short Psalm was sung; and pursuit started. Around 300-500 Scotsmen were killed and about 1,000 were wounded; 6,000 were taken prisoner. Cromwell claimed only 20 men killed. Monck's Regiment and the army received the silver Dunbar Medal, the first award struck for a victory in British military history.

The Battle of Waterloo – Hougoumont Farm 18 June 1815 (Napoleonic Wars)

Following his escape from Elba in March 1815, Napoleon's lightning thrust towards the Low Countries took the Allies by surprise. Many of Wellington's veterans were in America. However, the Duke had some experienced troops, including two Guards Brigades, in Belgium. When Napoleon attempted to knock out both Wellington, and Blücher's Prussians, south of Brussels in June 1815, he found the British vanguard, including Guardsmen, holding the key crossroads at Quatre Bras. The allies had time to deploy onto the ridge at Waterloo.

Hougoumont sits on rising ground and in 1815 the farm, its chateau and orchards concealed a sunken road offering a way to outflank the Waterloo position. Wellington regarded the Farm, forward of the Allied lines, as 'vital ground' which must be held. He sent four Foot Guards Light [infantry] Companies (400 men) under Lieutenant Colonel James Macdonell to defend it, and placed 900 German troops in woods nearby.

Napoleon's attack was opened against Hougoumont by a division of Lieutenant General Count Honoré Reille's 14,000-strong I Corps around 11.30 am on 18 June. By midday, the outposts had been pushed out of the orchards beyond the farm, but the first attack had been driven off. A second attack was mounted from the south and west, and French infantry forced their way into the farmyard through the north gate. Hand-to-hand fighting ensued, and Colonel Macdonell with three Coldstream officers, Corporals James and Joseph Graham (brothers) and four from the Third Guards, managed to reach the gates, closing them by brute force. Some 700 men of 2nd Battalion Coldstream Guards counter-attacked, pushing the French back, and reinforced Hougoumont. During the next hour two more French attacks were made, and a further assault was mounted between 2 and 3 pm. A crisis followed as French howitzers set the buildings ablaze, and ammunition ran short: two more attacks were mounted against Hougoumont.

Following the Imperial Guard's defeat, the defenders of Hougoumont, exhausted from seven attacks over nearly nine hours tended their wounded. The Coldstream had suffered heavily, losing 348 of all ranks, nearly 50 per cent of their strength: the Third Guards lost 236 men.

'The success of the Battle of Waterloo', Wellington said, 'turned on the closing of the gates at Hougoumont.' Colonel Macdonell, named 'the bravest man in England' shared his award with James Graham, by now a Sergeant. To this day Coldstream Sergeants hang a 'brick' from Hougoumont over the bar at Christmas to commemorate the extraordinary bravery shown at the Belgian chateau and orchard.

Right: Closing the Gate at Hougoumont, by Robert Gibb, c.1905.

The Battle of The Hindenburg Line 12 September–9 October 1918 (France)

Following its battering during the Battle of the Somme in 1916, the German Army made a strategic withdrawal of 10 miles in March 1917 to well-prepared defences codenamed 'Alberich'. The Hindenburg Line, as the Allies called it, comprised several defensive zones in depth with carefully sited reinforced concrete bunkers, barbed wire, trenches and artillery positions.

In August 1918 the Anglo-French counter-offensive at Amiens employed infantry supported by tanks, artillery and aircraft, and achieved a major victory: from then on the British Expeditionary Force of five armies was on the offensive, attacking the Hindenburg Line and beyond. On 27 September the Guards Division assaulted the Canal du Nord, a dry canal forming a significant obstacle in the Hindenburg support line, between Bapaume and Cambrai, after a short but intense bombardment.

The 1st Battalion Coldstream Guards (2nd Guards Brigade) were ordered to seize crossings across the strongly defended Canal between Graincourt and Havrincourt, but were immediately held up by machine guns firing down the Canal. Acting Captain Cyril Frisby's Company came under fire from a machine-gun emplacement – 'Mouse Post' – under a ruined iron bridge. Frisby called for volunteers, and sent a party to give covering fire. With Lance Corporal Thomas Jackson and two others, Frisby dashed forward into the canal, despite intense close-range machine-gun fire, and rushed the post. Twelve men and two machine

Left: Members of the Coldstream Guards put on their kit in preparation for Guard mount at Windsor Castle.

Above: Captain Ian Liddell VC in Lingen, April 1945.

guns were captured, although Frisby was wounded in the leg. Silencing the machine guns allowed two companies to cross the canal, but the barrage had moved forward, and the Battalion was under fire from enemy positions on their left. Captain Frisby therefore consolidated his gains close to his objectives: by 5 pm another 300 Germans surrendered to him with 30 machine- guns, while the other battalions of the Guards Division moved forward and captured the Divisional objective, the significant Flesquières–Premy Chapel Ridge (see Gort VC).

Captain Frisby and Lance Corporal Jackson were both awarded the Victoria Cross. Tragically, Corporal Jackson, who helped capture another machine-gun post that day was killed shortly afterwards: his award was made posthumously. The action of 1st Coldstream contributed to the seizure of the Hindenburg support line, and for 158 casualties, to an advance of four miles (6 km) that day; it helped to break a strong defensive zone, and with it, the morale of the German Army on the Western Front. On the very next day Field Marshal Paul von Hindenburg and General Erich Ludendorff agreed that Germany had to request an immediate armistice.

The Attack at Lingen 2–5 April 1945 (Germany)

On 23 March 1945 Field Marshal Sir Bernard Montgomery's 21st Army Group began crossing the Rhine for the breakout into northern Germany. The Guards Armoured Division advanced from Rees via Enschede in Holland in the direction of Bremen, and the Coldstream Battalion Group – the 1st (Armoured) Battalion in Sherman tanks and the 5th Battalion as lorried infantry – was poised near Lingen as operations to cross the River Ems and Dortmund-Ems canal were planned.

On 2 April the Household Cavalry Regiment reported an intact bridge just north of Lingen, and Lieutenant Colonel R. F. S. Gooch, commanding 1st Coldstream, planned to seize the crossing with an attack using surprise from a sudden heavy bombardment fired as the Guardsmen attacked. Captain Ian Liddell made a reconnaissance with his officers, and saw large aircraft bombs wired up as demolition charges on the bridge, and a ten-foot high log barricade on the western end. Captain Liddell's plan was for a personal dash to cut the charges while his Number 3 Company, a squadron of tanks and artillery, fired at the enemy bank: his platoon commanders did not question this, such was the confidence that they had in their company commander.

At 4.30pm Major Peter Hunt's tanks opened fire, some of them also using rockets 'borrowed' from the Royal Air Force, and the artillery barrage landed among the German defenders who were queuing for food. One of the tank gunners saw a battery of camouflaged 88mm guns, and fire was switched onto them. Ian Liddell climbed the barricade and ran forward under intense fire, cutting the wires connecting the bombs, finally throwing his wire-cutters at the German officer attempting to detonate the charges. The leading platoon followed and the first tank charged the barricade. Within a few minutes the bridge, largely undamaged, was in British hands, and Coldstream tanks were on the far side. Fifty German defenders were prisoners, and around 40 lay dead; only one Guardsman had been killed and four were wounded.

'How [the company commander] came through all that firepower unhurt was a miracle', Guardsman Laws said '… his heroic act inspired us all.' Captain Ian Liddell was awarded the Victoria Cross but, tragically, the news of the decoration came through just after he had been killed by a stray bullet near Rotenburg only 18 days later.

Lance Corporal Nicholas Straney, Coldstream Guards

Why I Joined The Guards

All my family (from Leeds) have been in the Army. My father was a chef in the Army Catering Corps and I was born in Germany in 1983. My uncle was in the Royal Signals for 35 years. He retired as a Major after rising through the ranks. He really wanted me to join the Coldstream, as they were the best regiment he had worked with. The sergeant in the recruiting office where I went was also Coldstream Guards. I didn't realise that the Guards wore tunic and bearskin. It was only when I got to training that I realised that I was an infantryman. I like the Army in general because of the security. I ski for the Army and the battalion ski team. My Dad was an army ski instructor. I've been skiing since I was about five years old. I go away four months every year to Val-d'Isère in the French Alps. Eight people normally go. The Coldstream Guards are very keen on skiing. I spent two years in Northern Ireland in Londonderry from May 2001 to

June 2003. I was there as a Guardsman within a patrol team. I went to Iraq on Operation TELIC 6 from April to October 2005 and we had the task of dealing with Al Amarah, capital of Maysan province on the Tigris. It was quite rough. Our battle group lost 10 killed and wounded. Number 1 Company was attached to 1st Battalion The Staffordshire Regiment. The Staffords obviously have a different way of doing things. We focus on appearance and want all standards to be high. I know other regiments say 'look at the bullshit they have to deal with' but we're not bothered. It's an all-round thing.

I'll definitely be in for as long as I can be. The way of life is too good. I don't know what I'd do if I left. I'm not friends with any of the lads I was at school with. I've got nothing in common with them. I'm waiting to get promoted to Lance Sergeant. It's definitely not dull. The ceremonial is a bit groundhog day but then you get away for a month. One company

went to South Africa for six weeks. The average Guardsman leaves after four years. I passed out with ten Coldstream Guardsmen and I am the only one left.

Operation TELIC 5, Al Jamyeat Police Station, Basra 2005 (Iraq)

In 2005 1st Battalion Coldstream Guards was deployed for six months 'keeping the peace' as the Basra City battle group on Operation TELIC in Iraq. The tour was characterised by high temperatures, and a volatile situation in which well-armed militia groups and terrorist elements mounted numerous attacks.

The dramatic pictures of a burning soldier jumping from a Warrior vehicle captured global news headlines, but few realised the background. The Coldstream battle group, under Lieutenant Colonel Nick Henderson, had been working closely with the Iraqi Police Service, which was inexperienced and heavily influenced by militias in Basra. On 19 September a 'Contact' involving two soldiers was reported to the Operations Room, and patrols were diverted to look for the men: it appeared that the two had been taken to the Al Jamyeat Police Station, in a hardline Shia area. A Company, the Staffordshire Regiment, the battle group Armoured Infantry Company, supported by dismounted Guardsmen, deployed to cordon the Police Station, containing the distrusted 'Department of Internal Affairs' (DIA) Police contingent, while a Brigade Negotiating Team went inside. The Iraqis responded by deploying 200 paramilitary police who levelled cocked weapons at battle group elements: a tense stand-off ensued.

It became clear that the DIA Police had asked the Mahdi Army militia to arrange a riot as a distraction, and 150 rioters with stones, timber and petrol bombs attacked the cordon, later attempting to kidnap soldiers. The angry mob increased to 500-1000 strong and

Number 2 Company advanced to push the rioters away from the Police Station, in temperatures of 50°C, with incoming small arms fire and buckets of petrol as well as petrol bombs being thrown. Reinforcements were received and casualties were evacuated by helicopter. Orders were later given to thin out the cordon, and to prepare for further operations as darkness fell: troops entered the police station only to discover that the detainees had been handed over to the Mahdi militia. The detainees and negotiators were found and the 'incident was closed' after midnight.

Coldstreamers and Staffords stood their ground in boiling heat against hostile crowds for over ten hours, displaying outstanding courage, determination, initiative and restraint. Despite 24 'listed' casualties and many minor injuries, the battle group Commander and the battle group to a man felt strongly that they had done the right thing to ensure the release of their comrades in a very tense situation.

Coldstream Heroes

George Monck, 1st Duke of Albemarle (1608–70)

Monck's family were Devon landowners and George, born a younger son, volunteered to fight under a kinsman on the Duke of Buckingham's expedition against Cadiz in 1625. He saw service on the Isle de Ré and in the Netherlands before distinguishing himself at the Siege of Breda (1637). He was given command of an English infantry regiment in 1639 and again in Ireland in 1642. He crossed to England to fight for King Charles I in 1643, but was captured at Nantwich in Cheshire the following January.

Below: General George Monck, c.1665.

dissolve and hold elections, and made contact with Charles II in exile. When the 'Convention' (Parliament) invited Charles to return, Monck welcomed the King at Dover: he was created Duke of Albemarle, a Knight of the Garter and Captain General. In 1661 Monck's Regiment, the last of the New Model Army, took up arms as the Lord General's Regiment of Foot Guards. When Monck died in 1670 his soldiers, who had enjoyed the contemptuous description 'Monck's men from Coldstream' became the Coldstream Regiment of Foot Guards; they felt it 'No Dishonourable Name'.

Monck demonstrated great bravery and tactical skill both on land and afloat. Resourceful, and with considerable influence in Parliament, Monck had a strong sense of duty to authority combined with an absence of personal ambition. He astutely judged the mood for change – and the King – rather than continued uncertainty in 1660.

Lieutenant General John, Baron Cutts of Gowran (*c.*1661–1707)

John Cutts was the son of an Essex squire born (probably) in 1661, and entered Catherine Hall (Cambridge) aged 15 although he did not take a degree. He joined the entourage of the Duke of Monmouth at the Hague, and became well known for his songs and verses. In 1686 he served in Charles, Duke of Lorraine's English volunteers against the Turks, showing great bravery at the capture of Buda. He then received his first Commission: as Adjutant-General to the Duke of Lorraine. He was commissioned as a lieutenant colonel commanding a regiment in the Netherlands in 1688, where General Hugh Mackay described him as 'an agreeable companion, with abundance of wit … but too much seized with vanity and self-conceit'.

Cutts, a regimental commanding officer, returned to England with William of Orange in 1688. In 1690 he served, again with distinction, at the Battle of the Boyne and was created Baron Gowran. He then commanded a brigade and received the surrender of Limerick. He fought and was wounded at Steenkirk in Flanders (1692), and took part in the unsuccessful 1694 Brest expedition. When Lieutenant General Thomas Talmash (Tollemache) died of his wounds from that venture, Cutts succeeded him as Colonel of the Coldstream Guards, and took command of a brigade at the siege of Namur, where his conspicuous courage in the final assault on the fortress earned him the nickname 'Salamander' for passing through enemy fire. Three years later, Whitehall Palace caught fire and Salamander again led his Coldstreamers into the heat to try to fight the flames.

Accompanying John Churchill, then Earl of Marlborough, to the Netherlands in 1701, Cutts was promoted Major General. A year later, as a Lieutenant General he led the storming party, 'like madmen without fear or wit' (Captain Robert Parker's description) against Fort St Michael (Venlo). However, he began to collect critics of his vainglory, including Dean (Jonathan) Swift who called Cutts as 'brave and brainless as the sword he wears'. In 1704 Cutts was the Duke of

After two years imprisoned in the Tower of London, Monck agreed to serve Parliament, and was appointed a Major General in Ireland from 1646–9. Forced to agree to an armistice, he was deprived of his command and censured by Parliament. Oliver Cromwell was impressed by Monck's abilities, however, and took him to Scotland where he commanded a regiment comprising loyal soldiers from an amalgamation of Sir Arthur Hazelrigg's and Colonel George Fenwick's Regiments. Monck and his regiment gave notable service at the Battle of Dunbar in September 1650 (see Coldstream Actions). During that decade he gained a reputation for efficiency and severity governing Scotland, while also becoming a successful 'General at Sea', destroying nine of Admiral Maarten Tromp's Dutch warships in 1653.

Monck was in Scotland during Cromwell's Protectorate, but supported Parliament when Major General John Lambert forcibly dissolved the Rump Parliament. On 8 December 1659 Monck moved to Coldstream, and, determined to avoid anarchy, set out for London with six regiments of Foot and four of Horse, 7,000 men in all, on 1 January 1660. On arrival Monck persuaded the Rump Parliament to

Marlborough's third in command, leading 12,000 British and German infantry in repeated attacks against the village strongpoint of Blenheim, pinning down 27 French battalions with his 16, a key role in the battle. In 1705 Cutts became Commander-in-Chief in Ireland; two years later this remarkable and colourful officer (who was also Member of Parliament for Newport and Governor of the Isle of Wight) died, not in the heat of battle, but of poor health.

General Sir James Macdonell GCB (*c.*1775–1857)

General Sir James Macdonell, a younger son of the chief of Glengarry in the Clan Macdonald, originally entered the army as an Ensign in 1793, and became a Lieutenant in the 78th Foot, the Ross-shire Buffs in 1794. He became a Captain in the 17th Light Dragoons in 1795, commanding a troop for nine years. Macdonell was appointed Major in the 78th Foot in 1804 and served under Sir John Moore at Hythe, Kent and then in southern Italy, at the Battle of Maida (1806). Macdonell received a gold medal for bravery at Maida; three years later he became a lieutenant colonel in the 78th.

In August 1811 Macdonell exchanged into the Coldstream Guards as a Captain and Lieutenant Colonel, and served with the 1st Battalion of the Regiment from May 1812 to January 1814 seeing action at Salamanca, Vittoria, Nivelle and Nive. He assumed command of 2nd Coldstream in the Netherlands in May 1814. On 17 June 1815 the Duke of Wellington directed Macdonell to take command of the Coldstream and Third Guards light [infantry] companies at Hougoumont Farm, on the right of the Allied position at Waterloo, with orders 'to defend the post to the last extremity'. The Farm was under attack for nine hours, but a critical moment occurred in the afternoon when French infantrymen fought their way in through the north gate. Macdonell rushed across with three other officers, the Graham brothers and four from the Third Guards, and being a powerfully built man threw his weight against the gates. The gates were eventually shut and barricaded, and Coldstream and other reinforcements moved up in support.

After Waterloo, when Wellington was approached with a sum of money for the 'bravest man in the Army', he nominated Sir James Macdonell. The latter felt strongly that the award should go to Sergeant James Graham, who duly received the accolade.

Macdonell was responsible for the successful defence and was knighted for his achievements at Waterloo. He continued in the Regiment after the War, becoming a Major General in 1825. In the 1830s he commanded Armagh District in Northern Ireland; he led a brigade in Canada during the unrest in 1834, and was later appointed Commander-in-Chief there. He was promoted full General in 1854 and raised to GCB in 1855, two years before his death.

Brigadier General John Vaughan Campbell VC, CMG, DSO (1876–1944) The 'Tally Ho' VC

John Campbell, the son of Ronald Campbell, a Coldstreamer recommended for the Victoria Cross (but who did not live to receive it) joined the Regiment in 1896 aged 20, and served from 1899 to 1903 in South Africa. He fought alongside 2nd Coldstream at the Modder River, Magersfontein and other actions, becoming Adjutant in December 1900. By 1903 he was a Captain, Mentioned in Dispatches and had received the Distinguished Service Order.

Guardsman David Underhill, Coldstream Guards

I am a 21-year-old from Cornwall who has served three and half years. My older brother worked in the officers' mess so I knew what it was all about.

I like a challenge. I fancied doing something different. I like the fitness side of things. I did a lot of sport before the Army and still do football and long-distance running. My speciality is 1,500m. A highlight so far was jungle training in Jamaica for six weeks. I was also part of the 2006 trials for the new Nuclear Biological and Chemical Defence respirator in Australia.

I was quite worried about Iraq before we went to Basra after seeing the news and everything but it wasn't too bad. I was a Light Support Weapon gunner. Most of the people were genuinely quite friendly. There was one little lad who came and chatted to us in our sangars [defensive positions] and would get us cans of coke.

I find drill the toughest thing. Two days on and one and half days off. It's the most draining. I didn't think I was going to make it through basic training so I'm proud I'm now in the Coldstream Guards.

Left: Brigadier General J.V. Campbell vc *(left, on the top of the tunnel arch) congratulates his 137th (Staffordshire) Brigade on capturing the St Quentin Canal, September 1918.*

Major General Sir George Burns GCVO, CB, DSO, OBE, MC (1911–97)

Several generations of Coldstreamers, from the Second World War to the First Gulf War and Bosnia eras, had the good fortune to know 'General George', who completed over 30 years regular service in the Regiment before serving another 28 as its Colonel.

George Burns was commissioned in 1932, joining friends in the Regiment rather than going into the City. After serving as ADC to the Viceroy of India, he returned to 1st Coldstream, deploying to France in 1939 and becoming Adjutant just before the German invasion of the Low Countries. The two Guards Brigades fought resolutely to hold the Dunkirk perimeter, and Captain Burns took over a company in action near Furnes (now Veurne), setting an example of coolness in danger and rallying its tired Guardsmen, for which he was awarded the Military Cross.

George Burns was later Brigade Major to 9th Infantry Brigade, and to the Divisional Support Group of the Guards Armoured Division when it was formed. In 1943 he was posted to Italy, where, shortly after his arrival, he took command of the 3rd Battalion in action on Monte Camino. Following another prolonged period under intense fire he was awarded the DSO. Guardsmen remembered 'Waggie' (his initials were WAGB) for his cheerfulness, disregard of danger, unlit pipe and invariable opening remark 'has anybody got a match?'.

Colonel George commanded 3rd Coldstream in the advance to Florence and on Monte Domini, until November 1944. After the war he was Brigade Major Household Brigade, and again commanded 3rd Coldstream in Palestine (1947–50). In 1955 he was commander 4th Guards Brigade in Germany, and then Major General commanding the Household Brigade and London District from 1959–62.

In 1966 he became 26th Colonel of the Coldstream. His contributions to the Senior Colonels Committee were much valued: he knew about leadership in action, and cared deeply about Guardsmen. He was also thankful to be able to stay on his horse during Queen's Birthday Parades. He always raised morale during Battalion visits, never failing to tease 'tail-end Charlie' Guardsmen guarding the rear, walking backwards on Northern Ireland patrols; Officers would stay up in relays during the night to entertain their tireless Colonel. He was equally enthusiastic in supporting the Regimental Association, the Jockey Club, and many other organisations near his Hertfordshire home. For very many George Burns epitomised the Regimental motto 'Second to None'.

During the First World War, Major Campbell joined 3rd Coldstream for the Battle of Loos (1915). In 1916 the Guards Division saw action during the Somme offensive in the Flers-Courcelette attacks (15 September) when tanks were first used. The 3rd Coldstream, under Lieutenant Colonel Campbell, was to advance with 2nd Coldstream on its left and the 1st on its right (for the only time in its history), over gently undulating, featureless ground from Ginchy to Les Boeufs village with a low ridge on the axis. Keeping track of distance or direction after the bombardments proved difficult.

Soon after Zero Hour (6.20 am) the advance was held up by machine guns. Colonel Campbell rallied the assaulting Guardsmen, who had become intermixed, with his Shropshire Harriers hunting horn, and charging the sunken lane position, captured several machine guns. Momentum took Campbell's men over three lines of trenches until they met resistance on the right. With few officers remaining, Campbell again sounded his hunting horn, and advanced another 800 yards, digging in with between 750 and 900 Guardsmen just short of the village by midday.

Colonel Campbell's Victoria Cross citation mentions that his personal gallantry and initiative at a very critical moment turned the fortunes of the day. Two months later, Campbell was promoted Brigadier General to command 137th (Staffordshire) Brigade (46th North Midland Division), which, on 29 September 1918, broke the Hindenburg Line at Bellenglise. The objective included a well-defended tunnel over the St Quentin Canal. Brigadier Campbell used ladders and a makeshift bridge: his men, wearing lifejackets from Channel ferries, crossed the canal with few casualties. The iconic photograph of New Army soldiers in a canal cutting being congratulated by their commander, captures 137th Brigade after this striking success.

Campbell was Regimental Lieutenant Colonel from 1923–27. He retired in 1933, and died on 22 May 1944. In addition to his courage, John Campbell was renowned for never asking people to do anything he would not do himself, his consideration for Guardsmen, sometimes contrary to 'normal form', and for his spontaneous warmth of friendliness.

LIFE ON THE FRONT LINE: 1st Battalion Coldstream Guards, 2007

Lieutenant Colonel George Waters

The 1st Battalion Coldstream Guards started to train in earnest for their deployment to Afghanistan on Operation HERRICK 7 in March 2007, six months before joining the counterinsurgency campaign in Helmand Province. The training embraced enduring low-level skills for all and the training of battle group Headquarters in running complex all-arms operations incorporating artillery, helicopters and close air support. It was also vital to ensure that all involved understood the nature of counterinsurgency and, in particular, how our actions would affect the perceptions of the local population – the key influence battle in which 'the population is the prize'. During the final mission rehearsal exercise with 52 Brigade, however, the Battalion received something of a shock: the Coldstream battle group was told that it was to be split up in order to allow the Danish battle group to take over the area previously assigned to the Coldstream. At the last moment, therefore, Coldstreamers prepared to deploy across Helmand Province and to Kabul.

Number 1 Company deployed into the high-threat environment of the capital as the Kabul Patrols Company tasked to provide security in Police District 9. The threat from suicide bombers has been particularly acute, which makes for a nerve-wracking atmosphere in which to patrol. Each additional bomb that explodes, particularly when combined with intelligence of yet more bombers in the city, adds to the tension. The Company in Kabul has undertaken daily patrols, Quick Reaction Forces and guard duties, interspersed with occasional Company surge operations. The importance of intelligence in counter-insurgency operations cannot be over-emphasised and the Company has devoted considerable efforts to this area: the arrest of Abdul Qader, a notorious Kabul 'bad hat', during a pre-planned Company operation on 16 January was a testament to their success in information gathering.

Number 3 Company has faced very different conditions in the 'Green Zone' of fertile ground near the Helmand River, north east of Gereshk, where the Company has been operating under command of the Danes. The difficulties of joint operations, poor communications, and paucity of helicopter flights, have left the Company somewhat isolated, much to the delight of Major Tom Charles, the Company Commander, who has his mission and Area of Operations, and has largely been left to get on with it. The Company received a very warm welcome from the Taliban on arrival, and Forward Operating Base (FOB) KEENAN was attacked on five days in the first week or so. The enemy have, however, steadily been pushed back to the degree that, halfway through the Coldstream tour, there is a secure zone of about five kilometres around the base. Fighting patrols in Company or Platoon strength have been combined with a strong focus on 'influence operations' to win the support of the locals. However, ultimately, no progress can be made without the willingness of Guardsmen to close with the enemy. Their courage and fighting

spirit, combined with their usual good humour in the most trying circumstances, has been inspirational. Every injured man whom I have visited in the superb (British) Bastion Field Hospital – thankfully very few have been wounded – has expressed a genuine desire to return to the Company as soon as possible, and certainly before the end of the tour.

Number 3 Company has been operating in genuinely austere conditions and, by and large, thriving on it. An obsession with the weather may be a peculiarly British phenomenon, but for soldiers on the ground it makes a huge difference; it can be of just as much significance as enemy action. Those in Kabul have been subject to the full severity of an Afghan winter with temperatures down as low as -30°C when wind-chill is considered. The Guardsmen have adapted well to operating in these temperatures and have been fortunate in being well equipped for the task: today's MOD-issued personal equipment is superb.

However, even first-rate kit cannot stop floods, and the inundation and mud in the Helmand valley in January had to be seen to be believed. The challenges of simply surviving, quite apart from fighting, in such conditions are enormous. Nevertheless, operations persisted throughout. The Reconnaissance Platoon were engaged in an operation to secure FOB ARMADILLO during the worst of the weather, and can empathise with their forefathers who fought across flooded areas of Holland and Germany in 1944–5. However, the enemy too are affected, and in truth the Taliban showed a marked reluctance to come out during the severe weather.

Major Chris Bell and Right Flank Company of the 1st Battalion Scots Guards have been operating in Warrior armoured vehicles, with a Coldstream Platoon under Andrew Joyce providing many of their dismounting infantrymen. Warrior has once again proved its capabilities in Afghanistan. Right Flank Company has been instrumental in two significant offensives. On arrival the Company was thrown straight into Operation PALK WAHEL, clearing the Upper Gereshk Valley, and it subsequently played a significant role in Operation MAR KARADAD, retaking Musá Qal'eh. Although Right Flank enjoyed a short period of stability at FOB ARNHEM, most of their time has been spent on the move around the Province in support of Brigade and battle group operations. Both vehicles and men have held up well under great pressure in arduous conditions although there will be more than a few Guardsmen who will be happy not to see a shovel for a considerable period once they leave theatre. Digging a new trench every night for weeks on end has been a necessary but not particularly popular task! The Taliban quickly gained considerable respect for Warrior's weapon systems and would usually melt away whenever the Company appeared, preferring to attack armoured vehicles with Improvised Explosive Devices (IED).

Coldstreamers have also been dedicated to Security Sector Reform tasks in Helmand, working with the Afghans to build the capability of their security forces. Those working in Operational Mentoring and Liaison Teams (OMLT) with the Afghan National Army (ANA) have built on the good work of our predecessors, 1st Battalion Grenadier Guards, although much remains to be done. The pre-eminent role of the Afghan National Army (ANA), supported by Captain Tom Bailey and other Coldstreamers, in the retaking of Musá Qal'eh, is a testament to the success of the OMLT work. The work of Major Guy Bartle-Jones (Welsh Guards) who deployed to Musá Qal'eh as the Military Stabilisation Advisor has been equally crucial. Such a title obscures the reality that he, almost single-handedly, administered a town of 20,000 people for two months, until local Afghans were prepared to take on the task.

The Battalion has also provided officers and seniors to the Joint District Co-ordination Centres, where the activities of Afghan forces, and those of International Security Assistance Force (ISAF) are drawn together. The first two months also saw the Reconnaissance Platoon take on the demanding task of 'mentoring' the Police: policing standards in Helmand were diabolical. Corruption, extortion and drug-taking are endemic and the narco-networks are all-pervasive, but, after less than a year of police reform, there are now grounds for guarded optimism. The Battalion is determined to nurture this optimism and support the reform programme, since successful reform of the Security Sector is the basis for our exit strategy from Afghanistan.

The Operation HERRICK 7 tour has been one of huge variety for the 1st Bn Coldstream Guards. There have been some constants which would have been as familiar to our forbears as they will be to our successors: the capricious turns of the weather, the lack of resources and the requirement to make do, the importance of leadership and sound training to prepare for the rigours of operations, and above all the sheer human endeavour and emotion involved in soldiering. The strength of bonds forged in adversity has been particularly important to everyone. Constant publicity has further impressed upon us the paramount importance of 'influence operations' in this information age.

The Battalion remains widely dispersed but in good heart. Coldstreamers, along with the Household Cavalry Regiment and Right Flank of the 1st Battalion Scots Guards have all contributed to 52 Brigade's efforts, which are delivering real tactical success on the ground. There is much of which we can all be proud, and now we wait to see the achievements developed into strategic success. Significant, but not insurmountable, challenges remain.

SCOTS GUARDS

Scots Guards Actions and Heroes

Actions

Waterloo (Hougoumont) 18 June 1815 (Napoleonic Wars, Belgium)

The task of holding this strategically vital farm fell to the light companies of the 2nd Battalion Coldstream Guards and the 2nd Battalion Third Guards (about 200 men). Although the first French attack was repulsed it was soon followed by another, and this time the enemy swept round both flanks, so that the buildings were under attack from three sides. The south gate came under heavy pressure but held, and was never forced open. To the north and west of Hougoumont, the Guardsmen still outside the walls now withdrew through the north gate. Sergeant Fraser of the Third Guards rode back on a charger belonging to Colonel Amédée Despans-Cubières, commanding the French 1st Light Infantry Regiment, whom he had wounded and unhorsed in personal combat. As the last men entered, the great gate was swung shut.

But before it could be properly barricaded, it was a rushed by a 30-man party from the 1st Light Regiment, led by a Lieutenant Legros, a huge man to match his name. Armed with an axe, he forced open the gate, and at the head of about a dozen men fought his way through into the courtyard. After a desperate hand-to-hand struggle, almost all the Frenchmen were killed. But more French troops were now attacking the gate, which had to be closed if Hougoumont was to be held. A 10-man party from the Coldstream and Third Guards fought to push back the wall of enemy who were pressing forward into the gap. While some stabbed and thrust at the desperate attackers, others heaved at the heavy doors. Very slowly they forced them back, pushing aside the pile of dead and dying Frenchmen on the other side.

An assault on the orchard at 1 pm was repulsed thanks to a counter-attack by the 2nd Battalion Third Guards, under Lieutenant Colonel F. Home. The Third Guards now replaced the First Guards light companies

Left: The charge of the Guards on the Heights of the Alma, 20 September 1854.

Scots Guards

Colonel of the Regiment: HRH The Duke of Kent KG, GCMG, GCVO, ADC (P)

Formed: 18 March 1642 – 3 September 1651; and reformed October 1660 to the present

Role Today: Armoured Infantry (Warrior). One Battalion with F Company on Public Duties.

Battle Honours: Namur 1695, Dettingen, Lincelles, Egypt, Talavera, Barrosa, Fuentes d'Onor, Salamanca, Nive, Peninsula, Waterloo, Alma, Inkerman, Sevastopol, Tel-el-Kebir, Egypt 1882, Suakin 1885, Modder River, South Africa 1899–1902
First World War: Retreat from Mons, Marne 1914, Aisne 1914, Ypres 1914, '17, Langemarck 1914, Gheluvelt, Nonne Bosschen, Givenchy 1914, Neuve Chapelle, Aubers, Festubert 1915, Loos, Somme 1916, 1918, Flers-Courcelette, Morval, Pilckem,

Poelcapelle, Cambrai 1917, '18, St Quentin, Albert 1918, Bapaume 1918, Arras 1918, Drocourt-Quéant, Hindenburg Line, Havrincourt, Canal du Nord, Selle, Sambre, France and Flanders 1914–18
Second World War: Stien, Norway 1940, Halfaya 1941, Sidi Suleiman, Tobruk 1941, Gazala, Knightsbridge, Defence of Alamein Line, Medenine, Tadjera Khir, Medjez Plain, Grich el Oued, Djebel Bou Aoukaz 1943 I, North Africa 1941–3, Salerno, Battipaglia, Volturno Crossing, Roccheta e Croce, Monte Camino, Anzio, Campoleone, Carroceto, Trasimene Line, Advance to Florence, Monte San Michele, Catarelto Ridge, Argenta Gap, Italy 1943–5, Mont Pincon, Quarry Hill, Estry, Venlo Pocket, Rhineland, Reichswald, Kleve, Moyland, Hochwald, Rhine, Lingen, Uelzen, North-West Europe 1944–5;
Post Second World War: Tumbledown Mountain, Falkland Islands 1982, Gulf 1991

Uniform: Thistle on the buttons, buttons grouped in threes on the front of the tunic, a thistle on the collar, no plume on the bearskin cap and a checkered or diced hat band on the forage cap.

Special Day: St Andrew's Day, 30 November

Recruiting Areas: Scotland, Cumbria, Corby

Marches: Quick: *Hielan' Laddie*
Slow: *The Garb of the Old Gaul*

Traditional Nickname: Jock Guards

Motto: *Nemo Me Impune Lacessit* (No one assails me with impunity)

Allied Regiment: 3rd Battalion Royal Australian Regiment

Website: www.army.mod.uk/scotsguards

Recent Operations and Highlights

2003 – Wellington Barracks, London. Required to retrain in order to cover the Fire Service while they went on strike. The Queen's Birthday Parade (Trooping the Colour).

2004 – Oxford Barracks, Münster, Germany. Conversion to Armoured Infantry. Having been a light role Battalion, the Scots Guards converted to the Warrior infantry fighting vehicle in five months. It was the first newly converted Battalion ever to get the highest grade on its first gunnery camp.

Exercise in British Army Training Unit Suffield (Canada). As part of the Royal Dragoon Guards battle group, Right Flank and Left Flank Companies completed Exercise 'Medicine Man'. Pre-Deployment Training for Iraq. Training in Germany in

preparation for deployment, included teaching Scotsmen to speak Arabic.

October **2004** to May **2005** – Operation TELIC 5, Iraq. As the Divisional Reserve their tasks were highly varied: boat patrols with the Royal Marines, foot patrols in Basra and Al Amarah, airborne operations, working with the US Navy Special Forces, interdiction operations and house arrests. They were present during the first democratic elections in the country.

2005 – Oxford Barracks. Adventurous Training. Training Support. Ranges in Sennelager and exercises in Poland. Supported the pre-deployment training for other brigades as they prepared to deploy to Iraq.

2006 – Oxford Barracks. Bowman combat radio conversion. Six months converting the Battalion to the new communications system. Exercise PRAIRIE EAGLE. Armoured infantry exercise in Poland, down to -27°C!

2007 – Oxford Barracks. Battle group training in simulators. British Army Training Unit Suffield (Canada) as above but this time as a Scots Guards battle group. Pre-deployment training as before. Operation HERRICK and Operation TELIC 11. Right Flank Company to Afghanistan and the remainder to Iraq.

2008 – Catterick, UK. On return from operations 4th Mechanized Brigade will move to Catterick, North Yorkshire which will be the future permanent home of the Scots Guards.

in the orchard. Nearly the whole of 2nd Guards Brigade under Lieutenant Colonel F. Hepburn of the Third Guards was responsible for the defence of Hougoumont for the remaining six hours of fighting. For nearly nine hours a British and German force of never more than 2,600 had withstood continuous attacks by 14,000 Frenchmen, almost a third of Napoleon's infantry. By doing so they prevented one corps from supporting Napoleon's four major attacks during the day.

The Battle of The Alma 20 September 1854 (Crimean War, South Russia)
The British Light [Infantry] Division crossed the River Alma and initially drove the enemy back. But the division was then forced back by Russian counter-attacks, and the 1st Division were called upon to advance to its support. All three regiments of 1st Guards Brigade crossed the river, and the Grenadiers and Coldstream then paused to reorganise. Markers were called out, and the lines were carefully dressed, as if on Horse Guards. The 1st Battalion Scots Fusilier Guards, however, having been delayed during the crossing, did not wait to reform, but was ordered forward up the slope. The other troops in front unfortunately withdrew at this moment, and confusion developed, as the two bodies met.

At a crucial moment, the two lieutenants and four sergeants forming the Colour Party of the Scots Fusilier Guards found themselves in the

Above: Company Sergeant Major MacKenzie and Guardsman Dickson engage in 'hearts and minds' in Basra.

Below: Company Sergeant Major L. Corbett, responsible for new Guards recruits at Catterick.

Left: Tumbledown Mountain by Terence Cuneo.

front of the fighting round the enemy strongpoint, the Great Redoubt. The Party was for a while almost surrounded, but stood firm, until the Battalion could rally round the Colours.

The Queen's Colour was found afterwards to have 23 bullet holes in it and the pole was shot through; two of the escort were killed. Two of the Colour Party (Lieutenant Robert Lindsay and Sergeant James McKechnie) were awarded the Victoria Cross, when it was instituted 16 months later on 29 January 1856.

The Battle Of Mount Tumbledown 13–14 June 1982
(Falklands War, South Atlantic)
On the morning of 13 June the 2nd Battalion Scots Guards was moved from its positions at Bluff Cove by helicopters to an assembly area near Goat Ridge near to their objective, Mount Tumbledown, which was defended by a crack Argentine unit, the 5th Marine Infantry Battalion. On the night of the 13th the main force of the Scots Guards began its advance on the western side of Mount Tumbledown. During the battle in the early hours of the 14th, men of the battalion launched a bayonet charge on the stout Argentine defenders which resulted in bitter fighting, and was a rare bayonet charge by the British Army. The battle raged on and by 8 am the final objective was taken and Mount Tumbledown was in the hands of the Scots Guards.

The battle had been bloody, yet successful, and the Battalion had proven the elite calibre and professionalism of the Regiment in taking a well-defended mountain, occupied by a top Argentine unit, for the Guardsmen had been performing Public Duties back in London only a few months before. The Scots Guards casualties were 8 Guardsmen and 1 Royal Engineer killed, and 43 wounded. Their Argentine opponents lost 40 men and over 30 captured. A troop of The Blues and Royals equipped with two Scorpion and two Scimitar armoured vehicles provided valuable 76mm and 30mm fire support during the battle.

Left: Each morning Non-Commissioned Officers representing each company report to the Regimental Sergeant Major to receive their instructions for the day.

Above: Members of the Scots Guards band on duty at Royal Ascot – note their Gulf War medals.

Scots Guards Heroes

Sergeant John McAulay VC, DCM

John McAulay, born in Stirling, won both the Victoria Cross and the Distinguished Conduct Medal (DCM) for acts of extraordinary bravery in the First World War. When he joined up as a private he was 26 and had already reached the rank of Police Sergeant in the Glasgow City Police. He served with distinction on the Western Front and was awarded his DCM 'for clearing pill-boxes at Ypres on 31 July 1917, accounting for several snipers single-handed and taking charge of his Platoon after his officer was killed'.

His Victoria Cross was awarded for valour on 27 November 1917 after he saw his Company Commander lying out in the open badly wounded near Fontaine-Notre-Dame in the Battle of Cambrai, under a hail of bullets. He carried the officer 500 yards. The official account appeared in the *London Gazette*, 11 January 1918:

John McAulay, Sergeant DCM, Scots Guards. For most conspicuous bravery and initiative in attack. When all his officers had become casualties, Sergeant McAulay resumed command of the company, and under shell and machine-gun fire successfully held and consolidated the objectives gained. He reorganised the company, cheered on and encouraged his men, and under heavy fire at close quarters, showed disregard of danger.

Noticing a counter-attack developing in his exposed flank, he successfully repulsed it by the skilful and bold use of machine guns, aided by his men only, causing heavy enemy casualties.

Sergeant McAulay also carried his company commander, who was mortally wounded, a long distance to a place of safety under a very heavy fire. Twice he was knocked down by the concussion of a bursting shell, but, nothing daunting, he continued on his way until his objective was achieved, killing two of the enemy who endeavoured to intercept him.

Major Sir V. Mackenzie, his Commanding Officer, wrote: 'He took command of the company after all his officers had been hit, cheered and encouraged them, brought back Arthur (Kinnaird) and many wounded men from positions of danger, beat back a counter-attack, killed several Germans, and was altogether splendid. I am recommending him for a VC but they are hard to get.'

Lieutenant (Temporary Captain) Charles Anthony Lyell, 2nd Baron Lyell VC (1913–43)

From 22 to 27 April 1943, Captain The Lord Lyell commanded his company, which had been placed under orders of a battalion of Grenadier Guards, with great gallantry, ability and cheerfulness. He led it down a slope under heavy mortar fire to repel a German counter-attack on 22 April. Led it again under heavy fire through the battalion's first objective on 23 April in order to capture and consolidate a high

point, and held this point [Point 226] through a very trying period of shelling, heat and shortage of water. During this period, through his energy and cheerfulness, he not only kept up the fighting spirit of his company, but also managed through radio telephony, which he worked himself from an exposed position, to bring most effective artillery fire to bear on enemy tanks, vehicles and infantry positions.

At about 1800 hours 27 April 1943, this officer's company was taking part in the battalion's attack on Djebel Bou Aoukaz. The company was held up in the foothills by heavy fire from an enemy post on the left; this post consisted of an 88mm gun and a heavy machine gun in separate pits. Realising that until this post was destroyed the advance could not proceed, Lord Lyell collected the only available men not pinned down by fire – a Sergeant, a Lance Corporal and two Guardsmen – and led them to

attack it. He was a long way in advance of the others and lobbed a hand grenade into the machine-gun pit, destroying the crew. At this point his sergeant was killed and both Guardsmen were wounded. The Lance Corporal got down to give covering fire to Lord Lyell, who had run straight on towards the 88mm gun pit and was working his way round to the left of it. So quickly had this officer acted that he was in among the crew with the bayonet [actually pistol and dirk] before they had time to fire more than one shot. He killed a number [five] of them before being overwhelmed and killed himself. The few survivors of the gun crew left the pit, some of them being killed while they were retiring, and both the heavy machine gun and the 88mm gun were silenced.

The company was then able to advance and take its objective. There is no doubt that Lord Lyell's outstanding leadership, gallantry and self-sacrifice enabled his company to carry out its task, which had an important bearing on the success of the battalion and of the brigade.

Lieutenant General Sir John Kiszely KCB, MC (1948–), 2nd Battalion

In 1982 Major Kiszely was commanding the leading Scots Guards Company – Left Flank – as it approached the craggy ridge feature of Tumbledown Mountain, seven kilometres west of Port Stanley in the Falkland Islands as it neared the last phase of the assault. The company passed through G Company under cover of darkness at 2230 and started climbing Tumbledown. Almost immediately two or three Argentine semi-automatic weapons opened up and despite an immediate section attack the company began to receive an accurate and increasingly heavy artillery and mortar bombardment, which continued throughout the night.

At 2.30 am after an artillery barrage a platoon attack was carried out on the forward enemy positions and Company Headquarters moved forward to join them after five enemy sangars (low defensive positions built of stone around a natural hollow) were taken. It then became obvious that there was a chance to maintain the momentum of the attack and with two sections of Number 15 Platoon an assault was made on the next group of enemy about 200 metres up the hill. About eight Argentines were killed, Major Kiszely personally accounting for two and bayoneting a third. One enemy round passed through his left pouch and bayonet scabbard before lodging in his compass. Although one Section Commander was shot dead and another man was wounded the assault

Right: Major G. Taylor, Second in command of 1st Battalion Scots Guards welcomes The Colonel of the Regiment, HRH the Duke of Kent, to an exercise.

continued up the hill with more enemy sangars and bunkers being taken at the point of a bayonet. With the demands of clearing those positions and guarding the prisoners as they were taken, only seven men initially arrived at the top of the mountain. Of those seven, three were immediately cut down by machine-gun fire. The Company Commander and three men were holding Tumbledown Mountain.

Although it was difficult to estimate the enemy dead, more than 30 bodies were removed from the battlefield. Twenty prisoners were taken and an unknown number put to flight.

Guardsman Tom Morris, Scots Guards

At the moment I am starting my pre-Non Commissioned Officers Cadre Training. We're expected to keep our fitness up and get our tactics sorted out.

This morning we had a six mile run, followed by map-reading all day. Then tomorrow is drill. With the map reading we use the compass to find grid bearings and magnetic bearings and learn how to recognise the features on the ground from a map. It's all part of becoming confident to lead men on the ground.

The week after we come back from leave we're going to go away for a couple of days to practice harbour routines, going into and occupying an area, the tactical advance into it, making sure you're not being followed. This involves setting up a snap ambush where you backtrack, wait for, say, ten minutes, see if you can hear anything or see anything and if anybody does come along you know that you've been followed. So you've got to extract. But obviously, if everything's OK, everything's sound, you go into the harbour that you've identified on the map. It'll probably be in woods at night time, so you set up your positions, where you're going to sleep for the night, where your sentry's going to sit, set up a trap line where you put a bit of string out so you know where you're going at night. You're going to identify all the likely enemy

threats where your enemy's going to be coming from, and also your extraction route, if he does come along – how you're going to get out of there quickly with the minimum fuss. It's going to go into things like how to deliver a set of orders which can take a long time, using models, using props, all sorts of different techniques.

The actual course at the Household Division Parachute Regiment Centralised Courses at Pirbright is two weeks of drill and four weeks of tactics. The drill will get you up to a teaching standard – you'll understand why you teach in that way. And then the four weeks tactics run in the Brecon Beacons is to enable you to command men in your team or section.

We start from the basics. You learn how to get down to a position behind cover all the way up to being in charge of the platoon, in charge of about ten men, giving quick battle orders and running through everything like ammunition, casualties, finding the enemy, destroying the enemy and then following up the contact with a SITREP making sure all your lads are alright. Just taking responsibility. We also do things like basic first aid. These days we are also doing something called Command Leadership Management, CLM for short, which gives you, recognised civilian qualifications, NVQs. It's the equivalent of being a junior manager and

the higher up the ranks in the army you go, the more of this CLM that you do. Now it's impossible to get promoted beyond a certain level without doing the CLM. It's a case of leaving the Army better educated.

LIFE ON THE FRONT LINE: 1st Battalion Scots Guards, 2007

Commanding Officer, Lieutenant Colonel Willie Swinton

This is the first update from Basra, just four days before Christmas and some three weeks after we assumed the role as the Manoeuvre battle group from the 2nd Bn Royal Welsh on 1 December. As I write, it pours with rain outside already testing the Technical Quartermaster's defensive earthworks of drains and ditches, and the longer-range forecast does not bode well for our ability to get about with our heavy armoured vehicles. At least it hasn't started snowing, yet.

Prima facie, much seems to have changed in Southern Iraq since the Battalion was last here. The Iraqi Army are now very much in evidence patrolling and generally providing a presence: to our collective surprise, six BMP tracked fighting vehicles rolled through the battle group last week whilst we were deployed in a holding area out on the outskirts of Basra. The Anti Tank platoon was understandably most disconcerted that its rules of engagement only allowed for a begrudged wave! The roads are routinely filled with Basrawis going about their daily business and most remarkable is the occasional roar of a Jordanian airlines passenger jet on its daily commute in and out from Basra bringing businessmen from all over the region.

So there are really positive and discernible signs of true progress although one doesn't have to look very hard to witness the almost biblical conditions that much of the population of Southern Iraq still endure. And then there is much more insurgent activity now than we ever experienced back in 2004. Daily our vehicle patrols encounter sophisticated improvised explosive devices, and the rocket attacks on our massive base at Basra airport continue largely unabated. There is however a broadly intact ceasefire that exists between Multi National Forces in Basra and Muqtada al Sadr's militia JAM who, until July, were the principal protagonists. Considerable effort is expended to ensure that no patrol or activity spooks or surprises the JAM for fear of precipitating a return to the violence seen over the summer months.

Last weekend, Provincial Iraqi Control was marked by ceremonies both at the airport and at Basra Palace, and responsibility for security in Iraq's southern city has now passed to the Iraqi Army and Police. A week in and there is no significantly apparent difference to our own routines although just yesterday our brigade, 4th Mechanized Brigade, announced that two of our four battlegroups would be returning home early, the first in as soon as six weeks. We are delighted to be staying for the long haul and I believe it is entirely to the battlegroup's credit that we will remain to the bitter end as the manoeuvre force for all of Southern Iraq, but the premature loss of half the Brigade clearly telegraphs a peace dividend of sorts.

The Brigade's stated Main Effort is monitoring, mentoring and training (M2T) the Iraqi Security Forces, and this attracts the lion's share of all available manpower and resources. Although prepared to support M2T, the Scots Guards battle group is much more routinely focused on providing physical protection for the force by

patrolling the rural/urban fringe of Basra, giving support to security within Basra airport and the provision of a potent and versatile reserve capability. We have grouped with us the Blackhorse Squadron, Royal Dragoon Guards, with whom we have worked closely over this past year in Sennelager and at BATUS, and they bring 14 CHALLENGER 2 main battle tanks. We are patrolling daily at company strength with a troop of tanks to deter or intercept the rocket teams targeting our base. These 'combat teams' will usually be preceded by the battle group's own DESERT HAWK UAV (Unmanned Aerial Vehicle) which is flown by a Gunner detachment under my tactical control. It has a very capable day and night video camera capability which can be downlinked straight to a laptop. This is one amongst many other new pieces of equipment out here that represent a welcome increase in capability. Our patrol progress is often covered by fast jets that hold high over Basra if the threat warrants their support, and a 155mm AS90 gun battery is also available at no notice to provide unequivocal fire support – and they have fired quite regularly, ie three or four times a week!

Two weeks ago we deployed Left Flank to the north of Basra, up towards the fabled Garden of Eden at the confluence of the Tigris and Euphrates. Their task was to re-establish a presence in the area over a four-day period and to deliver agricultural supplies and educational packs to a number of exceptionally poor Marsh Arab villages. They were welcomed and their supplies gratefully received, while the long 90km trip north and then back was uneventful. A small victory and possibly a bit late in the day, but it was great to be part of an enterprise that was so clearly well received. Piper Bennett managed a few tunes from the roof of his Warrior, too, which was met with surprising nonchalance.

Yesterday the battle group took part in an unprecedented joint operation with the Iraqi Army. Deployed at full strength to the west of Basra, we provided and demonstrated a significant armoured reaction force ready to assist a small ten-vehicle convoy comprising US Army Engineers with their Private Security Company protection from Tim Spicer's group Aegis, and a patrol of Iraqi Army armoured vehicles, as they moved into the city to visit a

reconstruction project in the Children's Hospital. Overhead, top cover was provided by a British Army Lynx and two Iraqi Air Force Hip helicopters, while above them lurked a pair of Tornado GR4s out of sight. This massive display of British combat power dwarfed the five-vehicle contribution by the Iraqis, but it signified that we are both willing and capable of working together.

Over to our east by a couple of thousand kilometres, Right Flank has been leading the well-publicised push to capture Musá Qal'eh in Helmand Province. Communication with the Company has been very difficult as they have spent almost all of the past three months entirely in the field. However, I know from the rare fleeting telephone calls that I have had with them that everyone remains in excellent form, their Warriors exceeding all expectations, and that they now have a fierce reputation with both the Taliban and the remainder of the British contingent in Helmand. Both parts of the Battalion are clearly experiencing two entirely different environments and sets of challenges. I sense that Right Flank will be drawing routinely on the war-fighting skills that we all honed this summer in Canada, and that their living conditions are devoid of the comforts we enjoy in Basra, and are as austere as those ordinarily experienced on exercise, but worse and sustained indefinitely. Resupply often has to rely on air delivery by parachute, and the stowage and carriage of such critical items as water is hugely problematic. They have been deployed at range throughout from their base at Camp BASTION, and with the paucity of helicopters in that theatre, simply getting soldiers back for R&R becomes an enormous problem. But I have heard at first hand from those back in Münster on their R&R that the whole Company is thriving on their work, and that we have every reason to be extremely proud of what they have achieved to date.

Guardsman Ferguson of the Mortar Platoon was tragically killed here in Basra last week when the Warrior he was driving slid into a canal, and he drowned despite the very brave efforts of his vehicle crew to rescue him. He was buried yesterday in Motherwell with a full Regimental funeral which was attended by the Regimental Lieutenant Colonel with a bearer and firing party provided by F Company. Fergie was a wonderful Scots Guardsman and a typical mortarman. Nine years a Guardsman, he was very well known throughout the Battalion for his big personality, a thoroughly inappropriate taste in T-shirts and his wickedly dry sense of humour. We will all miss him desperately and the Battalion will be less fun without him, but I am certain in the knowledge that we will never forget him – he was too big a character. This has been the second loss of one of our own in a very short space of time, and – so bitterly – both to tragic accidents. In each case, I can report that the accidents were freak and that there has not been any discernible lapse in training or competence. The confidence of those closely involved will always inevitably be shaken, but on the whole I have been so very proud of the way that the battle group has dealt with both tragedies.

It is now Christmas Eve and today we delivered two sets of battle group orders for operations over the next few days. We fully intend to mark Christmas properly, operations allowing, and we have been overwhelmed by the generosity of the Association, friends of the Regiment and the public with the veritable avalanche of parcels that have arrived here in the last week, on average 90 mail sacks a day! I wish to put forth to all those who read this update the assurance that this battalion continues to set the very highest standards and maintain its reputation for excellence.

En Ferus Hostis (Behold a Fierce Enemy)

IRISH GUARDS

Above: 'My Brave Irish' as Queen Victoria called them – The Irish Fusiliers in South Africa, by Caton Woodville.

Irish Guards Actions and Heroes

Actions

The South African War 1900

It was as a result of the bravery of Irish regiments in the disastrous early phase of the Boer War that the Irish Guards was formed. In the last year of her life Queen Victoria commanded that a fourth regiment of Foot Guards, the Irish Guards, be raised. The Regiment won its first decoration for bravery when Sergeant Hudson was awarded the Distinguished Conduct Medal for service with the Irish Guards Mounted Infantry against the Boers.

The Western Front 1914 (First World War, France and Flanders)

The Commanding Officer of the 1st Battalion (mobilised 997 strong), Lieutenant Colonel the Honourable George Morris, was killed in the first action of the Great War, an occurrence, which was cruelly repeated in the Second World War in Norway. After the bitter fighting on the Aisne in the early stages of the 1914–18 War (in the Irish Guards case at Soupir) the British Expeditionary Force (BEF) moved hastily north to the Ypres area to prevent the Germans reaching the sea on the Belgian coast. What happened to the Battalion during the First Battle of Ypres illustrates the kind of losses that all the BEF infantry battalions had to endure.

The 1st Guards Brigade had recently been taken over by Temporary Brigadier General Charles FitzClarence VC, the Irish Guards' former Regimental Lieutenant Colonel. The 'GOC Menin Road' as his troops called him was killed on 12 November after helping direct a successful counter-attack against an assault by the 9,000-strong Prussian Guard Division on 11 November and has no known grave.

The situation in early November was also so critical that the Adjutant was sent off to Brigade Headquarters to get help, which took some time to arrive. The dangerously thin line was holding out but had become perilously depleted. The 1st Battalion Commanding Officer, Lord Ardee, was wounded. On 2 November the Battalion reorganised into three understrength companies. On the 7th, the Battalion lost another Commanding Officer, Major Herbert Stepney. On the 8th the survivors reformed into two smaller companies. On the 9th only four platoons (160 men) could be mustered. On the 18th after further losses the Irish Guards were pulled back for the last time.

The 1st Battalion's losses were close on 1,000 all ranks killed, wounded or missing. The Battalion had been wiped out, partially rebuilt and nearly wiped out again. Even the famous Christmas 'truce' of 1914 brought it no succour. They were only 200 yards from the Germans under

Above: 4th Guards Brigade leaving 2nd Division for the newly formed Guards Division in which it became 1st Guards Brigade. No 4 Company 1st Battalion, Captain Sidney FitzGerald. Pipers visible, Lieutenant Colonel G.H.C. Madden (whose son and grandson both served in the Regiment) had taken over from Lieutenant Colonel Jack Trefusis DSO (promoted Temp. Brigadier General) the previous day. This was the day 2nd Battalion left Warley for France.

Irish Guards

Colonel of the Regiment: The Duke of Abercorn KG

Formed: 1 April 1900

Role Today: Light role infantry battalion and Public Duties

Battle Honours: First World War: Mons, Retreat from Mons, Marne 1914, Aisne 1914, Ypres 1914, 17, Langemarck 1914, Gheluvelt, Nonne Bosschen, Festubert 1915, Loos, Somme 1916, '18, Flers-Courcelette, Morval, Pilckem, Poelcapelle, Passchendaele, Cambrai 1917, '18, St Quentin, Lys, Hazebrouck, Albert 1918, Bapaume 1918, Arras 1918, Scarpe 1918, Drocourt-Quéant, Hindenburg Line, Canal du Nord, Selle, Sambre, France and Flanders 1914–8 **Second World War:** Pothus, Norway 1940, Boulogne 1940, Cagny, Mont Pincon, Neerpelt, Nijmegen, Aam, Rhineland, Hochwald, Rhine, Bentheim, North-West Europe 1944–5, Medjez Plain, Djebel Bou Aoukaz 1943, North Africa

1943, Anzio, Aprilia, Carroceto, Italy 1943–4 **Post Second World War:** Basra 2003, Iraq 2003

Uniform: The Irish Guards have a harp below the Crown on their buttons, buttons grouped in fours on the front of the tunic, a shamrock on the collar, blue plume in the bearskin cap and a green cap band on the forage cap.

Recruiting Areas: Northern Ireland, London, Liverpool and the West Midlands

Traditional Nickname: the Micks

The Presentation of the Shamrock: This tradition began soon after the Regiment was formed. It mounted guard with the Regiment's first King's Guard on 3 March 1901 and was on parade at Chelsea Barracks on St Patrick's Day the same month. Two Shamrocks were presented then. The first came from the Regiment and the second, which

arrived during the parade, was a gift from Queen Alexandra herself. The presentation of Royal Shamrock became a tradition, as did the intimacy and informality of the St Patrick's Day parade. In more recent years Queen Elizabeth The Queen Mother presented the Shamrock each year for more than 30 years confirming the close bond that she felt with the Regiment. The Princess Royal has now taken on the custom.

Freedoms: Liverpool, Windsor and Ladysmith, South Africa

Marches: Quick – *St Patrick's Day*
Slow – *Let Erin Remember*

Motto: *Quis Separabit* (Who Shall Separate Us?)

Allied Regiments: 4th Battalion The Royal Australian Regiment, Montserrat Defence Force (Leeward Islands, West Indies)

Recent Operations and Highlights

March **2002** to August **2003** – Based in Oxford Barracks, Munster, Germany as an Armoured Infantry Battalion, equipped with the Warrior Infantry Fighting Vehicle. Having just completed a training year (the enormous Exercise SAIF SAREEA in Oman had been in autumn 2001) the Battalion was poised on 'high readiness'.

The Langton Trophy (the Battalion's inter-platoon competition) was run just before St Patrick's Day. Irish Guardsmen formed the Bearer Party for The Queen Mother's Funeral in April and officers stood at the vigil.

During the summer, Numbers 2 and 4 Companies' predominant focus was trialling the new armoured vehicle simulator, the Combined Arms Tactical Trainer. Number 1 Company deployed to British Army Training Unit Suffield (Canada) for Exercises MEDICINE MAN 2 and 3 to act as the Opposing Force. In the autumn there was a Battalion Field Firing Camp in Sennelager (Germany) and having been stood down from Operation FRESCO (fire-fighting) the Battalion was stood by for possible deployment to Kuwait.

2003 – The Battalion deployed to Iraq in February, went 'through the breach' in March and was withdrawn from Iraq after the war-fighting phase in May. L/Cpl Ian Malone and Piper Christopher Muzvuru were killed in action. Three Military Crosses

and an MBE were awarded. The Battalion moved to Wellington Barracks, London, in August.

September **2003** to April **2006** – Wellington Barracks. The Battalion took over from the Scots Guards as a light role (Public Duties) Battalion. From December 2003 to April 2004 there was an Operation BANNER tour in South Armagh and in summer 2004 the Battalion was committed to Public Duties. In September and October the Battalion took part in Exercise GRAND PRIX in Kenya with the Guards Parachute Platoon attached.

June **2005** – The Battalion Trooped the Colour with the Iraq 2003 Battle Honour on the Colours. Number 1 Company formed the Escort.

August to October **2005**. A platoon was detached to join the Coldstream Guards in Basra. Commanded by Lieutenant Julian Roberts (eldest son of the Major General Commanding the Household Division), it was the same platoon that won the Langton Trophy in July.

February **2006** – The Battalion won the Infantry Ski Cup (combined Nordic and Alpine performance in the Army Ski Championships). April – Moved to Mons Barracks, Aldershot, as part of 1st Mechanised Brigade.

May **2006** to Present – Mons Barracks, Aldershot

Awarded the Carrington Drum for contribution to Airborne Forces. Won the Household Division Small Arms Ammuntion Maintenance competition.

June **2006** – Warcop and Otterburn, Northumberland. Battalion Field Firing Camp.

June to September **2006** Converted to Javelin anti-armour missile system and Bowman radio communications system.

October to December **2006**. Exercise TROPICAL STORM in Belize (Central America). A squadron of the Household Cavalry Regiment was attached.

2007 – (January to March) Pre-deployment training for Iraq. Operation TELIC 10 in Iraq (May to November). Lance Sergeant Chris Casey and Lance Corporal Kirk Redpath killed in action.

The Future?
At the moment there are possible tours to Iraq and Afghanistan. After that the Battalion is likely to return to 1st Mechanized Brigade in Aldershot.

2008 – Training year with possible overseas training, exercises and other operational tasks.

2009–2011 – Windsor. Presentation of new Colours and Queen's Birthday Parade in 2009. Followed by probable deployment to Afghanistan.

occasional heavy bombardment and two officers and six men were wounded on Christmas Day.

The Battles of Djebel Bou Aoukaz 27 April – 4 May 1943
(Second World War, Tunisia)

This action was an example of supreme bravery, dogged determination and success against the odds. The 1st Battalion in 24th Guards Brigade had embarked at Liverpool on board the P&O liner *Strathmore* in March 1943 as reinforcements to the British First Army. With the Eighth Army it was involved in a massive Allied pincer movement to drive the Germans and Italians out of Tunisia and North Africa.

The key to the town of Tunis, and ultimately to Tunisia itself, was the narrow neck of the Medjez valley, about 30 miles west of the town. At its eastern end the valley is about four miles across but dominated by a major feature, Djebel Bou Aoukaz, the 'Bou'.

Towards the end of 21 April, the Brigade, comprising 1st Battalions Irish Guards and Scots Guards and 5th Battalion Grenadier Guards were tasked to clear the corridor and the Irish Guards was ordered to capture two important features, Points 212 and 214.

The attack had originally been planned for the night of the 27th but was brought forward to 4 pm and preparations had to be made in a rush with platoon commanders giving orders on the move. The platoons

Sergeant Major P. Lally, Irish Guards

On being a Regimental Sergeant Major

My job as the Regimental Sergeant Major is to make sure the drills and skills laid out by the Standard Operating Instructions are passed down to the Guardsmen. I oversee the non-commissioned officer element in the Battalion. There have been huge changes since I joined the Army in 1987 such as health and safety issues. I think it's fair to say that the culture shock of going from Civvy Street, a young lad leaving school, and coming to this regiment, is probably greater now than it was, but we remain rigid on standards. We've been extremely hard from the beginning of this tour in Iraq on anyone stepping outside of the mark on the discipline side. We had a couple of issues with enemy indirect fire at the beginning of the tour. It's very erratic, but if you carry out the drills properly you have to be very unlucky to get wounded. The incoming rounds literally have to land on top of you. When the rocket/mortar shell is coming down you have to hit the floor promptly. We just haven't let anything go here.

On Northern Ireland

Its just getting over that initial boundary of chatting to people and making them realise you are not there to destroy their way of life. It is trying to go that extra mile to meet the local Sinn Fein councillor or to meet the local Loyalist representative.

On Irishness

Irishness is important to the Regiment and is something that we are constantly trying to develop. We can't recruit in southern Ireland but what we can do is recruit through family friends. We formed recently, in the last two or three years, a very strong bond with the Irish Defence Force. We visited them and we've had them visit us. I look back to 20 years ago and I think to myself 'thank God I did come and join the Irish Guards and not the Irish Army' which, being a Dubliner, I could have joined, because I would have been restricted to a tour of the Lebanon and a couple of other United Nations tours. We have formed very close bonds with them, which is to our mutual advantage. It might be a case where a young soldier in the Irish Army, he's done a bit so he's got a bit of experience but he wants to broaden that. And we're a good option, as an Irish regiment, to bring that forward.

Warrior Sergeant Major Glynn Crawley, Irish Guards

The Armoured Infantry Manning Increment was formed in 1994. These guys are very experienced in the armoured role. We have our own Guards AMI and they're all Household Division cap badges.

A Warrior Sergeant Major is the Company Commander's left hand man, because the right hand man is the Company Sergeant Major. I sit next to him in his Warrior; I gun and command and assist him. I'll try and take as much work off him as I can, so he can sit there and do other things. I'll advise him on his tactics, I'll plan and conduct all his Warrior ranges. I'll also help him to train his company up as Warrior drivers, gunners and commanders. And I make sure his company fleet of 19 tracked vehicles goes out the gate and his company fleet can move, speak and shoot. I'll assist in all the Warrior training. We also go away and instruct other battalions, other units before they go on operational tours and make sure all the training's going well. With Warrior you've got to deliver troops quickly, safely and effectively. It's an armoured taxi, we all get the people forward to deliver the troops on target, hopefully engage the target and destroy it so the guys get out and just do the outside areas and clean up. We'll use Warriors for fire support, we'll deliver troops, and launch the reserve platoon. It gives us more manoeuvrability around the battlefield. And we can get troops to wherever we want.

Captain Johnny Langton, Adjutant, Irish Guards

On recruiting young Officers

In the officers' mess we have this amazing broad spectrum of personalities from different areas, cultures and backgrounds. Yet for some reason we all seem to get on really well. The key criterion is that you must fit in. After potential officer visits there is a marking guide. There are points for manners, how he gets on with the Guardsmen and fitness. It is the platoon commanders who subsequently have to serve with them that make the final call; they can be quite ruthless. Sandhurst, by definition, should produce competent professional soldiers. We don't really have this 'you've got to be in the top ten of your platoon' business. Clearly it's great if you have done that but it's no great shakes if you haven't. It's all about when the young officer comes to the Battalion and how he performs and the effort that he makes to fit in. And doing your job just as a platoon commander and looking after your guys is fantastic but it isn't the be all and end all. You need to step out and you're really expected to play a full role in extra-regimental activities, whether that's running the Battalion rugby team, or sorting out the paintings of the officers' mess.

Captain Charles Williams, Irish Guards

On Visit to Ladysmith, South Africa

The Irish Guards were formed in 1901 as a result of the efforts of Irish soldiers in the Second Boer War. They really had a key role in relieving the 118-day Siege of Ladysmith. A lot of those regiments are now in abeyance so the Irish Guards were recently offered the freedom of Ladysmith to represent them all. I was tasked to organise a trip out there in 2005 including the Commanding Officer, soldiers from Ireland or people who had relations that fought in the Boer War. I had a variety of Catholics and Protestants, north and south, a real range. It incorporated a battlefield tour for about a week and we visited the graves and cleaned them up. In each place we had a ceremony and laid wreaths. We spent two days in Ladysmith preparing for and being awarded the freedom of the city. It went down really well and we marched the guys in red tunics and bearskins down the main street of Ladysmith to a couple of pipers. When was the last time they saw redcoats marching? A great thought. It's very easy to be involved in what we are doing now and to think it's all that matters. And in one respect it does. The safety of our men is paramount to do the job correctly but in the wider scheme of things, everything we do in the Army has come down from years and years of hard-earned experience and practice.

immediately came under intensive fire from the dominating ground to their left and the Battalion suffered appalling casualties in the cornfields and well-defended olive groves in the open ground.

Captain Desmond Fitzgerald MC, Adjutant 1st Battalion 1943–4, described the scene: 'the fire intensified and the whole cornfield was ripped and torn. Part of it was burning smokily. Amid the tall poppies that stood out over the corn there sprang a new crop – rifle butts. They appeared so suddenly, and so quickly, that it was almost a surprise to look beyond them and see the thin line of men plodding steadily on towards the olive grove.'

Afterwards a German prisoner was reported to have said. 'We could not believe it. We thought no one could cross that plain.' A Guardsman is recorded as saying: 'Thank god for drill. It keeps you going.'

Fitzgerald's description of the conclusion of the action emphasises what an achievement it was:

At dusk 173 men, all that had survived from four full rifle companies, and forward elements of Battalion Headquarters, struggled up the slopes of Points 212 and 214 beyond, and were promptly cut off by Germans swarming in behind them. Three days later, 80 men, which included a smattering of reinforcements who had been able to get through the German cordon to the little beleaguered force, were finally relieved having resisted incessant and persistent attacks to uproot them.

Lieutenant Colonel Andrew Montagu-Douglas-Scott (see Heroes) was awarded an immediate Distinguished Service Order, as was Captain Colin Kennard who had so dominated the defence of Point 214. Also given were two Military Crosses, four Distinguished Conduct Medals and seven Military Medals. In August it was announced that Lance Sergeant John Kenneally (see Heroes) had been awarded the Victoria Cross.

The North West Europe Campaign 1944–5 (Second World War, France, Low Countries and Germany)

The Irish Guards received the Battle Honours Cagny and Mont Pincon for the breakout battles from the Normandy landings bridgehead. On D+17 (23 June 1944) the 2nd Armoured Battalion (Sherman tanks) and 3rd Battalion (Infantry) had crossed the Channel as part of the Guards Armoured Division. After suffering heavy casualties in early August during the brigade advance, both battalions had a short period to refit and receive reinforcements. At the end of August the Guards Armoured Division battalions regrouped into regimental 'battalion groups', and the Micks 2nd (Armoured) and 3rd (Infantry) Battalion thereafter fought together. Thus came into being the Irish Guards group (including 74 tanks and 821 infantry when at full strength).

Highlights of this group following the advance to Brussels (1–3 September) included the taking of 'Joe's Bridge' intact across the Meuse-Escaut Canal by Lieutenant Desmond Lampard's three-tank troop of Shermans and Lieutenant John Stanley-Clarke's 30-man platoon who were

Left: Memorial Cross erected on Point 212 to commemorate those Irish Guardsmen who gave their lives taking and defending the Bou.

Above: Consolidating in the main square of Valkenswaard before resuming the advance. At that stage, Allied air superiority was total so 'bunching' was not such a sin as it had been.

Top: Defences against rocket attacks are upgraded at Basra airport with assistance from local civilian workers, 2007.

Above: Members of the sniper platoon fire their weapons in Basra, 2003.

Top: The Battalion tailor in his workshop in Basra, 2007.

Above: Supper in the cookhouse, Basra 2007.

detailed to capture it on 10 September under the covering fire of every tank in the Irish group commanded by Lieutenant Colonel J.O.E. Vandeleur.

The Irish Group initially led the ground forces from 'Joe's Bridge' into Holland for the link up with Operation MARKET GARDEN, the Allied airborne assault that aimed for Nijmegen, the bridge over the massive Maas–Waal Canal. However, it proved impossible in the end to link up with the British 1st Airborne Division at Arnhem because of the very narrow front and strong resistance. The Irish Guards Group managed to link with the US 101st Airborne Division at Zon, and reached Nijmegen.

Towards the end of the war as the battle moved across the Rhine, the 2nd and 3rd Battalions met fanatical resistance from German defenders. On 21 April 1945 a troop of Shermans and its supporting platoon were caught in a 15th Panzer Grenadier battalion counter-attack at Wistedt, a village between Bremen and Hamburg. With his tank disabled Guardsman Edward Charlton, the co-driver, dismounted his Browning machine gun in full view of the enemy and advanced firing from the hip to cover the withdrawal of the remainder of the little force. Wounded in the arm he propped the gun on a gate and carried on firing until, hit again, he fell, later dying of his wounds. Charlton, largely as the result of evidence provided by the Germans, was posthumously awarded the Victoria Cross, the last to be won in Europe during the Second World War.

Basra 6–7 April 2003 (Second Gulf War, Iraq)

The decision was taken by the Divisional and the Brigade Commanders that 7th Armoured Brigade would take the city. The Royal Scots Dragoon Guards and Irish Guards battle group had to press on to take the Institute of Literature. The plan was for Number 2 Company to attack securing a break-in point and then Number 1 Company was to pass through and secure the objective. Number 5 Platoon, under Lieutenant J. Plummer, pushed forward towards the objective. As Sergeant Whiteside led the platoon through the entrance an Iraqi playing dead sprang to life and hit Whiteside's Warrior with a rocket- propelled grenade (RPG). The enemy RPG man was fired at by numerous vehicles and had his *coup de grâce* from a high-explosive Challenger 2 tank round. As the break-in continued, Number 1 Company advanced and once the entrance had been secured Number 5 Platoon pushed on. Number 1 Company swarmed through, dismounted from its Warriors, breaking into the buildings and clearing the enemy from them.

In the mêlée of vehicles outside, Lance Sergeant Hanger, Coldstream Guards, noticed another Iraqi soldier come to life and pick up a weapon. Sensibly, aware of the risk of fratricide, or perhaps that his 30mm chain gun would not depress enough, he picked up his SA80 rifle and opened his turret exposing his head and torso and shot the man. Number 1 Company swept through and cleared a vast area.

The battle group began to reorganise in order to secure a zone from which 3rd Battalion Parachute Regiment could be launched into Old Basra where the streets were assessed as too narrow for armoured vehicles. As light failed Numbers 1 and 2 Companies consolidated around the Institute. An Iraqi soldier rushed forward from the shadows and fired into the back of a Warrior killing Lance Corporal Ian Malone

Right: RSM McLaughlin and Lance Sergeant Kenneally VC. On 27 August 1943 General Alexander made the presentation of the VC to Lance Sergeant Kenneally. The Battalion was formed up on three sides of a square and, after carrying out a full inspection, Lance Sergeant Kenneally was marched out to receive his ribbon. Then with Kenneally standing on the saluting base to his right, the Battalion marched past.

and Piper Christopher Muzvuru (from Zimbabwe), and wounding Lance Sergeant Holland, Coldstream Guards, and Lance Corporal Martin. A tense night followed: many were worried that more enemy remnants would try and take on the Micks.

The following morning a further clearance operation was conducted. The 3rd Battalion Parachute Regiment arrived and duly secured Old Basra – in about two hours without firing a shot. By lunchtime on 7 April British forces occupied the whole of Basra.

Irish Guards Heroes
Field Marshal The Right Honourable Earl Alexander of Tunis and Errigal KG, GCB, OM, GCMG, CSI, DSO, MC, DCL, LL.D (1891–1969)

'General Alex', as everyone fondly called him, joined the Irish Guards in 1911. From the start it was obvious he was a fine athlete; he won the Irish Mile in 1914. He went to France in 1914 in command of Number 1 Platoon of the 1st Battalion and served on the Western Front almost continuously (except when he was recovering from wounds). As a Platoon, Company and 2nd Battalion Commander he was almost incomparable, as his record shows: the Military Cross in 1915, the Distinguished Service Order in 1916, five times Mentioned in dispatches, and the immediate award in the field from the French High Command of the Legion of Honour, a very rare award for a British subaltern. In his obituary Lieutenant Colonel The Lord Nugent described Alexander's qualities as a Battalion Commander in the Great War: 'Courageous, decisive, and never rattled he had all the qualities of the Great Captains, qualities that remained with him throughout his service and which were to stand him in such good stead in the Second World War as a Commander in France, Burma, the Western Desert and Italy.'

He took command of the 1st Battalion in 1922; they were posted to Constantinople where he won the Brigade Sports mile with ease. Major General Alexander commanded the 1st (Infantry) Division, which he took to France in 1939, and his meteoric career in the Second World War culminated as Field Marshal and Supreme Allied Commander Mediterranean receiving the unconditional surrender of German forces in Italy on 2 May 1945. Eventually he served as Minister of Defence in Churchill's 1950s administration.

In 1946 when the Colonel of the Regiment, Field Marshal Lord Cavan, died, Alex was the obvious successor and the appointment was immediately approved by the King. Lord Nugent concluded: 'to say that All Ranks of the Irish Guards loved him is an understatement. They worshipped him.'

Right: A maquette of Field Marshal Alexander, on display in The Guards Museum.

Lance Sergeant John Patrick Kenneally VC (1921–2000)

Lance Sergeant John Kenneally, who died in 2000, was the last surviving Guards VC of the Second World War. He was considered to be a typical Mick. In his obituary in *The Guards Magazine* he was described as 'utterly loyal to his fellow Guardsmen, brave and relishing a good fight, kind and understanding, at times a rogue and rebel, yet modest, but always ready for a good laugh'.

He joined the Irish Guards in 1941 after obtaining the identity card of a John Patrick Kenneally who was returning to County Tipperary. He made his name during the Battalion's efforts to secure and hold the Djebel Bou Aoukaz during the final push on Tunis.

The battalion suffered terrible casualties during the assault and when holding the position; the Germans launched a series of savage counter-attacks. On 29 April 1943, on Point 212, Number 1 Company sighted an enemy company about to launch an assault. Kenneally, a Bren light machine-gunner in the company, decided that now was the time for him to attack. Alone, he charged down the bare, stony, forward slope, straight towards the German position firing from the hip as he went. The Germans were completely thrown off balance by this extraordinary attack and Number 1 Company was able to advance to finish them off.

The next morning the Germans again massed for an attack, and Kenneally repeated his remarkable exploit. This time, he charged, accompanied by a Sergeant from the Reconnaissance Corps, inflicting many casualties and broke up the enemy company which was forming up. It was only when he was seen to be hopping from one position to another with his Bren in one hand and supported by a Guardsman with the other that it was noticed he was wounded. He refused to give up his Bren gun, claiming that only he understood it. The final words of his citation read, 'his

Left: Dmr Lance Clerkin with Donnchad.

could have achieved what this one did in this battle. For Andrew, the trials and difficulties of the campaign were augmented by the tribulations that affect a command of such a family regiment when sending so many that he knew so well into such a fearful battle'.

At Anzio the battalion had its full share of the endless fighting, shelling and discomfort incurring 746 casualties. He was rarely out of the line and sustained the Battalion in many desperate situations by his courage and example and utter determination.

After the Battalion was withdrawn from Anzio in March 1944 and sailed for home he commanded a brigade in 4th (Infantry) Division and finally 1st Guards Brigade in 6th Armoured Division. Later on he returned to become Regimental Lieutenant Colonel Commanding the Irish Guards. This was an impressive record for an officer who began hostilities as a subaltern on the reserve.

Captain Hugh Everard J. Dormer DSO (1919–44)

Lieutenant Hugh Dormer was twice parachuted into France as leader of a Special Operations Executive (SOE) raiding party to damage a shale oil refinery, which was making fuel for the German Army. The second mission was successful and he was awarded the Distinguished Service Order. He turned down the offer of an enhanced role working with SOE on plans for the invasion of Normandy in order to return to his Regiment. On 1 August 1944, just 30 days after 2nd (Armoured) Battalion Irish Guards had joined the battle to liberate France he was killed in a tank skirmish in an orchard near the tiny village of St Martin des Besaces after apparently attacking a German anti-tank position.

A deeply religious man, he wrote in his diary (published posthumously in 1947) in his last entry before D-Day: 'God knows no man ever set out more happily or gladly before – and lead where it may, I follow the path in ever-mounting spirits. God grant me the courage not to let the Guardsmen down, knowing as I do how much they count on me.' The Guardsmen admired and loved him so much that they strewed his grave with flowers. He epitomises the unique relationship of a young officer for his Micks.

initiative and extraordinary gallantry in attacking single-handed a massed body of the enemy and breaking up an attack on two occasions was an achievement that can seldom have been equalled. His courage in fighting all day when wounded was an inspiration to All Ranks'.

On 13 May 1945, Churchill, exasperated with the Dublin Government's 'frolicking' with the Germans and Japanese, declared in his victory broadcast that all bitterness against the Irish race 'dies in my heart', when he thought of Irish heroes such as John Kenneally.

Brigadier (Claud) Andrew Montagu-Douglas-Scott DSO and Bar (1906–71)

Although from a great Scottish Border family, Andrew Scott's first love was always the Irish Guards, in which his father served in South Africa as one of its first officers. By the time the 1st Battalion sailed for North Africa in 1943 Lieutenant Colonel Scott was in command. They endured the terrible attack and defence of the Bou and as Brigadier Michael Gordon-Watson MC** says in his obituary, 'no battalion, unless inspiringly led,

---

Sergeant David Rodgers, Pipe Major, Irish Guards

On Music In The Irish Guards

Each of the five companies in the Battalion has its own march. When marching the Battalion on public duties in London the Pipes play them. The more traditional Irish set is what we call the 'Skins': 'Enniskillen', 'Tyrone Guards', 'Boy from Callaghan', 'Minstrel Boy', 'the Sash'. That is a well-known marching set that we

play within the regiment. Additionally we have a tune called 'El Basra' which my predecessor wrote in 2003 on Operation TELIC 1. On top of that there are many slow airs, jigs, hornpipes that we can play as well. That's done in a circle. We play those for entertainment purposes.

The Corps of Drums is a very similar scenario. It doubles as a machine-gun

platoon. Probably 75 per cent of our work is together. We'd always be together for the Trooping. The Corps of Drums was in the Battalion before the Pipes so when we are on parade together its called The Drums and Pipes. In the Scots Guards it's the other way round. People all think that pipers drink whisky. Personally I can't really stand the stuff.

LIFE ON THE FRONT LINE: 1st Battalion Irish Guards, 2007

Commanding Officer, Lieutenant Colonel Michael O'Dwyer

The two halves of the Irish Guards' recent tour to Iraq as part of Op TELIC 10 could not have been more stark. The battle group arrived amidst a cycle of violence that saw a constant fight in downtown Basra. The troops in Basra Palace, including Number 1 Company that were attached to 4 RIFLES, were under a constant barrage of indirect fire (IDF); simply resupplying them from the Contingency Operating Base (COB) had become a deadly operation requiring pretty much the rest of the Brigade, supported from the air, deploying into the city. The Manoeuvre battle group based in the COB was striking into the city nightly in an attempt to capture the perpetrators of the attacks against us. The more we were attacked, the more we struck. The result was unprecedented violence and the highest levels of casualties from enemy action seen during the Iraq campaign.

During the course of the first few months there were some outstanding displays of junior leadership, courage and initiative. Command wires used to initiate roadside bombs were found, at night, amidst flying rounds from the AK47s of the insurgents; cameras and other technical devices were recovered for exploitation having been found after the insurgent had placed them to record their devastating, deadly deeds. Many of these finds were down to the alertness and professionalism of the most junior Guardsmen, some of whom, having only been out of training for a matter of weeks, grew up very quickly; none were ever found wanting – all of them saved lives. There were heated and prolonged fire fights with the enemy who, invariably, came off worse.

The levels of violence took their toll. Vehicles from the battle group were hit countless times by roadside bombs and the near-constant barrage of IDF also caused immeasurable death and destruction. In the early part of the tour LCpl Carwright, LCpl Flowers and Cpl Edwards – all from Badger, our attached squadron from 2nd Royal Tank Regiment – died in the face of such threats doing their job to the best of their ability, and going beyond that expected of junior non-commissioned officers. Towards the end of the first half of the tour the battle group suffered its largest loss when LSgt Casey and LCpl Redpath were killed after their vehicle was struck by an IED from the side of the road. The vehicle was flung into the air, rolled on its side and spun around so that it was facing the direction of the remainder of the convoy. Carrying spare fuel, ammunition, red phosphorous and fragmentation grenades, it instantly caught fire. Showing a complete disregard for their own safety, the rest of the Pipes and Drums, together with other elements of the convoy were on the scene immediately and extracted the injured driver and commander. They battled against ferocious flames and the imminent threat of explosions to save the two non-commissioned officers in the back; sadly their efforts were in vain. They continued to control the situation, apply life-saving first aid and secure the immediate area until the convoy commander arrived. Throughout they displayed courage and initiative of the highest order with complete disregard for their own

safety to try and save their friends – they epitomised the example set by all Irish Guardsmen during the tour. LSgt Casey's and LCpl Redpath's death was a horrific event that will scar the hearts and minds of many for a long time but, led by the Battalion's quite outstanding Padre, Father Nick Gosnell, farewells were said and, after the most moving of repatriation ceremonies, the battle group determined to move on.

At the beginning of September the Brigade handed back Basra Palace to the Iraqis and reached an accommodation with the militia. The result was a break in the cycle of violence, a break which marked the end of the first half of the tour and the beginning of the second. A measure of the change in tempo is that in July there were 203 IDF attacks on the COB, each averaging between 3-6 individual rockets whilst the comparable figure for September was only 11. Half-time, however, was not an opportunity to sit down in the dressing-room with the oranges and admire the achievements of the first half, rather it was the opportunity for the Micks to focus on developing the Iraqi Army through monitoring, mentoring and training (M2T), something for which there had not really been opportunity to focus on up until this point. It was a great fillip to have Number 1 Company back in the fold and with two company/squadron groups the battle group was really able to forge ahead with what had always been its mission and the Brigade's main effort but which was now also the main activity. M2T suddenly was resourced, mentally and physically, and the Micks were at the vanguard of the Brigade's operations.

During the tour the Iraqi Army had formed a new Division for Basra Province and it was the battle group's job to turn it into a fighting force. Responsible, from Divisional Commander downwards, for the M2T of the Division whilst it moved from a standing start through to full operating capability the battle group was kept busy. The focus was on the force elements already in place whilst attempting to facilitate the Iraqis using their own chain of command to raise new elements and sustain those that already existed. It was an uphill struggle at times but immensely rewarding when it worked. In particular the establishment of an outreach programme, as detailed below, was the real sea change, enabling support to the Iraqi Army to be significantly ramped up.

The M2T Training Teams, each comprising an officer and three senior non-commissioned officers, worked within an American team living and operating alongside the Iraqi Army battalions. The specific role of the British contingent was to develop the low-level tactical skills whilst the Americans focussed more on the supporting elements and the operations room procedures. This meant that the small teams were constantly on patrol, either on foot or mounted in US HMMWV vehicles, instructing and cajoling the Iraqi Army soldiers or *jundi*. Both teams were instrumental in setting up schemes that saw local inhabitants (and in many cases former insurgents) become part of the official security apparatus and contribute to the security of their localities.

Number 4 Company ran the Divisional Training Centre (DTC) in Shaibah. They were a small outpost in a large Iraqi camp that had previously been an RAF airfield (1930s) and the main UK logistics base (until March 2007). The Blue Riband course of the DTC was a two-week package that took Iraqi companies up to and including company strike operations. This course was immensely popular with the local battalion commanders and *jundi* and although the standard of the companies, and their chains of command, varied enormously, all of them showed marked improvement as a result of the training. The adaptability, resourcefulness and patience of the training teams were amazing; they were extremely conscientious and put their heart and soul into the training, displaying considerable flair. They have gained the respect of the Iraqi soldiers who in turn have responded well to the instruction. Many of our team went over and above that expected of them to learn the language and culture, further forging the bond between trainers and their charges. This was often reciprocated and many of the Micks were given local names as a sign of their acceptance by the *jundi*.

The M2T role has been an immensely rewarding one and there is little doubt in my mind that the Iraqi Army in Basra is now in a much better shape to fend for itself and deal with the security in the Province without reliance on multi national forces. After a frustrating first half, the Micks have been able to make a real difference but there is still a long way to go and it will be many months and probably years before the Iraqi Security Forces are properly resourced and trained (albeit in line with regional norms) and, most importantly, show the will to take the fight to the enemies of Iraq. Our journey has had its ups and downs; it has been frustrating, comical, boring, exasperating, exciting, tragic and more. We leave much for our successors to do but have played our part in driving forward what is now the UK's main effort in Iraq.

WELSH GUARDS

Welsh Guards Actions and Heroes

Actions

The Battle of Loos 25 September – 8 October 1915 (France)

On 17 August 1915, the 1st Battalion sailed for France, where it was incorporated in the 3rd Brigade of the Guards Division being formed. After a few weeks training under war conditions behind the front, the Division was ordered to join in the biggest attempt to break the enemy front to date between La Bassée and Loos. The latter was a mining town overlooked by Hill 70 and both were in German hands. The chlorine gas-supported opening British assault on 25 September captured Loos and the hill behind it, but in a heavy counter-attack, the Germans recaptured the hilltop and two strongpoints supporting it.

The Welsh Guards, with the three other battalions of the 3rd Guards Brigade, arrived on the 26th at Vermelles, two miles from Loos. The village was under shellfire and little more than a ruin when the Battalion arrived after a gruelling march on roads choked by troops and traffic behind the battle. They bivouacked in the outskirts and at 2 pm on the 27th were ordered to recapture Hill 70, while the two covering strongpoints were also retaken. From a rise near Vermelles a long slope leads down to Loos in full view of the enemy. Their attack was to start from Loos and the Battalion in spreadout formation marched steadily through enemy fire and into the town. The Welsh Guards waited there under gas shelling until 6 pm when, on a report that the strongpoints had been recaptured, they were ordered to join the 4th Battalion Grenadier Guards and recapture Hill 70.

The hillside was under fire from an open right flank and climbing was slow work: it was dark before they reached the crest and the Prince of Wales's Company leading the Battalion had lost touch with the Grenadiers. The earlier report that the covering strongpoints had been retaken was found to be mistaken but orders to cancel the advance arrived too late to stop it. The leading troops reached the hilltop but met devastating machine-gun fire and were ordered to hold a line below the crest. Lying there under fire from an enemy they could not see, they dug in as well as they could and held the position until another battalion of the Brigade relieved them. Five of their officers had been killed and five wounded: 162 non-commissioned officers and men were killed, wounded or missing. Next day companies were reformed in trenches near Loos.

The Defence of Boulogne 22–25 May 1940 (Second World War, France)

On 21 May 1940, the 2nd Battalions Welsh Guards and Irish Guards, in 20th Guards Brigade, were sent from Dover to Boulogne to hold the port while troops were evacuated from Dunkirk and to delay the enemy's northward thrust. 2,400 Guardsmen held the German armour for a crucial two days before being ordered to return to England.

Left: Captain Osmond Williams leading the Regiment through London before they left for Hill 70, Loos, 1915.

Above: The Battalion being visited by President Lebrun of France in Boulogne, 1940.

Welsh Guards

Colonel of the Regiment: HRH The Prince of Wales KG, KT, GCB, AK, QSO, ADC

Formed: 26 February 1915

Role Today: Light role infantry battalion and Public Duties

Battle Honours: First World War: Loos, Somme 1916, '18, Ginchy, Albert 1918, Flers-Courcelette, Morval, Ypres 1917, Pilckem, Poelcappelle Passchendaele, Cambrai 1917, '18, Bapaume 1918, Arras 1918, Drocourt-Queant, Hindenburg Line, Ypres 1917, Havrincourt, Canal Du Nord,, Selle, Sambre, France and Flanders 1915–18

Second World War: Defence of Arras, Boulogne 1940, St Omer-La Bassee, Bourguebus Ridge, Cagny, Mont Pincon, Brussels, Hechtel, Nederrijn, Rhineland, Lingen, North West Europe 1940, '44–5, Fondouk, Djebel el Rhorab, Tunis, Hammam Lif, North Africa 1943, Monte Ornito, Liri Valley, Monte Piccolo, Capture of Perugia, Arezzo, Advance to Florence, Gothic Line, Battaglia, Italy 1944–5
Second World War: Falkland Islands 1982

Uniform: There is a leek on the button, buttons grouped in fives on the front of the tunic, a leek collar badge, a white, green and white plume on the bearskin and a black band on the forage cap

Special Day: St David's Day, 1 March.

Recruiting Areas: Anglesey, Bangor, Bridgend, Cardiff, Carmathen, Merthyr Tydfil, Newport, Pontypridd, Rhyl, Shrewsbury, Swansea and Wrexham.

Marches: Quick – *Rising of the Lark*
Slow – *Men of Harlech*

Motto: *Cymru am Byth* (Wales Forever)

Allied Regiment: 5th/7th Battalion The Royal Australian Regiment

Email Address: hjaww@yahoo.co.uk

Website Address: www.welshguards.net

Recent Operations and Highlights

2002 – From their base in Aldershot, the Battalion deployed to Bosnia for a six- month summer tour with the emphasis on disarming the local population. Some Scots Guards officers were attached.

2003 – Moved from Aldershot to Royal Air Force St Athan in South Wales and trained for Northern Ireland deployment to Londonderry. A Company group rotated through Northern Ireland for one year. The Close Observation Platoon was forward based in Ballykelly.

2004 – The peace process in Northern Ireland saw the draw down of the Battalion in Londonderry and it was immediately warned off for operations in Iraq. After intensive training for operations there, the Battalion deployed in September 2004 and returned in March 2005.

2005 – Training year in St Athan; Number 3 Company trained in Gibraltar.

2006 – Moved to Wellington Barracks, London. New Colours presented and the Battalion provided the Escort for the Colour on The Queen's Birthday Parade. Trained for deployment to Bosnia (deployed September 2006 and returned March 2007). Number 2 Company deployed as the surveillance company to Kosovo. A Platoon of Coldstream Guards was under command. The Mortar Platoon deployed to Afghanistan with 1st Battalion Worcester and Sherwood Foresters Regiment battle group.

It was a role that they had not been expecting: 20th Guards Brigade was commanded by Brigadier William Fox-Pitt, Welsh Guards. He told Lieutenant Colonel Sir Alexander Stanier, Commanding Officer of 2nd Welsh Guards, that the brigade was being sent to Boulogne on 22 May 'to protect the base. But there was no idea that the Germans were anywhere near and that we would be a reserve for the big counter-attack that we expected to go from Arras or wherever it was going to be', wrote Stanier later. The Battalion held a 3–4-mile front. The German war diary commented that 'the enemy is fighting tenaciously for every inch of ground'.

There were countless examples of bravery including that of Major Windsor Lewis. When he learnt on 24 May that the rest of the Battalion had gone he led the remainder of his company to the quayside in the heart of the town where he found several hundred British and French soldiers, not all of them armed and a host of refugees. He organised a position in the quayside railway station and held out for two days more. In the end he decided 'that the position was quite hopeless and that a massacre would ensue if we did not capitulate'. He was wounded and taken by ambulance to hospital. He later escaped and commanded the 2nd (Armoured) Battalion in the North-West European campaign of 1944–5.

Above: Members of The Prince of Wales's Company in Iraq, 2007.

Right: The Presentation of New Colours at the Quadrangle, Windsor Castle, 4 May 2006.

Opposite: 2nd Lieutenant Alex Bourne with The Queen's Colour.

Right: His Majesty King George V investing Sergeant Robert Bye with the Victoria Cross on 27 September 1917.

The Battle of The Fondouk Gap 7–11 April 1943
(Second World War, Tunisia)

When the 3rd Battalion Welsh Guards started to play its part in North Africa the Eighth Army had driven Rommel back through Cyrenaica and Tripolitania. From the west, the Axis forces were threatened by the British First Army and the United States II Corps. Encirclement of the enemy was almost complete. Rommel was in retreat along the coastal plain.

The 1st Guards Brigade was to capture the 700 ft Djebel el Rhorab hills to the north of the Fondouk Gap, which would allow 6th Armoured Division tanks to thrust through and meet Eighth Army. The opening assault was to be made by the Welsh Guards.

On 9 April the Battalion attacked. It soon came under heavy fire and took severe casualties. Though one section was able to push on towards the final objective, the rest of the Battalion was pinned down by fire in the foothills. The Commanding Officer called for further artillery and tanks. This support was forthcoming and a plan was made for a new attack to start at 1 pm.

Much of the credit for its success goes to the Adjutant, Captain G.D. Rhys-Williams, who went forward to explain the plan to the leading companies, in two of which all officers had been killed or wounded. He led the Battalion to triumphant success and, in ensuring this first victory for the Welsh Guards, he himself lost his life among the 114 casualties that it cost to capture the Djebel el Rhorab. 100 German prisoners were taken. Two days later the First and Eighth Armies joined hands 100 miles south of Tunis.

The Battle of Hechtel 7–12 September 1944
(Second World War, Belgium)

With Brussels and Antwerp in Allied hands, the decision was taken by Field Marshal Montgomery to advance and attempt to secure a bridgehead over the northern Rhine before the winter. Ten waterways had to be crossed in order to achieve this.

Having left Brussels, the Welsh Guards tank/infantry Group pressed on to the Albert Canal at Beeringen where the bridge had been partially destroyed. Under heavy fire, and with the gallant aid of the Sappers, the Group got across, surprised and destroyed a German battalion beside the road, forced its way through Helchteren and four miles beyond towards the town of Hechtel where they were held up by heavy and accurate anti-tank fire.

The Group first attacked Hechtel on 7 September but, after repeated assaults, it was finally captured on the 12th with 500 German paratrooper prisoners. Another 150 were dead and 220 wounded.

Hechtel was one of the bloodier battles fought by the 1st and 2nd (Armoured) Battalions Welsh Guards. Though on the last day the Group had the support of medium artillery and of the mortars and machine-guns of a company of the Northumberland Fusiliers, Hechtel was mostly a Welsh Guards battle. More perhaps than on any other occasion, the action was notable for individual acts of gallantry.

Welsh Guards Heroes
Sergeant Robert James Bye VC (1889–1962)

Sergeant Bye, a coal miner from Pontypridd, Glamorgan, won his Victoria Cross on 31 July 1917 a mere two years after he joined the new Regiment as a volunteer. During the opening attack of the Third Battle of Ypres (Passchendaele) he saw that two well-defended concrete blockhouses were hampering the advance. Using his own initiative he rushed one of them and put the garrison inside out of action with his grenades before rejoining his company, which then advanced in an assault on the second objective.

When the Welsh Guards had gone forward to the attack on the third objective, a party was detailed to clear up a line of blockhouses which had been passed. Sergeant Bye volunteered to take charge of this party, accomplished his mission and took many prisoners. Bye then returned to the third objective, again capturing quite a number of prisoners, which was a great help to the assaulting companies. All told he had accounted for over 70 German defenders. The citation in the *London Gazette* stated, 'He displayed throughout the most remarkable initiative.'

Lieutenant The Honourable Christopher Furness VC (1912–40)

Lieutenant Furness was in command of the Bren-gun Carrier Platoon, Welsh Guards, during 17–24 May 1940, when his 1st Battalion formed part of the garrison of Arras. During this time his Platoon was constantly patrolling in advance of or between the widely dispersed parts of the perimeter, and fought many local actions with the enemy. Lieutenant Furness displayed the highest qualities of leadership and dash on all these occasions and imbued his command with a magnificent offensive spirit.

During the evening of 23 May, Lieutenant Furness was wounded when on patrol but he refused to be evacuated. By this time the enemy, considerably reinforced, had threatened the town on three sides and withdrawal to Douai was ordered during the night of 23–24 May. Lieutenant Furness's Platoon, together with a small force of light tanks, were ordered to cover the withdrawal of the transport consisting of over 40 vehicles.

Captain David Basson, Welsh Guards

On Welshness

For somebody who isn't Welsh coming in, I was immediately struck by the Welshness. The Regiment really is a family. Whenever we get a new draft of recruits in from Catterick I see them first on Adjutant's memoranda. Because I know that they will have been away from home I like to point out to them that they have come home, and that it's a family regiment. The Welsh are so incredibly faithful to their families and the boys will go home for a weekend if they are based in London or Germany. They will go home any time they can. I have been in Canada after an exercise and been given one week off for rest and recreation, and the boys ask if they can pay for their own flights back to Merthyr for the week. When they arrive in the Regiment I always ask them who they know. They will always know at least four or five people. It's incredible because Wales is a small population and it is all word of mouth. They all know each other. If someone goes absent, for example, all you've got to do is chat to their friends or chat to one of the Sergeants and they'd say, 'oh I know somebody in that village and yes I heard that his mother was ill' etc. We've got this fascinating split between the North Walians and the South Walians. They get on very well but they are very different.

Major Edward Mellish, Welsh Guards

Number 3 Company Commander

I would say I know as many Guardsmen by number as I do by a name. For instance a Williams, Evans, Davis or Jones is more likely to be called 95. It's like a bit of a nickname, a nuance and no-one objects to it. In fact, there are quite a few guys who actually like to be known by their last two army numbers whether they've got an unusual surname or not. One of the most interesting jobs in the Welsh Guards is being a Platoon Commander. Just after we left London the last time in 2000 I got to go through the proper brigade training as a Platoon Commander. They simulate battle with lasers. Then I went to Canada to be a part of a brigade exercise where a Platoon Commander is at the coalface and sees what happens. It was a fascinating experience and it's the only place in the world that the British Army can really do that. Apart from that, being a Company Commander with the Battalion is something you aspire to do all the time.

Right: Members of the Welsh Guards band await the arrival of the Prince of Wales on St David's Day in Bosnia.

Below: Brigadier Sir Alexander Stanier Bt, DSO and Bar MC who commanded the 2nd Battalion during the fighting in Boulogne in 1940.

About 2.30 am, 24 May, the enemy [Rommel's 7th Panzer Division] attacked on both sides of the town. At one point the enemy advanced to the road along which the transport columns were withdrawing, bringing them under very heavy small arms and anti-tank gunfire. Thus the whole column was blocked and placed in serious jeopardy. Immediately Lieutenant Furness, appreciating the seriousness of the situation, and in spite of his wounds, decided to attack the enemy, who were located in a strongly entrenched position behind wire.

He advanced with three carriers, supported by the light tanks. At once the enemy opened up with very heavy fire from small arms and anti-tank guns. The light tanks were put out of action, but Lieutenant Furness continued to advance. He reached the enemy position and circled it several times at close range, inflicting heavy losses. All three carriers were hit and most of their crews killed or wounded. His own carrier was disabled and the driver and Bren gunner killed. He then engaged the enemy in personal hand-to-hand combat until he was killed.

His magnificent act of self-sacrifice against hopeless odds, and when already wounded, made the enemy withdraw for the time being and enabled the large column of vehicles to get clear unmolested. Lieutenant Furness was awarded a posthumous Victoria Cross.

Brigadier Sir Alexander Stanier Bt, DSO and Bar, MC (1899–1995)

Brigadier 'Sammy' Stanier joined the Regiment in 1917 and won the Military Cross on the Western Front. He was awarded his first Distinguished Service Order when commanding the 2nd Battalion, which had been ordered at short notice to cross to Boulogne as half of 20th Guards Brigade. The mission was to hold the port to cover the withdrawal of the British Expeditionary Force but the German 2nd Panzer Division fought its way into the port and the Brigade was ordered to evacuate.

With great skill and courage Stanier managed to get all but 200 of the Battalion down to the quay. The first Royal Navy destroyer to approach in an attempt to take them off was heavily shelled and, badly damaged, was forced to withdraw. When all seemed lost, another destroyer, HMS *Vimiera* crept in and managed to evacuate over 800 men of the Battalion on the quay.

There is a monument to Sir Alexander Stanier in Asnelles and Arromanches, Normandy. Shortly before the Brigadier died, he accepted the freedom of Arromanches. This was in recognition of his leadership of 231st Infantry Brigade in 50th (Northumbrian) Division which carried out the first 'Gold' Beach assault landing on D-Day, 6 June 1944. In spite of fierce opposition, he managed to capture all objectives by nightfall and continued in command throughout many hard-fought battles that summer and autumn and was awarded a bar to his DSO.

General Charles, Baron Guthrie of Craigiebank GCB, LVO, OBE (1938–)

General Guthrie was Chief of the Defence Staff between 1997 and 2001 and Chief of the General Staff, the professional head of the British Army, between 1994 and 1997. He had a glittering career starting in 1959 with the Welsh Guards, serving in most parts of the world where the British Army had a presence, either overtly or covertly.

It was during his operational tour as Adjutant of 1st Battalion Welsh Guards in Aden that Guthrie decided to serve with 22nd Special Air Service (SAS). He commanded a 12-man troop from G (Guards) Squadron in the Malaysian jungle before serving with the SAS in Aden and East Africa.

He subsequently commanded The Prince of Wales's Company in Munster, 1st Battalion Welsh Guards in Berlin, Pirbright and South Armagh and 4th Armoured Brigade in Germany. In 1992 he became the last Commander NATO Northern Army Group and Commander-in-Chief British Army of the Rhine.

Above: The Colonel of the Welsh Guards, HRH the Prince of Wales, meets members of the regiment and hands out leeks on St David's Day.

LIFE ON THE FRONT LINE: The Welsh Guards, 2007

From fighting fires in Birmingham to battling insurgents in Basra; from the bogs of Northern Ireland to the mountains of the Balkans; from the deserts of Afghanistan to the gravel of Horse Guards Parade. A Guardsman who has served with the Battalion since 2002 will have been on operations in every calendar year.

Bosnia 2002

At the beginning of 2002 the Battalion was based in Bruneval Barracks, Aldershot. It was from there that the Battalion deployed to Bosnia in March of that year on Operation PALATINE. The mission was to provide a safe and secure environment in which the country could progress towards normality. One of the main methods of facilitating this was to disarm the local population, a task that was conducted through a series of operations to remove weapons from the community. Many such operations were carried out, resulting in a staggering amount of illegally held weapons and ammunition found and handed in.

Her Majesty The Queen Mother died on the 30 March 2002 whilst the Battalion was in Bosnia. The Welsh Guards, along with the other regiments of the Household Division, provided a party of officers to stand vigil during the lying in state in Westminster Hall. This event highlighted the unique role of regiments of the Household Division; one moment patrolling the streets of a war-torn country, the next having the honour of providing officers for a poignant State Ceremonial event.

Fire Strikes 2002–3

By September 2002 the six-month tour to Bosnia was coming to an end and all ranks were looking forward to getting back home. However that was not to be the case, as the Battalion flew back to find that post-operational leave had been cancelled and instead they had to provide cover for striking firemen in Warwickshire and the West Midlands. On 11 February 2003, they handed over their fire-fighting commitments and prepared for a deployment to Northern Ireland.

Northern Ireland 2003–4

The public-order training and deployment to Northern Ireland coincided with the Battalion's move to RAF St Athan in South Wales, the first time that the Welsh Guards had been based in Wales since the Regiment's formation in 1915. The whole Battalion deployed to Northern Ireland in May 2003 to provide cover for the Marching Season. It was during this tour that Sgt Bennett was tragically killed while on an attachment to the Army Air Corps as a pilot. The successful Peace Process in Northern Ireland provided a Peace Dividend and the Battalion was withdrawn from Northern Ireland. The last company back from Northern Ireland was the Prince of Wales's Company who flew back to St Athan on St David's Day 2004 to be met by The Colonel, HRH The Prince of Wales.

Iraq 2004–5

At the end of the Battalion's commitment to Northern Ireland it was warned for operations in Iraq with 4th Armoured Brigade. After an intense period of training the Battalion deployed to Iraq in September 2004 for a six-month tour, returning in March 2005. The Battalion was split across Iraq with the main Welsh Guards battle group based in Camp Abu Naji, just outside the city of Al Amarah in Maysan Province, 185 miles to the north of Basra. The other elements of the Battalion were located in Basra; The Prince of Wales's Company was based in the Old State Building in the middle of Basra City whilst Number Two Company carried out Security Sector Reform, working out of the Shatt-Al-Arab Hotel in Basra; both companies were under the command of the 1st Battalion The Duke of Wellington's Regiment.

During its tour the Welsh Guards battle group had four main Lines of Operation; security, governance, economic development and communication. All told, the 1st Battalion Welsh Guards battle group enjoyed a most successful tour, during which they forged a strong working relationship with the local population and brought some significant improvements to Maysan Province.

Following a period of consolidation after the Iraq tour the Battalion was committed to a large number of training support tasks in 2005.

State Ceremonial and Public Duties

The Battalion moved from St Athan to Wellington Barracks, London in April 2006. The Battalion had been away from London and Public Duties for six years and so there was a lot of hard work required to reach the exacting standards required. Her Majesty The Queen presented New Colours to the Battalion on 4 May 2006 at Windsor Castle. A month later the Queen's Colour was Trooped in front of Her Majesty with the Prince of Wales's Company providing the Escort to the Colour – a parade all the more special owing to it being Her Majesty's 80th birthday. To mark the occasion a 'feu de joie' was fired by the Battalion in the forecourt of Buckingham Palace at the end of the Parade.

The Balkans 2006–7

No sooner had the dust settled on Horse Guards Parade than the Battalion had to switch its attention to training for the imminent deployment to Bosnia and Kosovo. Some men were on Parade on the Saturday in tunic and bearskin, and in combat clothing on the Sunday starting their training in Kent for the deployment to the Balkans. The Battalion was to be the last British battalion to serve in Bosnia and their departure was marked by a parade on St David's Day in Banja Luka during which The Colonel, HRH The Prince of Wales, presented leeks to the Battalion and then met Bosnia's political and religious leaders.

The Welsh Guards finally returned from Bosnia on 29 March 2007 and were met by the Armed Forces Minister, Adam Ingram,

Left: The Welsh Guards battle group in Iraq 2005.

and the Bosnian Ambassador to the UK, Her Excellency Ambassador Tanja Milasinovic. Mr Ingram said:

'This marks the end of an era. It is all too easy today to forget what a dire and desperate situation our forces faced when they first went into Bosnia in 1992 ... Successful elections took place last year. Most of those who left their homes have returned ... You and those who have gone before you have done a tremendous job helping people who could not help themselves'.

Some of the Welsh Guardsmen opted to turn down the flight home in favour of a more gruelling journey back. Captain James Westropp formed a team of Welsh Guardsman to cycle from Bosnia to Calais, kayaking across the channel, and finally running three marathons back to back from Dover to Wellington Barracks before taking up their cycles again and cycling from London to Bangor in North Wales prior to laying up the Battalion's old colours. The Colonel, HRH The Prince of Wales and HRH The Duchess of Cornwall started the Iron Guardsman Challenge on St David's Day 2007 in Bosnia. The team of ten hand-picked men arrived in Wellington Barracks 30 days after setting off. It was a fantastic physical and mental achievement for all who took part, and the Challenge raised over £34,000 for charities.

Afghanistan 2007

The mortar platoon was back in the UK only for a brief period before a six-month deployment to Helmand Province in Afghanistan in support of the 1st Battalion The Worcestershire and Sherwood Foresters. They took part in some of the heaviest fighting that has been a feature of the British presence in that region, providing mortar fire control throughout and firing an unprecedented number of mortar rounds. Every man returned safely in October 2007.

State Ceremonial and Public Duties

On return from the Balkans the Battalion prepared for The Queen's Birthday Parade. Although the Colour being trooped was from the Coldstream Guards, the bulk of the troops on parade were from the Welsh Guards and the parade was commanded by a Welsh Guardsman. Owing to the pressure of operations the Battalion only had four weeks to prepare for the Parade, and it is testament to the hard work and effort of all the Guardsmen involved that the standard of the Parade drew widespread praise.

The Battalion provided the bulk of the troops for the State Opening of Parliament on the 6th November 2007 dressed in greatcoats and bearskins: barely a day later, the Battalion was on exercise in Belize in jungle hats coming toe to toe with tarantulas and sharing their space with scorpions and snakes. There is plenty of variety and excitement in the life of a Welsh Guardsman.

Sport and Adventure Training

Throughout the previous six years the Battalion has made sure that there is time for Sport and Adventure Training. Being Welsh, Rugby plays an important part in Battalion life. Every year each company fields a 15-man team for a gruelling and hard-fought inter-company competition with every company playing each other on the same day. The Battalion's Rugby team plays at a high standard with four men playing in the Army team in the 07/08 season and three of them also play for the Combined Services Team. A Welsh Guardsman also coached the Army's main rugby team. A number of Adventure Training Exercises have been run in the past years including an annual skiing exercise for over 100 men to France, parachuting expeditions to America, diving in Belize, kayaking and climbing in the Pyrenees to name just a few.

Conclusion

There hasn't been a dull year in the new millennium for the Welsh Guards. Operations have driven activity but there have been plenty of opportunities elsewhere. The ceremonial role has been executed to the highest of standards throughout and the Battalion is looking forward to Trooping its Colour again in 2008.

THE GUARDS IN ACTION

THE POST-WAR YEARS: 1945 TO THE 1960s

Colonel Simon Doughty

Palestine – Malaya – Cyprus – Suez Canal Zone – Oman – Kuwait – Aden – Borneo

Late 1945 brought peace at the end of six years of war. In previous centuries, Household Troops might have expected a period of service at home. They had always been ready to fight the King's enemies wherever they might be, but, except for the 1920s and 1930s, were never far from the Sovereign in times of peace. The post-Second World War era was, however, to be very different, as the Guards deployed frequently overseas, playing their full role as occupying troops in Germany, as garrison troops in outposts around the world, and in Britain's difficult drawdown from the days of Empire.

With the war in Europe over in May 1945, attention turned to the Far East, with plans to dispatch the 1st Guards Brigade. But with the Japanese surrender in August, the Brigade soon found itself bound for Palestine, and a quite different type of soldiering. The British Mandate in Palestine had remained a dormant issue during the war, but with thousands of Jewish refugees making their way to the Middle East from all over Europe, trouble was inevitable. British policy was a balancing act: promoting self-government while allowing some Jewish immigration and also protecting Arab civil and religious rights. As a policy, it was fraught with difficulty.

Above: Tripoli Corps of Drums GOC Parade, 1948.

1st Guards Brigade sailed from Southampton in early October 1945, bound for Haifa. Life was uncomfortable but bearable, while the Brigade's tasks were a far cry from the mechanised campaigns of North-West Europe. Cordon and searching, roadblocks, low-level patrolling – these were all to become very familiar to troops in years to come.

The security situation deteriorated in mid-1946, and in July the King David Hotel in Jerusalem was blown up by members of the Jewish Stern Gang with great loss of life. Early in 1947 1st Guards Brigade moved south, to conduct the cordoning and searching of Tel Aviv, a considerable task. A successful operation was inevitably followed by reprisals against the Brigade units. 3rd Battalion Coldstream Guards were attacked in their base on the outskirts of the city, with one Guardsman killed. The Colours, hanging in the Officers' Mess, came under fire for the first time in nearly a century, and might have been lost had they not been quickly removed by the Adjutant.

Britain relinquished its mandate in 1948, with the United Nations partitioning the country in pursuit of a solution. British troops were now a target for both Arabs and Jews, while also trying to protect one group from the other. In January 1948, a company of Irish Guards, in the town of Safad in the north, was holding the ring prior to the British withdrawal. An Irish Guards officer was offered a substantial bribe by the Jews to give them details of the plan, but he refused. When the moment came to withdraw, the Guardsmen, 'looking deliberately unconcerned', leapt into their vehicles, and the town was cleared in under five minutes. Soon, Arabs and Jews were fighting for possession of the police station.

The final withdrawal was now fully underway. On 14 May 1948, a troop of The Life Guards escorted the departing High Commissioner as he made his final drive from Government House in Jerusalem to the airfield. At Haifa, 1st Battalion Grenadier Guards mounted another guard of honour, with the Pipes of the Irish Guards. The Mandate expired at midnight, but 1st Guards Brigade was required to hold the Haifa enclave for a further six weeks. Just after midday on 30 June, the Union flag was lowered for the last time, bringing to an end Britain's 30-year presence in Palestine. 1st Guards Brigade were the last troops to leave.

As the British presence in Palestine ended, the Malayan campaign was just beginning, a state of emergency being declared on 17 June 1948 in response to the growing threat from the Chinese Communists ('bandits' in the nomenclature of the time). A newly formed 2nd Guards Brigade

Left: Battalion transport on flight deck.

Below: 1st Battalion Coldstream Guards in Portsmouth dockyard, en route to Cyprus in 1951. HMS Illustrious is in the background.

was raised for operations there, sailing for Singapore in early September. One of the battalions, 3rd Battalion Grenadier Guards, had only returned four months earlier from a two-and-a-half year tour in Palestine. The 600-strong 3rd Battalion Grenadier Guards, one of the first to arrive in Singapore, travelled 200 miles north by train, to Kuala Lumpur. On arriving at Sungei Besi Camp in Selangor state, the Sergeant Major asked a small gunner, perched on a pile of canvas, where the camp was. 'I'm sitting on it' was the helpful reply.

For 2nd Guards Brigade, operating in the jungle was entirely different. Some of the battalions had recently been on Public Duties, and National Service meant that a good number of their Guardsmen were new to the Army, with little training and no operational experience. Jungle warfare required new skills and tactics, and also placed a heavy reliance on junior officers and non-commissioned officers.

The Brigade's role, to restore confidence and round up bandits, seemed a simple one, but it was to be more challenging. The bandits concealed themselves well in the jungle, and the British troops had yet to be equipped with radios and helicopters. Patrols, assisted by local trackers, had to be entirely self-sufficient, with soldiers carrying loads of 60 lbs or more. On the rare occasions when patrols made contact with their elusive enemy, the fighting was violent and fleeting. In March 1949, a platoon of Grenadiers was ambushed by some 15 bandits, well dug-in. Despite reacting instantly with a counter-attack, five Grenadier Guardsmen lost their lives. Later that year, the Grenadiers' fortunes were reversed, when, in the space of a month, they had killed or captured 11 armed bandits, and wounded 9 others.

In early April 1949, a non-commissioned officer and four Guardsmen of the Coldstream Guards set off on a patrol that was intended to last two or three hours. Dressed in light jungle clothing, they left their camp equipped with just one Sten sub-machine gun, four rifles, a few grenades,

a local map, and a compass. Soon, they made contact with a group of bandits, and in attempting to reconnoitre around them, the patrol found its route back to camp barred to them. They were forced to move east rather than west, and for seven days and nights, with no food and little sleep, they made their way through thick jungle. On the second day, they shot dead a lone bandit, probably a scout. On the following day the patrol encountered six bandits, killing one and wounding another. Finally, on the seventh day, soaking wet, cold and tired, they met a friendly British patrol, and safety was at hand. The section commander, Lance Sergeant Gulston, received the immediate award of a Military Medal, while the *Malay Tribune* described the patrol as 'Unquestionably the most staggering feat of human endurance seen in Malaya during the emergency.'

The concept of 'Hearts and Minds' was a product of the Malayan Emergency. Indeed, one of its earliest operations was planned by the Commanding Officer of 2nd Battalion Coldstream Guards, Lieutenant Colonel (later General Sir) Victor FitzGeorge-Balfour, who identified the

Left: (l to r): Noel Baker, Field Marshal Sir John Harding, Governor of Cyprus, Nicos Kranidiotis, Archbishop Makarios, and Alan Lennox-Boyd at a meeting in Cyprus in 1956.

targeted by the terrorists. In November 1956, 33 casualties were inflicted by EOKA, the highest throughout the campaign.

3rd Battalion Grenadier Guards, on a quiet posting in Malta, soon found themselves moving east to Cyprus. One of the battalion's early 1957 missions, in the Troodos mountains, was to kill or capture Colonel Grivas's second-in-command, Gregoris Afxentiou. Following a large cordon and search operation, a group of terrorists were flushed out of a cleverly concealed underground hiding-place. Then, suddenly, a voice in English was heard to say 'Come in and get us out', and Afxentiou burst out, firing a Sten gun and killing a soldier from The Duke of Wellington's Regiment. He scuttled back into his hide, and there followed a seven-hour siege, with the Grenadiers forming the cordon and members of the press watching with interest. The siege finally ended with a combination of grenades, explosives, tear gas and petrol. Afxentiou's charred body was later recovered from the hiding place.

The Blues were deployed in Cyprus from 1956 to 1959. Soon after arriving, the Regimental Medical Officer was shot dead in his car while visiting families in Nicosia. In 1958, a young Blues officer and a trooper, both National Servicemen, were shot in the back in Famagusta in reprisals following the accidental death of a woman three days earlier.

In the same year, National Serviceman Cornet Auberon Waugh (son of the novelist Evelyn who had served in The Blues 1942–5), while on patrol, managed, as he described later, 'in a moment of absent-mindedness' to cock his .30 Browning on his Ferret scout car and then, noticing 'an impediment in the elevation of the machine gun', decided to 'dismount, seize the barrel from in front and give it a good wiggle. A split second later I realised that it had started firing. No sooner had I noticed this, than I observed with dismay that it was firing through my chest.' Waugh bled profusely and was convinced that he would die, so much so that he asked his Corporal of Horse Chudleigh to kiss him. Since Chudleigh 'did not spot the historical reference' (to Lord Nelson's famous request to Captain Hardy at Trafalgar) he 'treated me with some caution thereafter.' Waugh was lucky to survive the accident.

Although The Life Guards had briefly deployed a squadron to Cyprus in 1955, their main effort was in Egypt, where the Regiment was based from 1954 to 1956. The 'Essential Duty' allocated was a rather tedious one: patrolling the unmarked perimeter of the Canal Zone to prevent pilfering of Army equipment, and to patrol the Canal itself to prevent the locals from stealing the copper telephone lines. Organised sports helped to reduce tedium (athletics, cricket, football, for the soldiers; polo for the officers) while Regimental Headquarters worked on contingency plans for a range of rather alarming threats, including an advance of the Soviet Army on the Suez Canal.

By the time the real crisis began in Egypt in 1956, with its President, Colonel Gamal Nasser, seizing the Canal, The Life Guards had returned to Windsor. Soon, the advance party with vehicles were on their way back to Port Said, but by the time they arrived, a ceasefire had been ordered,

support of the squatters as worthy of effort. These squatters had illegally cleared land and were now occupying it, and since they had no right to be there, they also bore no allegiance to either the government or the Communist bandits. They were easy prey to the bandits, unless the security forces could provide something more appealing. By the end of 1951, some 35,000 squatters had been moved by the Guards alone into 30 new 'Kampongs' or villages in Malaya. The names of two of these villages were to be 'Coldstream Village' and 'Balfour Village'. The latter was still flourishing in 1994.

Cyprus was to be the next challenge. It was once a pleasant Mediterranean posting, but this all changed in April 1955, when the EOKA (after the Greek initials for 'National Organisation of Cypriot Struggle') campaign, led by former Greek army Colonel George Grivas, was launched to force the British Government to agree to Enosis – the union of Cyprus with Greece. The campaign began with minor bomb attacks and the littering of streets with propaganda leaflets. By June the first deaths had occurred, with British administrators and soldiers being

Left: D Squadron Royal Horse Guards (The Blues) in Malaya, 1966.

Left: D Squadron Royal Horse Guards (The Blues) in Malaya, 1966.

Bottom: Scots Guards in Malaya monitoring an area of jungle they have mined to see whether there are any communist bandits hiding in the long grasses, 23 April 1949.

and the Anglo-French attempt to retake the Canal was over. It was only the swift intervention of The Blues, based in Cyprus, that prevented all the vehicles, bar one, from being unloaded. The one vehicle to make it ashore was, of course, the Officers' Mess truck, and it took the intervention of Field Marshal Sir John Harding to recover it!

The following year, The Life Guards were warned for an accompanied tour in Germany, only to be told later that it would be, instead, an unaccompanied tour to Aden. Shortly after arriving, in late 1958, a squadron was dispatched, by air, to Oman, to support the Sultan's Forces against the rebels in the Jebel Akhdar. Soon, the squadron was working with the SAS, in a short and highly successful operation.

Looking back, today's generation of Household Cavalrymen and Guardsmen might well conclude that their post-war forbears had it pretty easy during the 1950s when compared to the era of Iraq and Afghanistan. The truth is that regiments and battalions were frequently on the move, and often deploying to yet another new posting that nearly always brought unexpected dangers, requiring a complex hybrid of tactics and techniques that needed to be acquired at first-hand before they could be taught. Overseas deployments tended to be longer than today, and the postings appeared much more remote than now.

There was to be no let-up in the 1960s, as terrorist campaigns for independence intensified and Britain's withdrawal from the residual Empire quickened. The ending of the Aden campaign in 1967 marked the conclusion of a chapter, while the more home-grown terrorism of the Ulster Troubles was barely two years away. The lessons learned during that era still, of course, have a currency today.

In describing the contribution of the 2nd Battalion Scots Guards, the last of the three Guards battalions to leave Malaya in 1951, the then General Sir John Harding, Commander-in-Chief of Far East Land Forces, (and later to be the Colonel of The Life Guards), summed up their contribution thus: 'They have confounded the critics and proved again, if further proof was needed, that there is nothing Guardsmen cannot achieve when they put their minds and hearts to it.' He could have been writing about any regiment or battalion of the Household Division, before or since.

GERMANY 1945–2008

Colonel Oliver Lindsay

On 4 July 1945 1st Battalion Grenadier Guards was among the very first British troops to enter Berlin, the ruined capital of Germany. Burned-out tanks littered the roads. Dark crowds of Germans lined the pavements, clustered in knots on the uneven rubble. The smell of death and dust was everywhere.

Almost two months earlier, following Victory in Europe Day, Guards Battalions had each become responsible for vast areas. The first priority was disarming and the demobilisation of German soldiers and the second was helping the displaced people.

One Guards battalion found 3,000 Russians in its area; they were among the fortunate few surviving Soviet prisoners of war. Thousands of their compatriots had been fed to Auschwitz's gas chambers, while the Russians had starved to death in the East over, according to some accounts, two million German prisoners of war.

The Blues, close to the Soviet Zone, saw the Russians and Communist Germans erecting watch towers. Like others, The Blues endeavoured to control the Black Market and maintain internal security.

In December 1947 negotiations between Russia, America and Britain over the future of Germany finally broke down. Fears were raised that the Russians would impose their solution by force.

Across Eastern Europe key members of the non-Communist parties disappeared, kidnapped at night. Slowly the Communists eliminated the opposition, edging each satellite country towards their goal of one party Communist rule, under Soviet hegemony. The situation deteriorated further with Stalin's claim that capitalism made war inevitable.

To meet the threat, the North Atlantic Alliance with an integrated military command organisation, soon known as NATO, was agreed in 1949 by America and the West European nations. The British Army of the Rhine (BAOR) changed from an occupation force of two divisions into a field force of initially four. This was to become a permanent commitment which, at its height, amounted to 77,000 men.

All Guards battalions were frequently in Germany; the Grenadier Guards alone having 11 tours there, despite crises elsewhere and the maintenance of Public Duties in London. The Household Cavalry were Corps troops and patrolled the inner German border. Many of the lengthy training exercises by the early 1960s were interesting, testing and worthwhile. All phases of war in a nuclear setting were usually covered including river crossings at night. On their conclusion, the Commander

of 4th Guards Brigade held a debriefing, usually in a pub, attended by most officers. Criticism was levelled and lessons learned. Reputations were made or marred.

Guards Battalions always served in 4th Guards Brigade or in West Berlin until that city garrison brigade was disbanded in 1994. The 4th Guards Brigade was generally acknowledged to epitomise the high standards that are the hallmark of the Household Division, as well as having a formation pride unmatched by any other Brigade in BAOR.

The equipment was largely obsolescent and battalions were under strength as the last of the admirable National Servicemen had left us in 1962. Many barracks were in need of refurbishment and there were never enough married quarters. On the other hand there was plenty of sport; battalions also rented ski huts in the German Alps and adventurous training was much encouraged.

Above: Russian commander Marshal Georgi K. Zhukov, inspecting the Guard of Honour of 1st Battalion Grenadier Guards with Field Marshal Bernard L. Montgomery at a ceremony held at the Brandenburg Gate in Berlin in 1945.

Above: Warriors of the 1st Battalion Coldstream Guards in Germany, 1995.

The Coldstream and Welsh Guards in 4th Guards Brigade in the early 1960s found that the whole NATO strategy was based on the threatened use of atomic weapons in order to cope with the numerical superiority of the Russians. Tactics changed as the equipment and mobility improved. 1st Battalion Scots Guards in Münster in 1972 found that the concept of static, immobile defensive positions of ten years before had gone. Instead, battle groups of all arms were based on tanks and mechanised infantry; they consisted of between two and five sub-units called combat teams. The battle groups occupied a series of planned alternative positions in depth to check, canalise and destroy the Warsaw Pact forces by aggressive contact, using mobility and all available firepower, still including nuclear weapons.

By the late 1980s the British Corps in Germany consisted of two forward and a reserve armoured division. There was also a reinforcing division available from the United Kingdom. The tasks of the forward ones was to delay the enemy, while the reserve division, which included Guards battalions, was trained to carry out a series of counter-moves – counter-attack, counter-penetration and the counter-stroke. The Household Cavalry were equipped with Chieftain main battle tanks from 1969 and maintained a regiment permanently in BAOR until the major reorganisation of the Army in the early 1990s. From the early 1970s onwards operational tours in Northern Ireland often totally disrupted a regiment's or a battalion's annual training cycle in Germany.

The collapse of Communism in Russia, East Germany and elsewhere surprised everyone. East Germans were suddenly permitted to travel to the West; the Berlin Wall was rapidly demolished, paving the way in 1990 for German reunification. War in Europe, which had so long been central to all Western military thinking and procedures, ceased to be a threat to our very survival. BAOR, together with its allies, had provided the cutting edge for the protection of West Germany and Europe. The professionalism and dedication of those so closely involved, together

with our families accompanying us, was a fundamental that should always be remembered.

Although none deployed to fight in Germany, in the role for which they had prepared, the armoured divisions of BAOR were very capable and one of them, the 1st Armoured Division, was deployed most successfully to liberate Kuwait after Saddam Hussein's invasion of that country in 1990. Subsequently British formations and units based in Germany have served in a variety of conflicts. Before deploying to Kosovo, 1st Battalion Irish Guards was there having trained, like many other units, in Canada where from 1971 the Suffield prairie practice area provided more space for realistic all-arms training.

The Household Division was probably better represented among the senior commanders in BAOR/Berlin than was any other part of the Army. From the 1960s the Household Division officers who served there in the ranks of major general and above included Erskine-Crum, Nelson, Norfolk, Bowes-Lyon, Cathcart, Fraser, Worsley, Gow, Gordon-Lennox, Scott-Barrett, Redgrave, Guthrie, Hobbs, Corbett, Naylor, Denison-Smith, Mackay-Dick, Drewry, Kiszely and Watt, among others.

The 1st Battalion Scots Guards has been based in Münster since 2003 (although it is now in both Iraq and Afghanistan). The Battalion will move to Catterick in 2008.

The peace dividend, following the collapse of the Warsaw Pact in 1991 and the end of the emergency in Northern Ireland, has led to dramatic reductions in the number of infantry battalions, armoured and artillery regiments. The Army today is the smallest it has been since 1828, despite wars in the Middle East and the threat of international terrorism.

No Regiment or Battalion of the Household Division is expected to be stationed in Germany again. It is the end of an era, reflecting optimism that there will be 'peace in our time', in Europe, as Prime Minister Neville Chamberlain put it 70 years ago.

BRITISH ARMY OF THE RHINE

General Lord Guthrie

The second British Army on the Rhine was formed on 25 August 1945 from 21st Army Group. Its original function was to control the army corps districts which were running the military government of the British zone of occupied Germany. After the assumption of government by civilians, it became the command formation for the troops in Germany only, rather than being responsible for administration as well.

As the Soviet threat increased, BAOR became more responsible for the defence of Germany than its occupation. It became the primary formation controlling the British contribution to NATO after the formation of the alliance in 1949. Its primary combat formation was 1st (British) Corps. From 1952 the commander-in-chief of the BAOR was also the commander of NATO's Northern Army Group (NORTHAG) in the event of a general war with the Soviet Union and the Warsaw Pact.

The 1993 'Options for Change' defence cuts resulted in BAOR being replaced by the 25,000-strong British Forces Germany (BFG) in 1994.

I was stationed in Germany in 1961 when 1st Battalion Welsh Guards was part of 4th Guards Brigade. During my service of 44 years I spent 14 years in Germany, eventually becoming Commander-in-Chief BAOR and Commander of the Northern Army Group. During my time there

Above: 1st Battalion Coldstream Guards fighting through its objective on an exercise in Germany in 1997.

Captain Paddy Shields, Irish Guards

Life In British Army Of The Rhine

I joined the Regiment in 1977 at Münster, then in West Germany. Life revolved around the vehicles and going on long exercises. We had 'Active Edge' scenarios – where people from independent headquarters would come around and inspect our readiness and they then used to tip us out to battle position areas.

The Picquet Officer would get a signal or a telephone call to say 'activate now'. There would be a hive of activity while the information cascaded down and the married men were summoned from their married quarters. Our kit was already packed and ready to go and the vehicles would be lined up, ready to move out of the main gate. We would get a couple of hours before a team would land on our doorstep and we would be

inspected in our vehicles. When the inspection got down to Guardsman level they would say things like 'let me see your water bottle, let me see your washing and shaving kit'. We had pre-arranged assembly areas scattered about the local area and we'd all trundle out and sit in the woods and set up our radio nets and just hang about and get a cup of tea on and then by about 2 pm they'd collapse it all and we'd all come back to Headquarters and they'd tell us how we had done.

In the late 1980s we were in Berlin, which was a fantastic posting. We were there when the Wall came down and that was a really interesting time: to be in the centre of Europe in a cultural city with its music and arts and then to see the comparisons in the East.

Left: Spandau Prison in 1947.

were many changes and the Germany of 1961 was very different to that of 1994.

When I was an Ensign and a Platoon Commander in Hubblerath the Second World War was still very much in people's minds and our commanders had all, without exception, fought in the war. Many had very mixed feelings about the Germans. Although the policy of non-fraternisation had been abandoned some years previously, there was not a great deal of contact between the local Germans and the British Army and not much effort was made by us to change the situation. In the early 1960s Germany was a drab country and the economic miracle was yet to bear visible fruit. The Germans were still fearful of a possible Soviet attack and nearly every family had some story to tell about disasters which had befallen their relations. During the Cuban missile crisis, I well remember a number of German businessmen turning up at our barracks pleading for a passage to the United States as they feared the Third World War was about to begin.

But Germany changed and in the 1980s and 1990s became prosperous. Contacts between the Army and the local civilians became close. I always thought it interesting that, when we were first in Germany and members of the Armed Forces were married to Germans, the Germans always wanted to settle eventually in England. But by the time the 1980s and 1990s came that was rather different. Life in Germany was nothing like as hectic for soldiers as it has become today. A great deal of sport was played and officers were able to shoot, ride, hunt with the Weser Vale and sail in Army yachts from Kiel.

4th Guards Brigade was much involved in training and taking part in exercises which, in some cases, lasted for as long as six weeks. Training took place in the open countryside and was not restricted to training areas. The local farmers were surprisingly tolerant about the damage which was done to their land but they felt it acceptable because of the threat from the East for which we must be prepared. The officers got to know their area of potential operations extremely well and contingency planning for war was taken extremely seriously. Germany was popular for many as one felt financially rather better off than being at home. The Status of the Forces Agreement allowed duty-free goods to be purchased and one was able to buy a very much nicer car than if one was at home. Once they had settled in Germany, many of the families would like to have stayed on when the time came for them to return to the United Kingdom.

I was lucky enough to command 1st Battalion Welsh Guards in West Berlin which was a particularly popular station. We had a very different role from the Army in mainland West Germany and being surrounded by East Germany and the Russian Army gave life a certain edge. Berlin was an exciting city during the Cold War and our role, which included guarding Spandau Prison and Rudolf Hess, was quite different from anything else we had been asked to do. The Household Cavalry, who were not in 4th Guards Brigade, were the armoured reconnaissance element for 1st British Corps and spent much of their time patrolling the border and became great experts on the Iron Curtain in the British sector.

As Commander-in-Chief from 1992 I had to reduce the size of the British Army of the Rhine and Berlin from some 60,000 to 26,000 within two years. This was quite a challenge as the British Army of the Rhine, apart from its soldiers, had some 250,000 dependants. In many ways the reduction in size was a sad operation but certainly was necessary once the Cold War was over and troop reductions had taken place due to various Ministry of Defence savings exercises.

Germany was good to many of us. I commanded a Platoon, Company, Battalion, Brigade, Corps and Army Group there and I was very fortunate to have served at such a time.

Above: Lance Sergeant S. Smith, 1st Battalion Scots Guards dismounting from a Warrior.

NORTHERN IRELAND 1969–2007

Major General Anthony Leask

For 37 years the British Army fought a campaign to defeat terrorism and restore law and order to Northern Ireland. In this the Household Division played its full part. Units were deployed to the Province on resident tours of up to two years with their families and unaccompanied roulement (movement of troops or equipment) tours of up to six months. The regiments and battalions of the Household Division served eight resident and the equivalent of 64 roulement tours. These tours of duty, and the training required before them, took everyone away from their primary roles of general war and Public Duties. Yet the standard of The Queen's Birthday Parade improved markedly during these years; and the actions of those who fought in the Falkland Islands in 1982 show that operational skills remained as high as ever.

It was the commitment of officers and men at platoon level that was most remarkable. Initially they were required to deal with civil disorder, rioting of savage intensity: then the gunmen appeared on the streets. Over the years terrorist tactics and weaponry became more and more sophisticated. Many of the best small arms were available to them, and they became expert in the use of all types of improvised explosive devices and home-made mortars. Their attacks became ever more deadly. Every day, discipline, alertness, endurance and leadership were tested to the full. The terrorists also carried out their attacks in the rest of the United Kingdom and overseas. Everyone became involved, with increased levels of security and alertness required in barracks, married quarters, on training and even when off duty.

In October 1969 B Squadron The Life Guards was the first Household Cavalry to be deployed to Northern Ireland. Thereafter both Regiments served numerous tours in the armoured car and in the infantry roles. Their involvement will also be remembered for two incidents that occurred outside Northern Ireland. On 27 August 1979 Earl Mountbatten of Burma, Colonel of The Life Guards, was killed by a terrorist bomb in the Republic of Ireland. Then on 20 July 1982 The Queen's Life Guard, mounted by The Blues and Royals, was attacked in Hyde Park. Four officers and men were killed and three wounded; seven horses were also killed and three wounded, including Sefton who won the heart of the British people.

An outline of a few incidents gives some idea of operations by the Foot Guards over the years. On 8 November 1971 a roundabout in West Belfast was deliberately blocked by burning cars. A platoon of 1st

Battalion Scots Guards approached the area from the hillside above and took up covering positions. Another group moved to clear the roundabout. As they approached they came under fire from the flats overlooking the area and withdrew to the covering position, pursued by petrol and blast bombs. Over the next three hours a fierce gun battle took place with numerous gunmen. Ammunition ran short and had to be resupplied. Lance Sergeant Allan Ball used his sniper rifle to full effect, until he was blown off his feet by a blast bomb. For his courage he was to receive the Military Medal.

The next night a further operation was mounted to clear the roundabout and another equally fierce battle took place. Subsequent information indicated that up to 11 terrorists had been killed during those two nights. This was the beginning. The bombing of commercial and industrial premises was one terrorist tactic designed to bring the Province to its knees. On Friday 21 July 1972 no fewer than 16 bombs went off in the centre of Belfast. The last of many calls indicated a bomb in the Oxford Street Bus Depot, packed at that time on a Friday with hundreds of women and children. 1st Battalion Welsh Guards was fully stretched. The only men available were a four-man team commanded by Sergeant Philip Price, who had just got to sleep having been deployed the

Captain Smith, Irish Guards

Life In Northern Ireland

I first went there in 1982. We did a lot of vehicle checkpoints, a lot of patrolling, and a lot of helicopter operations. We would start at one end of the county where the helicopter would drop us off and we would stop somebody in a car on a particular road. We would then fly around four or five different locations and we'd be spotting the same bloke about 20–25 minutes later at the other end of the road so it would give the impression to the opposition that we were everywhere. In the main our relations with the local people were very good because we had the soldiers from the south of Ireland and you keep the banter going.

previous night. On arrival at the depot Sergeant Price identified the most likely vehicle to contain the bomb and started to clear the area, regardless of his own safety. During the clearance the bomb exploded, killing him instantly. His courage and selfless action saved many lives that day.

An example of the alertness required of all ranks at all times was demonstrated by Lance Corporal Rodney Clayden, 2nd Battalion Coldstream Guards, at that time serving on a resident tour in Londonderry. On the morning of 17 November 1977 he was opening a checkpoint on the Craigavon Bridge, a routine and repetitive task. There were a number of traffic cones set out to control vehicles but that morning he noticed there was an extra one. Subsequent clearance of the additional cone revealed a deadly booby trap consisting of a pressure switch, Semtex explosives and 1.5lb of ball bearings.

On the morning of 21 December 1978 Sergeant Richard Garmory, 1st Battalion Grenadier Guards was commanding a patrol of two four-man teams in Crossmaglen, South Armagh when he saw a suspicious van with boxes piled in the back. Checking with his magnifying sight he spotted firing slits in the boxes. At that moment his team was engaged by four automatic weapons. Bullets passed through his sleeve but he was unhurt. However, all three of the Grenadiers in his team were hit and subsequently died. Despite being under heavy fire Sergeant Garmory continued to fire back until his ammunition was expended; he checked and assisted his men as best he could, and used their weapons to continue the fight until assistance arrived. It seems likely that he hit some of the terrorists before the van sped off. For his exceptional courage in countering this well planned attack on his patrol he was awarded the Military Medal.

Such incidents and acts of skill and courage were sustained throughout the campaign. The 1st Battalion Irish Guards was prevented from playing its part until 1992. The Battalion, recruited from all parts of Ireland, brought local knowledge and sensitivity to the task, and was highly effective from the outset. But its members will most remember 10 September 1981.

Left: A patrol of The Queen's Company Grenadier Guards near Crossmaglen, November 1983.

Above: Members of D Squadron The Life Guards training for an independent squadron tour, 1981/2.

On that day terrorists attacked the coach returning from the Tower of London Guard to Chelsea Barracks. As the vehicle approached the barracks a nail bomb was detonated wounding 23 men. Sergeant Danny Cullen was badly wounded in the shoulder. Despite this he secured and rallied his men until help arrived. Guardsman Ian Trafford had recently joined the Battalion and was in the barracks when he heard the explosion. Without waiting for orders he rushed to the scene and administered first aid. Eighteen years old and with only rudimentary medical training, he saved at least six lives that day. Both their British Empire Medals were well earned.

Above: CSgt Sutcliffe from the MILAN Platoon, 1st Battalion Coldstream Guards, pauses while leading his multiple in the Newtownhamilton area of South Armagh, 1996.

Many individual officers and soldiers served in the Guards Independent Parachute Company, in Headquarters Northern Ireland, in the Ulster Defence Regiment of which 8th (County Tyrone) and 9th (County Antrim) Battalions were affiliated to the Household Division, and in other units, and played their part in the campaign. But it is those who served in the covert units that deserve special mention. Their operations among the terrorists required extraordinary skill and courage.

On the night of Friday 14 May 1977 Captain Robert Nairac, Grenadier Guards was abducted by at least seven men whilst on a covert operation in South Armagh. For his exceptional courage Captain Nairac was awarded the George Cross (see Heroes).

On Friday 2 May 1980, intelligence was received that a terrorist group armed with an M60 heavy machine gun and other weapons, and responsible for numerous murders and attacks, was in a house in north Belfast. They were ordered to assault the house. The speed, aggression and courage of the Special Forces team stunned the four terrorists, so much so that they surrendered within a few minutes. The capture of this group had a profound effect on terrorist morale in Northern Ireland. However, Captain Westmacott was killed giving covering fire during the assault. He received the first posthumous Military Cross ever to be awarded.

During the campaign 38 officers and men of the Household Division were killed and 162 wounded as a result of terrorist action in Ireland and in London. There are no victors in such a campaign. Nevertheless terrorism was defeated and peace returned to Northern Ireland. Officers and men of the Household Division played their part in this achievement.

THE FALKLANDS WAR 1982

Major General Michael Scott

The war to retake the Falkland Islands, known as Operation CORPORATE lasted some ten weeks. The Household Division contributed a significant part of the Task Force Land Element and included both 2nd Battalion Scots Guards, 1st Battalion Welsh Guards as well as two troops from the Blues and Royals. In addition, the Division had guardsmen serving with 22 Special Air Service. 1st Battalion Welsh Guards were hit badly on 8 June by Argentian aircraft resulting in a heavy casualty toll. The article below describes the Scots Guards hard fought, gruelling and courageous battle for Mount Tumbledown on 13/14 June.

Before 2nd Battalion Scots Guards left for the South Atlantic on 12 May in the comparative luxury of the famous liner *QE2*, the 2nd Battalion Scots Guards had undergone intensive training with 5th Infantry Brigade in Wales. But the inclement weather of Sennybridge was nothing compared with what awaited them when they arrived on the Falklands.

After landing at San Carlos on 2 June, three days later the Battalion was taken initially in the assault ship HMS *Intrepid*, and then in four landing craft to Bluff Cove. In appalling weather the Battalion dug-in and awaited the expected order to move forward to Stanley. During the week the Battalion was there, good intelligence was received from the reconnaissance platoon in a covert patrol base well forward in Port Harriet House, which had a profound effect on the brigade plan for the advance on Stanley. During this week the Battalion defended against two, if not three, enemy planes which attacked the landing ships logistic *Sir Galahad* and *Sir Tristram* at Fitzroy, with small arms fire.

The first phase of the battle for Port Stanley, the island's capital, was successfully completed when, during the night 11/12 June, 3rd Commando Brigade captured Mount Longdon, Two Sisters and Mount Harriet. The next phase involved 5th Infantry Brigade whose plan was for 2nd Scots Guards to take Mount Tumbledown from the west and, when firm, to provide fire support for 1st/7th Gurkha Rifles to assault Mount William. 1st Battalion Welsh Guards was subsequently to be prepared to take Sapper Hill.

Tumbledown Mountain

The Battalion plan was for a silent night attack in three phases, supported by a fire plan, nine 105mm light guns and naval gunfire from the frigates HMS *Active* and *Yarmouth*. The mortars of 42 Commando and 1st/7th Gurkhas were also made available.

Each phase was to involve a company attack on a different part of the objective. Phase One was for G Company to take the first part of Tumbledown. Thirty minutes before G Company crossed the start line, there was to be a diversionary attack from the obvious southerly approach along the line of the Darwin–Bluff Cove–Stanley track. Phase Two involved the Left Flank Company moving through G and assaulting the main part of the mountain, and in Phase Three Right Flank Company would secure the final part.

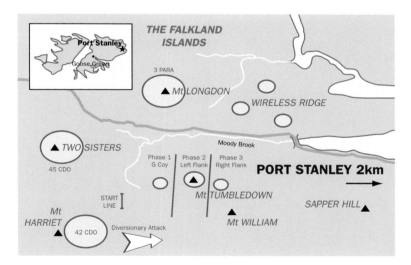

Above: Military and construction equipment in Port Stanley, left behind by retreating Argentine forces in the Falklands, 13 July 1982.

On the morning of 13 June, the Battalion moved by helicopter to an assembly area to the south-west of Goat Ridge, well out of sight of the enemy, and dug in. Enemy shellfire was sporadic and ineffective although one casualty was taken.

Detailed reconnaissance and orders took place throughout the day and rehearsals for the move into the forming-up point were held. The recognition signal 'Hey Jimmy' was adopted in the knowledge that Argentines were incapable of pronouncing a J!

The diversionary attack, led by Major Richard Bethell of Headquarter Company, started on time and, after initial success, ran into trouble because the Argentines were much stronger than anticipated. After being mortared in a minefield, the attackers withdrew with eight wounded. However it was discovered after the battle, in an interview with the captured Argentine battalion commander, that the 90-minute diversion had the desired effect.

G Company crossed the start-line at 9 pm (local time) with one platoon and company headquarters leading to secure the first half of the company objective, to be followed by the other two platoons to secure the second half. Progress across the open ground was slow through sporadic mortar and shellfire and the occasional star shell. The cold was intense. The company secured its objective by 2230 hours and gave supporting fire when and where it could to Left Flank, which was coming under heavy machine-gun and sniper fire.

Left Flank Company advanced with Second Lieutenant James Stuart's Number 13 platoon taking the high crags on their left and Lieutenant Mitchell's Number 15 Platoon the enemy positions in the lower slopes on the right. Company Headquarters and Lieutenant Anthony Fraser's Number 14 Platoon were in depth. In addition to small arms fire, the company began to come under increasing mortar and artillery bombardment. Enemy snipers, with high-grade night sights, killed two Guardsmen and mortally wounded a sergeant.

Against the enemy sangars (low defensive positions built of stone around a natural hollow), many of which were cleverly sited under the

rocks, 66mm, 84mm and M79 grenade-launcher rounds were only partially effective. However, the leading sections of the left forward platoon had some success against them with grenades, flushing out the forward snipers and, following a communication cable, locating and destroying several sangars and sniper positions despite fierce enemy resistance. At this stage the Battalion was having difficulty in bringing mortar and artillery fire to bear on a confused situation, but at approximately 0230 hours, artillery rounds landed accurately in front of the right forward platoon and the platoon commander, together with the company commander and company headquarters, led an attack on the forward enemy positions. This assault was successful and the momentum

Above: Members of the 2nd Battalion Scots Guards on parade at the Falklands War commemoration, London, 17 June 2007.

Far left: Guardsman Pengelly on QE2.

Left: RAF Sir Galahad under attack.

of the attack was regained. About eight enemy were killed with grenades, rifles and bayonets, the company commander John Kiszely himself killing two and bayoneting a third.

Although one section commander was killed, the assault continued up the hill, with sangars and bunkers being taken at bayonet point. The demands of clearing these positions and guarding prisoners, resulted in only seven men of Left Flank reaching the top of the mountain and the end of their objective. Three of these were immediately cut down by machine-gun fire from Right Flank Company's objective. Below them were the lights of Stanley.

Major Simon Price, commanding Right Flank Company, came forward, assessed the situation and, leaving Second Lieutenant Lord Dalrymple's Number 1 Platoon to give covering fire, approached the enemy with his other two platoons from the right. The assaulting sections moved forward firing 66mm and M79s as they went. The attack became fragmented, and groups of four to six men moved through the rocks, covering each other and destroying the enemy with grenades and bayonets. The enemy positions were well prepared and supported each other, making the assault a hazardous affair, but, by about 0815 hours the company was secure, and Tumbledown Mountain was in the hands of the Battalion. Soon afterwards, the ceasefire was declared and fighting ended.

Why did the Battalion win? Tumbledown epitomised the regimental spirit. Men went forward under fire because they were part of the Family (section, platoon, company, battalion) and because they were with their friends. This spirit coupled with leadership from the front, overcame heavy odds and gave men a depth of confidence and togetherness that the enemy could never beat.

But 2nd Scots Guards' tasks in the Falklands were not yet over. It was the last of the infantry battalions to leave, after being responsible for the guarding of Argentine prisoners and establishing company bases in both West and East Falkland. It was relieved by the first garrison battalion at the end of July, returning to a Regimental welcome at Brize Norton and Chelsea, that all who experienced it will never forget.

Above: HRH Prince Charles at RAF Brize Norton Air Base in Oxfordshire to welcome back Welsh Guards who survived the Bluff Cove disaster in the Falklands, 29 July1982.

Above: HRH Prince Andrew addresses the congregation at the Falklands War commemoration at Horse Guards Parade in 2007.

THE GULF WAR 1990–1

Colonel Hugh Boscawen

Soon after the decision was taken in August 1990 to deploy British troops to Saudi Arabia on Operation DESERT STORM (the British Operation name was GRANBY) 1st Battalion Grenadier Guards, in the WARRIOR Armoured Infantry role in Münster, provided 99 men to the 1st Bn Staffordshire Regiment battle group (7th Armoured Brigade, although some individuals served elsewhere). On 16 November 1990, the Grenadiers were ordered to provide two formed companies to 4th Armoured Brigade. The Queen's Company under Major Grant Baker, were to join the 1st Battalion Royal Scots battle group, and No.2 Company under Major Andrew Ford, the 2nd Battalion Royal Regiment of Fusiliers battle group. The companies were formed and prepared in 14 days, and a fortnight's training ensued: the companies included members of all the other Guards Regiments (including The Blues and Royals) from the Grenadiers' integral Armoured Infantry Manning Increment.

The Queen's Company fought as the Armoured Infantry Company in the 14th/20th Kings Hussars battle group, and No 2 Company remained with the Fusiliers apart from a brief attachment to the 14th/20th battle group for one phase. The ground offensive was short and sharp as the Grenadier companies in their battle groups successively overran 10th Iraqi Armoured Division and other troop positions on Objectives STEEL, BRASS, TUNSTEN and COBALT; following an exhilarating drive at speed across Wadi al Batin into Kuwait early on 27 February 1991, the Ceasefire was called. Overall 420 Grenadiers served in 14 different organisations on Operation GRANBY, and their regimental spirit and ability to reconstitute the two companies so quickly was remarkable. In December 1990 the blue, red, blue tactical flash was introduced so that the Guards serving in other battlegroups in the desert could maintain their sense of identity as Guardsmen.

A Squadron The Life Guards under Major James Hewitt deployed in their CHALLENGER tanks in December 1990 to the 14th/20th Kings Hussars battle group. The Squadron took part in 4th Armoured Brigade's actions, ending on the Basra Road, North of Kuwait City. After Christmas 1990, Regimental Headquarters, B and C Squadrons (under Lieutenant Colonel Anthony De Ritter) together with 1st Battalion Scots Guards (Lieutenant Colonel John Cargill) joined the force as the In Theatre Replacement (Armoured Delivery) Group to provide vehicles and crews: the Scots Guards rapidly converted to WARRIOR vehicles in the desert. Other individual Guardsmen (including Lieutenant Colonel Robert

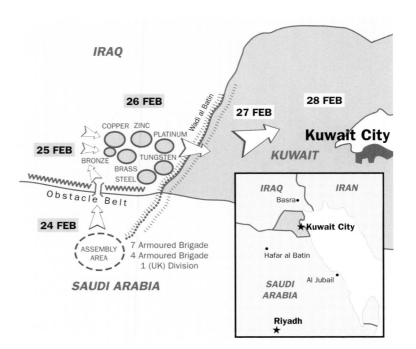

Above: Evacuating prisoners of war by RAF Chinook helicopters.

Right: Lieutenant Ashton Radcliffe, Kuwait, March 1991.

Cartwright, commanding 1st Grenadiers) served in theatre, and the Scots Guards Band (under their Director of Music, Lieutenant Colonel David Price) did sterling work in 33 Field Hospital in Saudi Arabia. The Household Cavalry and Coldstream Bands deployed as medics in the United Kingdom. The 1st Battalion Coldstream Guards was selected to join Operation GRANBY in late December, and their story is described below.

The Life Guards and the Grenadier Guards gained the battle honour 'Wadi Al Batin'; they, and the Coldstream and Scots Guards were awarded the theatre honour 'Gulf 1991'.

News of Saddam Hussein's invasion of Kuwait, on 2 August 1990, took most in the West by surprise. Six weeks later 7th Armoured Brigade was sent to the Gulf, under the codename Operation GRANBY.

1st Battalion Coldstream Guards was in Wellington Barracks preparing to move to Germany. However, in November the government agreed to send 4th Armoured Brigade and 1st Armoured Division troops to the Gulf: eventually about 45,000 Servicemen and women deployed. The 1st Coldstream went on Christmas leave having heard the Commanding Officer, Lieutenant Colonel Iain McNeil, say 'they won't need us in the Gulf – if they do, I'll eat my hat'.

Less than a month later the Battalion was in the Gulf: a month after that, on 26 February, the Battalion was moving into Iraq.

The task initially given was to guard prisoners of war taken by British troops (consistent with the Geneva Convention). Lieutenant Colonel McNeil was given command of the Prisoner of War Guard Force comprising 1st Coldstream, 1st Battalion Royal Highland Fusiliers and 1st Battalion King's Own Scottish Borderers.

The Battalion moved into the desert to acclimatise on arrival in Saudi Arabia. Battle shooting, navigation, NBC and tactics all had to be adjusted to desert conditions. Keeping the Mark 1 SA80 Rifle and Light Support Weapon firing in sandy conditions needed continuous effort. Some in the Battalion (recalling pictures of 1940s Desert Rats) brought combat jackets, but many found the weather cold and wet.

Desert training was interspersed with time in Al Jubayl on the Gulf coast, where Lieutenant General Peter de la Billière, Commander British Forces Middle East, visited the Battalion. The nearby detonation of a Scud missile one night caused the Battalion hastily to don respirators, and those who had not prepared their NBC equipment learned good lessons. A Household Division Dinner (with alcohol-free beer) was held with the Officers of The Life Guards and Scots Guards.

On 18 February the Battalion vehicles drove 300 miles to Al Qaysumah where the Prisoner of War camp, 'Maryhill Camp', was being built. Route DODGE was packed with the transport of three army corps; thousands of vehicles fought for road space. The Battalion flew by C-130 Hercules aircraft to a nearby airstrip, and training continued while politicians considered President Mikhail Gorbachev's last-minute peace initiative. Night bombing and artillery raids were audible in the north,

reminiscent of the First World War. Allied air supremacy was immensely reassuring.

On 22 February the Battalion joined 1st (British) Armoured Division in its Forward Assembly Area. The ground war started at 0400 hours on 24 February (G Day). General H. Norman Schwarzkopf's plan envisaged that VII (US) Corps would attack on G+1: 1st (US) Infantry Division would breach the Iraqi defences to allow three armoured divisions, including 1st (British) Armoured Division to attack enemy tactical, operational and strategic reserve divisions, including the Republican Guards, simultaneously.

The weather was overcast with rain and a sandblaster wind, and the Battalion Orders Group took place in a sandstorm:

'this was the real thing … Lives depended on one getting it right … Orders were crisp, business-like and positive. But as I looked round these men, whom I genuinely liked,' Colonel McNeil wrote. 'I wondered how many I would see again … We all wore Arab head-dress, wrapped around the head, face and nose, so it was hardly a conventional sight.'

The need to provide close support to the armoured brigades had been acknowledged, and Support Company Group (Major Simon Vandeleur) joined 4th Armoured Brigade. The Battalion Group was due to move on G+2 with the Divisional Administrative Area group – 6,000 vehicles – but 48 hours 'Notice To Move' became two hours at a stroke. The Divisional Harbour Party followed the brigades through the minefield: the brigades then fanned out, looking like a most impressive battlefleet with their rear lights.

The Battalion moved, but heavy rain and inky darkness led to delays and bogged vehicles: surrendering Iraqis suddenly appeared, terrified and hungry. When Major Jonathan Bourne-May's Land Rover drove over a mine, the Battalion halted until daylight. The Battalion Harbour Party under the author, encountered more Iraqis while on reconnaissance in poor visibility next morning. After 'dry fire and manoeuvre' by the Second in Command and Lance Sergeant Teague, Grenadier Guards, the London District photographer, a starving enemy group, small and elderly compared with Guardsmen, surrendered. On 26 February (G+2) the Battalion halted 30 miles inside Iraq, setting up a Prisoner of War cage. The move, 50 miles, had taken 14 hours.

Above: Company Sergeant Major Ric Howick and Lance Corporal 'Lennie' Lenthall organising Iraqi prisoners of war, February 1991.

Number 2 Company (Major Jonathan Bourne-May) and Number 3 Company (Major Peter Hicks) moved forward by air and vehicle to collect prisoners. Navigating in featureless terrain in sandstorms amid minefields and unexploded bomblets was challenging. Later that day, Major Simon Holborow's Number 1 Company platoons flew forward to corral 300 prisoners taken by 7th Armoured Brigade. That afternoon, Number 2 Company took the surrender of numerous Iraqis from infantry and 12th (Armoured) Division, some in firefights.

Platoons and sections moved by helicopter, Land Rover or 4-ton truck to collect prisoners that night and on 27 February (G+3) the Brigades approached Wadi al Batin, marking the Iraq–Kuwaiti border. Prisoners were generally so hungry, thirsty and demoralised that a single 4-tonner with a machine gun proved sufficient to guard them.

On G+3 the Battalion drove 40 miles up Route FOX past abandoned trenches and destroyed armoured vehicles. Mines and bomblets marked previously occupied positions. The desert was so flat that the curvature of the earth could be seen, and Companies again sent out parties to collect Iraqis: one platoon took 1,300 prisoners.

The news, early on 28 February (G+4) that a ceasefire was planned for 0800 hours (local) was a surprise, but the need to collect prisoners remained. Just before the ceasefire 1st Armoured Division cut the Basra–Kuwait road, after a land campaign lasting just 100 hours. Coldstream tasks continued: Number 2 Company collected 1,000 prisoners from 32nd Heavy Regiment Royal Artillery. On 1 March the Battalion met up with Support Company, itself with many prisoners, and drove into Kuwait.

Many junior Non-Commissioned Officers with a few Guardsmen had looked after large groups of prisoners. Lance Corporal Lenthall and his section were guarding one group, when a Company Officer arrived and saw Corporal Lenthall teaching a huge phalanx of bedraggled Iraqis foot drill to keep them warm. He heard him end the lesson, Pirbright-style, with 'and what's my name?' Hundreds of Iraqis shouted in unison – 'Lennie'!

The Battalion Group drove back to Al Qaysumah on 4 March via the Basra–Kuwait City 'motorway' over the Mutla Ridge, littered with thousands of destroyed vehicles caught attempting to escape from Kuwait. The route crossed minefields, wire entanglements and trenches of First World War proportions near the Saudi border. Evidence of a crushing defeat lay everywhere.

The Battalion then settled down to training, and 'sizing and selection' for The Queen's Birthday Parade, at Al Qaysumah and then in Al Jubayl, to which the Battalion returned on 13 March. Competitions were held with our US Allies, and Coldstreamers were convincing winners in March and Shoot competitions before flying back to the United Kingdom during 3–8 April. Tragically, just before the Battalion returned, Guardsman Christopher Napier was killed in a road accident in Al Jubayl, the only Coldstream fatality in the Gulf.

Lance Corporal of Horse Richard O'Connor, The Life Guards

Lance Corporal of Horse Richard O'Connor of The Life Guards was a 24-year-old tank commander when the call-up for the First Gulf War came in 1990. He was a member of A Squadron The Life Guards that took part in the assault with Challenger Main Battle Tanks to drive the Iraqi army from Kuwait. He is now a Captain and serving at Hyde Park Barracks.

Having eventually deployed just after Christmas, the main effort was getting the squadron of Challenger main battle tanks ready prior to deploying for what we thought would be a relatively short time in the Saudi Desert just to train and acclimatise. In the event we remained deployed throughout the tour.

The personal equipment we had at that time bears no comparison to what we have today and I recall the extreme cold we had to endure for the initial part of the operation. I can remember writing letters in the freezing rain from inside the bivouac with an old style parka on, trying to stay warm. The weather had made the training very difficult and I do recall having to dig one or two tanks out from hull-down sunken positions.

As time went on we all became aware by listening to the BBC World Service that what we had been training for would now become a serious reality. The air bombardments were continuing and our time was fast approaching to take part in the ground offensive.

Having been given the word we were moved up to our start-line and from that point on morale and camaraderie became a massive part of our efforts. You became especially close to your own crew and there was a sense of combined effort during what was to come. All of us were scared, anxious and yet excited at the prospects. We kept ourselves busy playing cards while waiting for the call, as sleep just seemed impossible.

Once the time came to move through the enemy breaches, all five days seemed to roll into one big event. The leadership displayed by our squadron leader Major James Hewitt was immense and he had a great way of keeping his men focused throughout the operation. The effect of our own artillery on the enemy became very clear during our advance, with some horrific sights. That said, our main focus was to move and strike with momentum, using our thermal imagery. For the first time in my own mind the thought of killing the enemy became a reality. There was hardly time to reflect on this. Survival and the sense of care for each other pushed us through with little sleep. We caught the odd forty winks whilst replenishing between objectives while the other tanks took turns to provide protection. During the first two days this was tiring as we were all in Nuclear Biological Chemical (NBC) conditions, closed down and suited. Once the threat of NBC decreased morale soared.

The scariest time was when we came across what was believed to be a Republican Guard Division, many kilometres away during darkness. We were in a good position to force an engagement but remained controlled under the leader's direction, which was just as well as it turned out to be a friendly battle group and a Blue on Blue ('friendly fire') incident was avoided. As the operation went on, we became more and more proficient with our techniques and drills. Long range and short range engagements were performed. However, you would not have wanted to hear the verbals. We were now focusing on catching up with the Republican Guard force fleeing back to Iraq. Fear had disappeared. We were not far from overhauling them when the halt was called. There was a great sense of relief coupled with frustration but also an incredible sense of pride at what we had achieved.

We had all learnt many lessons, including compassion towards the enemy at the time of their surrender in the objectives. Just as important, team work in maintenance, the duty of care to one another, hygiene and morale. The focus then returned to family. My wife had given birth to my second son during my absence. For that and the thought of what may have happened to me, I felt guilty. I was however able to return shortly after hearing the news. As a young soldier, I thought the job had been done.

Most of the Battalion found the Gulf War experience fascinating. We had seen Grenadiers in 7th Armoured Brigade, and The Life Guards and 1st Battalion Scots Guards on occasions; the Scots Guards Band had made its name in the hospital in Al Jubayl. Although the role of collecting prisoners and 'Divisional Troops' had sounded unexciting, there was no shortage of other tasks, and danger, armed Iraqis, and millions of mines. Fortunately there was little fight in most of the Iraqis: the Battalion collected some 7,300 prisoners, about 2,000 of which it took itself.

Lasting impressions included listening to BBC World Service and American Forces Network news every hour, poor weather, monotonous rations, wonderful support in letters and parcels from home. Bottled water, and plastic plates, knives and forks were war winners. Coldstreamers certainly experienced the 'frictions', and sights and smells of war. Dejected, near-starving prisoners, charred tanks and guns, and the litter of discarded ammunition and rubbish – the signs of defeat – were never far away. Talking to Sandhurst-trained Iraqi officer prisoners was interesting: their Army had been totally outclassed, out-thought and outfought. General Schwarzkopf's achievement in masterminding the destruction of so many Iraqi divisions in 100 hours equalled that of some Great Captains in history.

1st Battalion returned home after nearly ten weeks, with terrific morale and proud to have helped liberate Kuwait. Coldstreamers duly provided a Guard for the 1991 Queen's Birthday Parade. Several months later, Lieutenant Colonel McNeil addressed the Battalion, and was disconcerted when Officers and Guardsmen did not fall out when expected. Major Yorke, the Quartermaster, stepped forward and, recalling Lieutenant Colonel McNeil's words, gave the Commanding Officer a hat to eat, which he did; fortunately it was made of meringue.

THE BALKANS 1994–2007

Major General William Cubitt CBE

Regiments of the Household Division were deployed to the Balkans on numerous occasions from 1994 to 2007. Operations started in 1994 in Bosnia with 1st Battalion Coldstream Guards – under command of Lieutenant Colonel Peter Williams – deploying as armoured infantry from Germany to protect humanitarian aid convoys. Being under command of the United Nations (UN) with a peacekeeping mandate, they wore the light blue UN beret and travelled in white armoured vehicles. At that stage, peace was an illusion with fighting between factions occurring on a regular basis. Consequently the activities of the UN Protection Force (UNPROFOR) – as it was called – extended well beyond that envisaged. The UNPROFOR commander was Lieutenant General Michael Rose, Coldstream Guards, a former Special Air Service commanding officer. NATO intervened in 1995 and subsequent deployments of the Household Cavalry – commanded by Lieutenant Colonel William Rollo – and 1st Battalion Grenadier Guards – commanded by Lieutenant Colonel David Russell-Parsons – were as NATO troops. The Bosnia commitment ended with 1st Battalion Welsh Guards under European Union command (the EU's first military operation) in 2006/7. The Commanding Officer was Lieutenant Colonel Richard Stanford.

As the situation in Bosnia improved in the late 1990s, that in Kosovo deteriorated significantly so that NATO intervened in 1999 with 4th Armoured Brigade (commanded by Brigadier William Rollo, The Blues and Royals) comprising, among others, D Squadron Household Cavalry and 1st Battalion Irish Guards, commanded by Lieutenant Colonel William Cubitt. By 2007, the commitment in Bosnia had reduced to the provision of an Intelligence, Surveillance and Reconnaissance Task force provided by 1st Battalion Welsh Guards.

Bosnia 1993/94

Number 2 Company 1st Battalion Coldstream Guards

From November 1993 to May 1994, 1st Battalion Coldstream Guards was deployed in Bosnia as part of the United Nations Protection Force (UNPROFOR).

Number 2 Company spent the first three months of the tour in Vitez as one of the two companies in the area that gave security to humanitarian aid convoys. This involved many hours in static positions on the designated routes and patrolling. At the time, there was extreme hostility between the Bosnian Croats in the Vitez pocket and the Bosnian Muslims outside which frequently flared up into active fighting. The activities of patrols often went beyond mere security for the aid route and the Company rescued civilians from the midst of fierce fighting and treated civilian casualties injured by mortar fire.

The company moved to Sarajevo on 17 February becoming the first British company into the besieged city, the Company Commander's Warrior having struck an anti-tank mine en route. The Bosnians had defended Sarajevo for nearly two years against Bosnian Serb forces who surrounded it and bombarded it with artillery. The Serbs were being coerced under threat of NATO air attack to withdraw their heavy weapons 20km from the city centre or to give them up to UNPROFOR control. Troops were required to establish and run Weapon Collection Points in Serb territory.

The Company deployed in deep snow, on 19 February, as the first armed UNPROFOR units to be deployed in a Serb-held area, to three separate platoon positions: Number 5 Platoon in a village at Osijek, 6 Platoon with a grandstand view of Sarajevo at Poljine and 7 Platoon with Company Tactical Headquarters on a hill at Krivoglavci. The task was to corral the heavy weapons and then to deny their repossession by the Serbs. There followed a few tense days as the Company cajoled the Serbs into handing in their weapons despite their understandable reluctance as an unbeaten army acting under duress. However, the firm actions and vigorous charm offensive mounted by the Company bore fruit as all known heavy weapons in the platoon areas were under UNPROFOR control in time to satisfy the NATO ultimatum.

Despite some difficult incidents with resentful Serb troops, this first close contact with the Serbs was largely cordial. At the low level, Serbs frequently expressed their liking for the British which resulted from British assistance to the Yugoslav partisans in the Second World War. This period also saw the Company's first exposure to the French-dominated command structure in Sector Sarajevo which fully stretched the linguistic ability of members of the Company.

In late February, the Bosnian Croats and Muslims signed a peace agreement which brought the fighting in Central Bosnia to an end and imposed extreme demands on UNPROFOR manpower to implement the ceasefire. Number 2 Company was called back to Vitez on 3 March to assist in this process. This involved the establishment of checkpoints on designated routes as they crossed the now dormant front line, and observation posts from which to monitor the ceasefire. Once again, low-level diplomacy resulted in the first free movement across the confrontation line since the fighting had begun.

On 16 March, the Company was on the move again to Sarajevo and was placed under operational control of the 3rd *Régiment d' Infanterie de Marine*. The Company's tasks were to open a road through the front lines by which civilian movement could be established, and to monitor the ceasefire within an area some 5km north of Sarajevo city centre. A busy programme ensued of negotiation with Bosnian Serbs and Muslims, removal of defensive obstacles, clearance of mines and munitions, the construction of a UN checkpoint and the establishment of observation posts from which to monitor the ceasefire. The first busload of Muslim civilians travelled under Warrior escort from Sarajevo to Visoko through Serb-held territory on 23 March. The situation seemed to improve daily until 6 April when a Scimitar tracked vehicle of the Reconnaissance Platoon careered off a hill track between the front lines. While reconnoitring a recovery route, the Company Commander's team was fired on by a sniper and the locally-employed civilian interpreter was wounded in the leg.

During this time, Serb forces began to attack the Muslim-held town of Gorazde some 80km south-east of Sarajevo which resulted, on 11 April, in NATO air strikes. An immediate consequence of this was that all routes through Serb-held territory and the airport were closed thereby cutting Number 2 Company off from Vitez until 28 April. Up to 120 UNPROFOR personnel (including 33 British) were being taken hostage by the Serbs which gave cause for concern over the safety of the Company's observation post on the Serb front line.

Above: Number 2 Company 1st Battalion Coldstream Guards armoured vehicles in central Bosnia, 1994.

Indeed, before dawn on 17 April, the Observation Post came under attack by automatic fire and grenades. Lance Sergeant Waterhouse was to be awarded the Military Cross for his conduct during this action. That day the Company was also placed at one hour's notice to move to Gorazde and was to be relieved in place by the French battalion. In the event, the Company never deployed to Gorazde due to Serb objections to the passage of Warrior fighting vehicles.

On 28 April, Number 2 Company recovered via Vitez to Gornji Vakuf and thence back to Germany bringing to an end a period of intense and varied activity.

Staff Corporal Henry Newton, The Life Guards

Bosnia 1994, 1996 and 1999

The role was drastically different each time. In 1994 it was United Nations. At the time I was a Trooper, just a driver with the troops. There was still a lot of ethnic cleansing going on. We tried to monitor it as best we could, and stop it happening but obviously with the United Nations, there was only so much you could do and you had to stand back being under the law where you could only fire if you were fired upon. Otherwise you would get dragged into it yourself. Our Squadron had Scimitar.

It was very difficult. Lots of poverty, lots of orphans. Which for a young Trooper was a bit of an eye-opener. We used to get supplies to them but the supplies disappeared before they got to us. Also any building we did for schools, again stuff was taken.

For the next tour in 1996 we were in Banja Luka at the Wood Factory as an independent squadron. Our main task was at a place where refugees of all ethnic groups in Bosnia went. One of our missions was to try and sustain that village with resupply, help them through the winter, such as getting logs from the woods. Help them as best we could. Lots of hearts and minds: playing football with the kids; getting to know the locals. In the period of time that I'd been away it had got a lot better.

I was the troop leader's operator so I gained a different aspect. With knowledge, the mission becomes clearer for you. It was a very good tour.

For the UN tour we were in white vehicles and sky blue berets. It took a bit of getting used to. For the second tour we were in the British Army green and black with regimental add ons.

With the first tour we were far more standoffish. There were lots of Mujahadeen who didn't like us being there. They wanted to get about their business. On the first tour we used to get stoned by the kids.

On the second tour we used to pull up and all the kids would have prepared a makeshift football pitch because they knew that we played football. We played a lot of football. I didn't come away being David Beckham but by the end our skills were a lot slicker than at the beginning.

We also provided protection within the town of Banja Luka. In the town centres there were lots of people going around with small arms and anything could kick off at any time and so it was policed. We were working a lot with the local police trying to get them to do the business. But there was a lot of corruption.

In 1999 the tour was again completely different. We were taking out foot patrols but in a very relaxed posture. You'd go up to get a coffee, mingle with the locals and they liked that.

Kosovo 1999

1st Battalion Irish Guards

On 12 June 1999, 1st Battalion Irish Guards entered Kosovo in the largest Western armoured operation in Europe since the Second World War. The Micks had the key roles of securing the Kosovan capital, Pristina, and (in the case of Number 1 Company in The King's Royal Hussars battle group) the northern town of Podujevo.

For the Battalion in Münster, Germany, it all started on 5 February with a warning to make ready to deploy to Macedonia – a country of which many had never heard. Number One Company deployed with The King's Royal Hussars in late February. They trained in severe weather on the Krivolac training area in central Macedonia until the NATO bombing of Serbia and Kosovo started, when they moved rapidly north to assist in the defence of Macedonia against Serb retaliation. The Company helped construct refugee camps for Kosovar Albanians, in which a camp for 30,000 was constructed in 48 hours.

The main part of the Battalion deployed to Macedonia in late April supported by D Squadron The King's Royal Hussars, A (King Harald's) Company 1st Battalion The Green Howards, 52nd Battery Royal Artillery and 26th Armoured Engineer Squadron. D Squadron Household Cavalry Regiment deployed at the same time. The Irish Guards battle group trained for a month at Krivolac and then moved north to Petrovac near Skopje where it became the 'High-Readiness battle group'.

It will probably never be known for sure what caused Yugoslav President Slobodan Milosevic to agree to the deployment of NATO troops in Kosovo. It may have been the 11 weeks of aerial bombing or the influence of Russia. But many commentators believe that it was the indication by late May that NATO was countenancing a ground invasion. At this time, the Micks were training in the full glare of publicity in Macedonia. In *The Times* on 24 September 1999, it was judged that 'it was the switch of strategy to a land assault, made credible in the fields and valleys of Macedonia and Albania, that did the trick'.

On 12 June, NATO ground forces designated Kosovo Force (KFOR) to enter Kosovo as Yugoslav forces withdrew. The Parachute Regiment and The Royal Gurkha Rifles took control of the Kacanik mountain gorge through which The King's Royal Hussars and Irish Guards battle groups then passed. The King's Royal Hussars moved north towards Pristina and sent their Micks (Number 1 Company) to secure Pristina airport. On arrival, they found the Russians had arrived before them. They then waited in a high profile stand-off until Pristina was secured by the Irish Guards battle group and then were sent further north to liberate Podujevo in scenes of great Albanian jubilation. Number One Company ran Podujevo until their return to Münster in August. They made a huge difference to the lives of the community in Podujevo which had suffered very badly at the hands of the Serb forces.

Returning to 12 June, the Irish Guards battle group took up the charge some 10 miles south of Pristina. A small team was sent ahead to locate the Serb commander in Pristina to ensure that there were no misunderstandings between the withdrawing Serb forces and the battle group. The battle group arrived at the outskirts of Pristina in the evening of 12 June and Number 4 Company entered the city early on 13 June, followed by the Anti-tank and Mortar Platoons. Battle group Headquarters established itself on the southern edge of the city. The Albanian Kosovar community was ecstatic. Triumphant crowds showered the Guardsmen with flowers. However, the Serb community became increasingly alarmed and the withdrawing Serb soldiers and policemen were heavily-armed. Patrols started to discover the darker side of life in Pristina in the form of dead bodies and stories of atrocities. As well as enjoying the euphoria, the battle group set about the task of maintaining law and order as the Serb forces withdrew. That afternoon, the Reconnaissance Platoon secured the landing site for the helicopters which brought in the Parachute Regiment to take over the eastern half of Pristina.

As well as trying to establish law and order from the chaos in the western half of Pristina for a fortnight, the battle group deployed into a 600 sq km area around Pristina. This area was to be the battle group's area of operations until 12 October. In the east, the area ran up to the boundary with Serbia where a boundary post was established by the Anti-tank Platoon. In the west it included Kosovo Polje – a town of great sensitivity to both Serbs and Albanians – and Obilic with its two strategic power stations. The battle group's area contained a Serb community of some 18,000. The inter-ethnic violence that this implied was the main focus of activities throughout the tour.

Corporal of Horse Adams, The Blues and Royals

On Kosovo 1999

We were the lead call sign. At my level initially, as a Lance Corporal, we were somewhat in the dark – we didn't know if we were going to take a war footing or peace-keeping. I well remember going through Macedonia with the crowds cheering and shouting 'NATO'. And then as we went on to the road that took us into Kosovo there was a refugee camp.

All the children came running down the hill towards the fence line, cheering. Our main jobs were securing the roads, to allow the militias to leave Kosovo itself. So we were lining routes, just making sure they were leaving. That lasted for about four weeks. On entering one village all the children and adults clustered around the vehicles and threw roses and chocolates on them.

On Taking James Blunt's Guitar To Kosovo

We got his guitar in the back bin which was a bit of a struggle. I was quite annoyed. I thought 'Where the hell am I going to put this thing'. When we all got together, I'd light a bit of a fire and we'd do a song – I didn't think he was going to become a famous Pop Star.

In the first six days, many encounters were had with Serb troops who were still well-established, especially in the urban areas. Hostilities could have resulted from any misunderstanding or hasty move on either side.

Above: The Commanding Officer and RSM 1 Irish Guards receive flowers from Kosovar Albanians, 1999.

The combination of boldness and preparedness to talk to the Serb Army and Police paid dividends so that they withdrew on schedule without major incident.

The Kosovo Liberation Army came out of the hills. An 'Undertaking' was established whereby they would demilitarise over three months and then transform into a civilian Kosovo Protection Corps charged with civil defence-type activities. This was a bitter pill for them to swallow. 'Demilitarisation' and 'transformation' were hard tricks to pull off and involved much negotiation backed up by a firm hand. In the background, extremists persisted in trying to drive out the Serb community.

The Albanian community returned rapidly in their hundreds of thousands from Macedonia, Albania and the mountains. Many of their houses had been destroyed in the fighting and many atrocities had been committed against them. There was deep hatred for the Serbs. The hardest aspect of the tour was keeping the lid on inter-ethnic violence while coercing both sides to sit down and talk about the future. This process turned company commanders (and to an extent platoon commanders) into district commissioners until the arrival of the UN administration in August. An important strand in the operation throughout was the humanitarian assistance to the Albanian community, especially the preparation for winter.

A key part of KFOR's mission was to enable the Kosovo Serb community to stay there so that Kosovo would remain multi-ethnic. On 23 July, 14 Serbs were killed while harvesting just south of the battle group area. This firmly switched the operational focus of the battle group onto protecting the Serb community. From then, every Serbian village and Serbian Orthodox Church had a residential guard. Perhaps some of the strangest tasks ever to befall Irish Guardsmen were the long vigils in fourteenth century Serb Orthodox Churches and the Reconnaissance Platoon's stay in the ancient monastery at Gracanica.

Above: Battalion Headquarters 1 Irish Guards Pristina, Kosovo on the first day, 1999.

On 12 August, a patrol from Number 4 Company encountered an Albanian raiding party in a Serb village. In the ensuing action, three gunmen were wounded and three others captured. This action sent an unequivocal message to extremists on both sides.

In late August, anti-Serb violence intensified with the bombing of the monument to the 1389 Battle of Kosovo and the mortaring of the Serb town of Gracanica. The Serbs of Gracanica rioted causing major problems for the artillery battery (by then 16th/159th Battery had replaced 52nd Battery) and sucking in two platoons of Micks. The town remained barricaded until 26 September. Three attacks on Kosovo Polje followed, culminating in the bombing of a Serb market, killing three and wounding 37. This caused the Serbs of Kosovo Polje to riot and to block the main road from Pristina to the airport. The Green Howards, supported by the anti-tank platoon of the newly arrived Norwegian battalion, weathered the storm. The roadblocks were removed in a battle group operation early on 5 October involving Green Howards, Irish Guards, Royal Green Jackets, Norwegians, Carabinieri and UN Police. This was the first time that KFOR had forcibly removed a major roadblock and was the flagship operation in a new drive to maintain freedom of movement.

One of the interesting features of the tour was working closely with so many different nationalities. At various times, the UK 4th Armoured Brigade included British, Canadian, Finnish, Czech and Norwegian troops. Also, for a time there was a distinct Irish flavour manifested in cooperation between the Micks, The Royal Irish Regiment, an Irish Army transport company and a Royal Ulster Constabulary reconnaissance party. The battle group worked closely with D Squadron Household Cavalry Regiment and with Lord Strathcona's Horse (Canadian reconnaissance). We developed a close association with the UN Police from many different nationalities, and the Italian *Carabinieri* and with Russian forces. A Russian field hospital was located in Kosovo Polje, so Soviet-era vehicles and Russian soldiers were common sights in the battle group area.

The Russian contingent lent us a troupe of the Russian Army Chorus and Dance Ensemble for a show in early October. Earlier in the tour, we were fortunate that the Regimental Band was deployed in its medical role to Kosovo and was able to provide some musical entertainment.

Another interesting aspect was the variety of indigenous weaponry and equipment that was encountered. This included large numbers of Yugoslav Army tanks seen withdrawing in the early days, the military training aids at a Yugoslav Police training centre, large amounts of abandoned ammunition and stores, and the 3,000-plus weapons seized by the battle group. Among the weapons handed over by the Kosovo Liberation Army were Thompson sub-machine guns and a Sten gun which presumably came to the region with the Special Operations Executive in the Second World War. From the bombing, there was little evidence of destroyed armour but many examples of precise bombing of fixed installations. There were also signs of excellent concealment by Yugoslav armour.

The Irish Guards battle group had the reassuring experience of handing over to *two* battalions of Scandinavians, the Norwegian Telemark Battalion and the Swedish Rapid Reaction Battalion. For a two-week period in October, C Company Telemark Battalion was under command of 1st Battalion Irish Guards.

The greatest sadness of the tour was the loss in a road accident of Trooper Holt, D Squadron King's Royal Hussars. He died on 25 July 1999.

AFGHANISTAN

Major General Barney White-Spunner

3.08

The British Army was involved in Afghanistan on three separate occasions in the 19th and 20th centuries, and not always with conspicuous success. The first two expeditions were mounted by the then British government of India, worried about Russian influence on successive Afghan Emirs who might have sided with our then great rival for imperial domination of Central Asia.

Our first military foray was in 1839, when Lord Auckland, then Governor General in Calcutta, dispatched a force 'in order to repel the shadow of Russian aggression ... and to force Shah Shuja, a weakened worthless exile, upon the Afghan people, till then well disposed towards us; and this great and unprovoked injustice, the cause of all our subsequent troubles in Afghanistan, was to be effected by military measures of which the rashness and folly seem at the present day almost inconceivable', wrote the great imperial servant Sir Henry Durand. Although the force managed to occupy Kabul, it was forced to withdraw in January 1842, with the loss of 4,500 British and Indian soldiers and their families in the now infamous Retreat from Kabul, known to us today largely from Lady Elizabeth Butler's dramatic painting *Remnants of an Army* (1890) of the supposedly sole survivor, Assistant Surgeon Dr William Brydon of the Bengal Army, riding into Jalalabad. Subsequent impressive British tactical victories there, at Ghazni and at Kabul under Colonel Sir Robert Sale, Major Generals Sir George Pollock and Sir William Nott, which also rescued British hostages, did not alter the strategic outcome of the war.

The second expedition was launched in late 1878, allegedly in response to the failure of the Emir Shir Ali to respond to Viceroy of India Lord Lytton's emissaries, but really because Britain feared once again that the Russians might come to dominate the government in Kabul. This expedition was better led and Kabul was occupied fairly easily. The rebellion in southern Afghanistan was, however, more difficult to put down and in July 1880 a tribal leader called Ayub Khan lured the British garrison out of Kandahar and defeated them at Maiwand, known to this day as one of the British Army's least glorious defeats, where Brigadier General George Burrows's force was only just saved from annihilation by the very distinguished conduct of the Royal Horse Artillery. It was in response to Maiwand that the future Lord Roberts marched south from Kabul to Kandahar, covering 313 miles in 22 days of blistering heat to relieve the city garrison including Maiwand survivors and defeat Ayub Khan on 1 September.

Above: Locals greet members of the Grenadier Guards on a dawn patrol.

Right: The Household Cavalry on patrol in Helmand Province.

Regimental Quarter Master Sergeant Chant, Grenadier Guards

Operational Mentoring Liaison Team Officer, Afghanistan
In Afghanistan, the Grenadiers were all over the place. Around 250 doing their operational mentoring liaison team with the Afghan National Army, a job that itself takes you everywhere. There were at least five Grenadiers in Kabul processing the recruits to the Afghan Army from Kabul to Camp Bastion. We had a whole company of Grenadiers, Number 3 Company, attached to the Royal Anglians in Garmsir. We provided two mortar sections with the Royal Anglians and we had Grenadiers attached to the American Army with the Task Force. It is just amazing how we just found a Grenadier everywhere doing a good job there.

Every time there was a big operation, I would go out. The Afghan National Army company of 90 soldiers would have roughly 25–30 Grenadier mentors with them. We would go out with GPS so we could track where we were and have communications with the Commanding Officer, so we could tell him how things were going.

There was, briefly, a Third Afghan War in May and June 1919 but this time it was Afghan inspired when the then Emir thought he would capitalise on British disorganisation after The Great War to annex parts of the then North West Frontier Province. The Empire mustered, impressively, 140,000 soldiers on the Khyber Pass within a fortnight and a single Royal Air Force aircraft bombed Kabul, so the Emir withdrew.

There were no Household Division regiments involved in these campaigns as such, although the odd individual participated on the staff. It would not be until just over 82 years later that we would have a more formal involvement and by then the circumstances would be very different. Between 1919 and the mid-1970s Afghanistan enjoyed a long period of peace under the comparatively stable government of the successive Emirs. However, the overthrow of the Emir in 1975 led to what Auckland and Lytton had always feared, and in 1979 the Russians invaded. The bloody ten-year war that followed eventually succeeded in

removing them, but only after severe loss of life and damage to the economy, which was made considerably worse in the ensuing civil war. It was during this fighting that Kabul was largely destroyed, as were the ancient irrigation systems, which had been developed over many centuries to keep the rain-starved country from drought.

The bitter fighting of the 1990s resulted in the Taliban seizing power in 1996, a cruel and repressive regime who used an extreme and cynical interpretation of teachings of the Prophet Muhammad to dominate what was by then an impoverished country whose infrastructure had been largely destroyed. They relied on terror to suppress dissent and exploited the ease with which the opium poppy could be cultivated to finance their terror by exporting drugs. They also actively supported Osama bin Laden's Al Qae'da, so after the 9/11 attacks in the USA the American government joined with their many internal enemies to remove them, which was accomplished in a remarkably swift and effective campaign between October and December 2001.

Once the Taliban had been removed, Afghanistan faced a formidable challenge in constructing a new government. This was headed by President Hamid Karzai, and it was to support his fledgling administration that British troops returned to Kabul in December 2001. The first troops there were 16th Air Assault Brigade, then commanded by Brigadier Barney White-Spunner, The Blues and Royals, who had several Household Division soldiers on his staff. They restored order to Kabul, and the north and east of Afghanistan fairly easily, but it was not until 2006 that the international community was ready to face up to the challenge of helping President Karzai, by then confirmed in office by democratic vote, to establish the authority of his government throughout the more troublesome south.

It was here that the effects of a very severe drought had been felt most seriously, and the Taliban had capitalised on this to encourage farmers to grow the resilient poppy instead of the more thirsty cereals which they had previously cultivated and which had made Afghanistan self-sufficient in food by the 1970s; by contrast, in 2001 the country could only produce about one third of its annual cereal consumption. About 70 per cent of the opium sold in the United Kingdom originates in Afghanistan.

The 16th Air Assault Brigade therefore returned to Afghanistan in the summer of 2006, deploying into Helmand Province to provide security for the redevelopment effort designed to provide alternative livelihoods

Above: Vehicles of Squadron Headquarters of D Squadron, the Household Cavalry Regiment give members of the Parachute Regiment a lift in Musá Qal'eh, Afghanistan, similar to one of the roles they had performed in the Falklands 25 years before.

to the farmers so that they would no longer need to grow the opium poppy, and to remove the residual Taliban threat, fuelled by the madrassahs in Pakistan. The original deployment saw the Guards Parachute Platoon deploy with 3rd Battalion the Parachute Regiment together with D Squadron the Household Cavalry Regiment, which suffered three killed in what developed into severe fighting with the Taliban during July and August (see below). Colonel Charles Knaggs, Irish Guards, ran the Reconstruction Team in the Helmand provincial capital Lashkar Gar.

In March 2007 1st Battalion Grenadier Guards deployed with the 12th Mechanised Brigade mentoring and helping the Afghan National Army as it tried to establish the authority of the Kabul government. Future plans in Afghanistan have yet to be confirmed but it seems likely that several of our regiments will be deployed to support a campaign that has become a priority for NATO and the international community.

D Squadron the Household Cavalry Regiment on Operation HERRICK 4, Afghanistan, 2006 by Major William Bartle-Jones, The Blues and Royals (D Squadron Leader)

Once the decision had been made that D Squadron would be part of the Helmand Task Force, preparations went into overdrive at Thetford, Norfolk and on Salisbury Plain. The Scimitar-family tracked armoured vehicles taken to Afghanistan were not the ones used in pre-deployment training as the 16th Air Assault Brigade radio communications required a differently equipped set of vehicles. Five days of intensive simulation training on the Combined Arms Tactical Trainer at Land Warfare School,

Warminster, Wiltshire, ultimately proved critical once we were deployed on the ground. 3rd Battalion the Parachute Regiment battle group required the Squadron to step into the Afghans' sandals and role play Taliban insurgents in the Salisbury Plain exercise.

The Squadron enjoyed a challenging firing camp at Lulworth Gunnery Ranges on the Dorset coastline. The usual firing tests were completed for the crews. Each of the four Troops was pushed through a series of interconnected scenarios, testing awareness, ability to fight dismounted alongside vehicle weapon systems, casualty treatment, reaction to improvised explosive devices (IEDs) and shoots on a fleeing enemy. The Squadron experienced all of these in the field so they were not only pertinent but potentially life-saving.

The Coldstream Guards ran an informative patrol awareness and public order package with many crossovers from Northern Ireland. Lance Corporal Hamnett Royal Army Medical Corps ran a superb in-depth team medics course for a third of the Squadron which again proved life-saving on operations. Immersion included the worried families. Families Officer Captain Paul Maxwell, The Blues and Royals, and the Squadron Leader briefed them and updates continued throughout the tour. Two of the mothers collected enough goodies and money so that a comfort box and an electric fan could be sent out to Afghanistan, for which every soldier was extremely grateful.

Following a staggered deployment the Squadron found itself at Camp Bastion in a staggering average of 115 degrees Fahrenheit. Captain Alex Greenwood, Royal Scots Dragoon Guards, on attachment as the Squadron Logistics Officer met and shepherded the unit to its accommodation. Wearing body armour, helmet, carrying their luggage

Left: Covert observations in Helmand.

Below: Corporal Kingshott and Captain Allan 1st Battalion Grenadier Guards waiting for the dust to settle after an airstrike near Kajaki, Afghanistan, 2007.

The vehicles arrived in good time, and none of our containers had been broken into during the journey from Pakistan. Apparently the thieves were so cunning that they actually cut holes in the roofs of the containers before stealing the equipment, re-welding the plate removed back onto the containers and repainted the area they had damaged. Nearly $1m of fuel had been stolen en route to the Camp and, worryingly, the thieves had used oxyacetylene cutters to get at it.

Initial days were spent planning both at Camp Bastion with battle group Headquarters and Kandahar where Brigade HQ was located. Harrier jet pilots from Number 4 Squadron Royal Air Force were flying many sorties in support of the Helmand Task Force. The first draft operational order arrived, necessitating a change in the Squadron order of battle. The four Troops were reorganised to have three 30mm-gun Scimitars and one Spartan multi-role armoured personnel carrier apiece. The Squadron fitted bar armour, trained on Electonic Counter Measures equipment, zeroed all weapon systems and conducted mandatory briefings on all conceivable tasks.

and weapon just the shortest of distances was more than a little demanding. The purpose-built Drash tentage was perfectly liveable, in fact positively plush in comparison to the temporary accommodation and although hot due to the broken air-conditioning units, this helped the Squadron to acclimatise much faster. Camp Bastion at the time was expanding at a rapid rate. Six months previously the area was nothing more than a piece of desert. It now housed a 40-bed field hospital, a Joint Operations Centre, a runway, helicopter park, limited Internet facilities, a gym and all the other facilities needed to support a battle group.

Below: D Squadron the Household Cavalry Regiment information signs at ANP Hill, Afghanistan.

To further acclimatise men and vehicles, the Squadron took on the task of force protection to the Royal Engineers as they repaired the Camp Bastion runway. This freed the much put-upon Gurkha Rifle company for perimeter defence, something that unit came to love over the next five months! Many of the vehicles were experiencing problems; we had already used three gearboxes which could be blamed on aggressive driving, although the viscosity of the oils and lubricants also gave concern. Environmental Health Offices visited the tank park to ascertain the heat levels within the vehicles, but as it was morning they got a reading of only 128.4 degrees, nowhere near the 158 degrees Fahrenheit in the drivers' compartments operated in from June to early August.

For political reasons 16th Air Assault Brigade had to minimise its initial plan and send platoon-sized units to be forward based in northern Helmand towns, Now Zad in the west, Musá Qal'eh in the centre and Sangin in the east with a huge impact on Squadron operations and dispositions. Each town boasted a hard core of Taliban fighters, tenacious, extremely courageous often to the point of insanity, persistent and well armed with plenty of ammunition, although many a Quartermaster would have winced at their storage discipline. Initially the Taliban moved freely between the towns, surging in areas they felt they could have an effect.

The Squadron's training was cut short by a task out of area to the east of Lashkar Gar, providing an armoured screen in support of the Regional Task Force plan. The task was uneventful but the heat took its toll on both vehicles and men, the most serious of whom (Trooper Goodyear) was a near fatality, with an inner core temperature of 41.7 degrees Celsius (107 degrees

Right: Members of the Grenadier Guards clearing a compound during 12 Mechanized Brigade Reconnaissance Force's attack into Lwar Malazay in 2007.

Below: Squadron headquarters of D Squadron of the Household Cavalry camped up in Kandahar.

Fahrenheit); 42 degrees is deemed irrecoverable. Two other heat casualties had to be evacuated by Chinook escorted by an Apache attack helicopter.

While The Squadron conducted this initial operation, Corporal of Horse Shaun Fry, The Life Guards, who was attached to 7th Parachute Royal Horse Artillery (7 Para RHA) as a Joint Tactical Air Controller, was wounded by a 107mm recoilless rifle attack in Sangin. Corporal of Horse Fry was sent home to the UK for further treatment to a wound on his hand, but not before he had called in crucial US air support at Now Zad to cover A Company 3rd Battalion the Parachute Regiment and at Sangin.

Support to battle group operations took the form of securing helicopter landing sites, lines of departure and securing/holding ground in support of infantry and logistic assets. On the move north-east from Gereshk to Sangin up the Helmand valley, the convoy was attacked by an IED. The last vehicle, carrying four policemen, was destroyed killing all its occupants and wounding a further three nearby. The vehicle was only 30 yards behind a Squadron Spartan which was undamaged. The priority was the convoy so we had to leave the Afghan National Army to get on with its own casualty treatment and evacuation, following orders to do so. Number 2 Troop was left in Sangin to protect the Engineer teams that were improving the District Centre defences and perimeter. The Troop ended up staying almost five weeks until mid-August, having packed for a six-day recce exercise.

Having sortied to look for suspicious activity north of Camp Bastion and found nothing, the Squadron next rapidly deployed to Now Zad to take much-needed ammunition to the Gurkha Rifle Company stationed there, following reports of a heavy machine gun being seen in the area and therefore it not being safe to fly the ammunition in by support helicopter. The Gurkhas had exchanged hand grenades across the wall with the Taliban at times and were under pressure. Following a period of patrolling and direct fire support from 'The Shrine', to become known as 'ANP Hill' to the south of the town, the Squadron was able to shut down attacks by the Taliban and gave the Company a well-earned respite from fire, having lasted 17 days.

This lull was followed by C Company 3 Para relieving the Gurkhas, with Scimitars engaging targets in depth as support to the infantry.

Unfortunately there was not time to cement this success, as Brigade ordered D Squadron and the Gun Group to Musá Qal'eh, adding to the frustrations of Lieutenant Colonel Stuart Tootal, Commanding Officer, 3 Para.

This was a precursor to the most significant action of the Squadron's tour, as Number 1 Troop was left behind in Now Zad to support C Company while the remainder pushed towards Musá Qal'eh escorting 1st Battery 7 Para RHA. Their joint task was to cover the extraction of the Danish Recce Company and Pathfinders from Musá Qal'eh. Once the 105mm guns were in position the eight Squadron vehicles advanced to gain the ridgeline overlooking the town from the west. Initially, minefields and fog hampered this; Callsign 21 was manoeuvring near the ridgeline when it struck an anti-tank mine. The explosion destroyed the running gear and gearbox, removed the engine decks and buckled the chassis. Fortunately, and testament to the new mine-blast protection, Corporal of Horse Moses, The Life Guards, and the other two members of his crew were unharmed. The vehicle was subsequently destroyed using Apache Hellfire anti-armour missiles to prevent the enemy capturing it.

Following the mine strike, the Squadron manoeuvred to try and achieve its mission, but tragically was caught in a well-executed Taliban ambush. The initial command-wire operated IED destroyed callsign 41, killing Second Lieutenant Ralph Johnson, The Life Guards, Captain Alexander Eida (7 Para RHA) and Lance Corporal Ross Nicholls, The Blues and Royals, immediately. Trooper Martyn Compton, The Blues and Royals, survived the immediate attack but suffered 70 per cent burns to his body having crawled from the wreckage. Corporal of Horse Michael Flynn with his crew of Troopers Minter and Leach (all The Blues and Royals) were caught in the ambush killing area, their path blocked forward and back. They managed to extract themselves under heavy enemy fire back to the relative safety of the other vehicles. Lance Corporal of Horse Andrew Radford showed tremendous bravery extracting Trooper Compton with the aid of covering fire from Corporal of Horse Flynn and Number 3 Troop callsigns. The Taliban ambush was defeated only by the initiative of Lance Corporal of Horse Anderson using the

51mm mortar and the second-in-command coordinating fire from all surviving callsigns.

The Initial Reconnaissance Team and the 3 Para Commanding Officer's Tactical Headquarters deployed within 22 minutes of the contact report. While they were en route, Lance Corporal of Horse McWhirter, The Blues and Royals, used air assets to further dissuade the Taliban from interfering with the destroyed vehicles and the equipment on them. With its Number 1 Company, supported by the Scimitars and Spartans, 3 Para took control of the area, extracted those killed and ensured both Scimitars, severely damaged in the contact, were destroyed.

A memorial service was subsequently held back at Camp Bastion, hugely supported by the battle group, and the dead soldiers were repatriated to the UK via Kandahar where over 1,000 members of the International Security Assistance Force paid their respects.

The Squadron was given a short time to reflect before pushing on, with more deliberate operations into Musá Qal'eh and Now Zad. I arrived in the immediate aftermath and agreed with Major Alexander Dick that the command handover should take place as planned. This was nearing completion when news from Sangin came that Lance Corporal Sean Tansey, The Blues and Royals, had been killed while attempting to change the torsion bar on a Spartan. A further memorial service was held and Lance Corporal Tansey's body repatriated to the UK. The Commanding Officer Household Cavalry Regiment, Lieutenant Colonel Edward Smyth-Osbourne, The Life Guards, visited and delivered some critical morale-boosting in the immediate aftermath, and made seven richly deserved promotions.

In the wake of these tragedies, a handover of command and being split into three separate locations, the Squadron displayed a vast amount of courage and professionalism. The Second-in-Command led two significant infantry-support operations on routes used before where the Milan anti-tank missile was fired for the first time from a Spartan. Under the direction of Sergeant O'Farrell, 3 Para, we felt particularly competent, and he was somewhat taken aback as to our enthusiasm and ability with this infantry weapon system. It proved extremely useful in protecting us against Taliban attacks against static targets. On these two operations Lance Corporal of Horse Scott, The Blues and Royals, Lance Corporal Hamnett Royal Army Medical Corps and Trooper Smith, The Blues and Royals in the Squadron ambulance extracted casualties in the built-up areas under the direction of the Second-in-Command.

The resupplying of the outstations was becoming increasingly difficult, especially Musá Qal'eh and Sangin. The threat to aviation assets had risen dramatically and Chinooks had taken direct hits from small arms fire. This had a knock-on effect on our outstation support as vehicles requiring repair were remaining off the road as much needed supplies could not be brought forward quickly. The lack of spares was also affecting our capabilities, a reoccurring theme throughout the tour. Only twice did we deploy from Bastion without at least one vehicle breaking down before

we had reached the highway which was not more than 6km from the camp. In late August and early September vehicle reliability improved as the heat died down. A Relief in Place of Now Zad could be easily achieved and we often accomplished a sub-unit move, changing vehicles and crews. In Sangin this had to be accomplished by helicopter.

The Squadron, less the vehicles awaiting spare parts (always two or more), was more frequently used to test the 'Maneouvre Outreach Group' (MOG) theory. This entailed pushing into the wider expanses of the desert to dominate the ground and transit routes, and also allowed for more interaction with the local people, often between Musá Qal'eh and Now Zad. A ceasefire was agreed at the former due to the heavy losses and casualties on both sides. It was negotiated in the desert by Commander British Forces and Helmand Task Force, Brigadier Ed Butler, Lieutenant Colonel Stuart Tootal, Commanding Officer 3 Para, and Colonel Charlie Knaggs, Irish Guards, Commander of the Provincial Reconstruction based at Lashkar Gar. D Squadron maintained the security for this 'shura' (council) and subsequently held mini-shuras to enable carriage of supplies into Musá Qal'eh by the elders of the town.

The largest threat to the Squadron and MOG came from land mines either washed down the wadis or legacy mines littering the desert. They

Left: A commander's eye view from a Household Cavalry Scimitar in Now Zad.

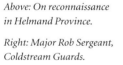

Above: On reconnaissance in Helmand Province.

Right: Major Rob Sergeant, Coldstream Guards.

suffered six mine strikes between them; the most serious destroyed a Weapons-Mounted jeep providing flank protection to one of our convoys. All three occupants survived although Lance Bombardier Parkinson, 7 Para RHA, lost both his legs and suffered a severe head wound. Corporal of Horse Hoggarth, The Life Guards, and his crew had a lucky escape four days later when their Scimitar triggered an anti-tank mine on the extremities of the track, blowing the bar armour off and disabling the vehicle in a Taliban area. The Royal Electical and Mechanical Engineers worked tenaciously to ensure the vehicle was not only drivable but could return to Bastion without further repair.

We were retasked following some essential maintenance in Bastion to resupply Now Zad once again. This was followed by an extremely difficult extraction of Number 4 Troop from Sangin as part of the battle group's handover to fresh troops of 3 Commando Brigade. Intelligence had identified a possible route across the River Helmand north-east of Sangin but what seemed like deliberate insurgent ambush tactics warned us off this plan. Eventually excellent recce skills and judgement by vehicle commanders marked out a route across four tributaries of the river. Leaving Sangin 4 Troop came under fire that was suppressed by 30mm cannon, 105mm high-explosive shells and Milan missiles (11 in all). The Squadron drove back to the Musá Qal'eh area to continue MOG activity.

Our last foray was into Now Zad as part of deception operations to allow a Company of 2nd Battalion The Royal Regiment of Fusiliers to conduct some deliberate operations of its own. This foray proved successful despite intense Taliban infantry and mortar fire. Although 1 Troop remained on ANP Hill for the final four days, while the rest of the Squadron containerised the vehicles in camp, our formal support to the Brigade (now 3rd Commando Brigade built round 42 Commando Royal Marines) ceased on 18 October.

The remainder of the tour saw an extensive handover to C Squadron Light Dragoons commanded by Major Ben Warwick. The key message was that the Scimitar-series tracked armoured vehicles provided rapid mobility, firepower and protection for the battle group and Brigade. The Taliban had been successful in defeating this armour only once and by sheer luck rather than judgement. This tour reinforced old lessons and will aid further developments. A fitting memorial to those who lost their lives stands outside the Joint Operations Centre at Camp Bastion.

The Squadron returned to Windsor for a medal parade taken by Major General Barney White-Spunner, formerly The Blues and Royals, who also attended a memorial service held at the Garrison Church, before speaking to family members at a reception held in the Warrant Officers' and Non-Commissioned Officers' Mess.

The Squadron's tour was a huge success for the Scimitar reconnaissance vehicle and the Household Cavalry as a whole. However the loss of Second Lieutenant Ralph Johnson, Lance Corporal Ross Nicholls and Lance Corporal Sean Tansey has been felt across the entire Regiment, battle group and Brigade.

IRAQ

3.09

Colonel Ben Bathurst, Formerly Welsh Guards
(Commanded 1st Battalion Welsh Guards 2004–6)

I can only comment on 1st Battalion Welsh Guards having commanded its battle group in Al Amarah, Maysan Province from October 2004 to May 2005. This will give a flavour of what operations in Iraq are like and the supreme professionalism of the Guardsmen in very demanding circumstances.

The Welsh Guards took over from 1st Battalion The Princess of Wales's battle group which successfully dealt with two uprisings in Al Amarah from the Muqtada al Sadr militia or 'Mahdi Army', firing more ammunition in six months than the whole of the British forces did in the first warfighting phase. Our job was to exploit the opportunity that they had created and our main effort was to ensure that the democratic national and provincial elections were held in January 2005.

Our first task was to ensure that a change of approach was not mistaken for weakness. We set about creating a large number of jobs (19,000 by the end of the tour) and reinvigorating reconstruction projects put on hold by the fighting, as well as conducting a series of search and detain operations to unhinge some of the key insurgents.

For everyone who might think that the Household Division are 'just ceremonial troops', their opinion will be sharply reversed by the scantest glance at the Guards' record in Iraq. Every Regiment has seen service there since 2003, during the most recent operations in that country. The initial phase of the campaign, Operation TELIC 1 in 2003, saw 1st Battalion Irish Guards and the Household Cavalry Regiment in action in what was then termed the 'war fighting phase'. However, operations have continued with varying degrees of intensity and no less danger. The 1st Battalions Scots and Welsh Guards served together in 4th Armoured Brigade in Operation TELIC 5 in 2005 with 12th Mechanised Brigade and 1st Battalion Grenadier Guards served on Operation TELIC 7 in 2006. 1st Battalion Irish Guards returned to complete a TELIC 10 operational tour in Basra province by November 2007. Each Regiment and Battalion has its own unique story to tell and each would be a fascinating book in itself.

Above: Lance Sergeant Scarf on patrol with Iraqi Police.

Left: An Irish Guardsman makes last minute checks before a range firing period.

Aside from our Welsh Guards light infantry companies, we had a Warrior Armoured Fighting Vehicle Company from The Duke of Wellington's Regiment, a Challenger 2 tank squadron from The Royal Dragoon Guards, Scimitar reconnaissance vehicles from B Squadron The Queen's Dragoon Guards and a plethora of other assets from Phoenix Unmanned Aerial Vehicles or drones, Chinook, Merlin, Sea King, and Lynx helicopters, along with their maintenance teams, logistic support

detachments, bomb disposal teams and medical teams. When we were further reinforced by Left Flank Company, and then Right Flank Company, Scots Guards, we numbered over 1,000 in Camp Abu Naji.

One operation in particular characterised the nature of operations in Maysan and that revolved around the town of Majar al-Kabir where six Royal Military Policemen were brutally murdered on 24 June 2003. Our predecessors were fully occupied with the fighting in the provincial capital city, Al Amarah, and had taken the sensible decision not to spread themselves too thinly by operating everywhere in a province the size of Northern Ireland. The District Council leader, an immensely brave man, was determined that control should be restored and the power to the militias and tribal leaders should be reined in. A straightforward operation into the town was out of the question as all it would have led to would have been more fighting, this time involving us. A more manoeuvrist approach was required and therefore we set about providing reconstruction projects – generators, water-purifying units, road and school building – in the smaller towns all around. Within a week, a deputation of 30 tribal sheikhs came with the District Council leader to demand equal treatment for Majar al-Kabir. They frequently

Trooper Jason Glasgow, The Blues and Royals

From Trinidad And Tobago

In the regiment we have Fijians … some Australians, South Africans. It's diversified. It's good because it's different cultures. Listening and hearing the Fijians talking, it's all part of the experience. I came from Trinidad and Tobago and moved to America with the family. So I thought I'd join the US Marines. I signed up, and it came to Monday morning and I went into the Equipment Office – and on the wall was a chart with the casualty rates between the different nationalities in Iraq and Afghanistan: and the British was lowest. And I tell myself there and then that they have to be doing something right: I was accepted because I had a military background in the Defence Force in the Caribbean.

It's proper hard graft sometimes – but it is worthwhile. Once you work the work, it's no problem. I have no complaints whatsoever. I am happy. If your lives are happy, then everyone's happy with your performance. Out here in Iraq, the temperatures, as a driver are horrendous. The temperature is something like plus-55 degrees Celsius. The vehicles have no air-conditioning. So you're driving, and it's literally plus-55 on the outside, it's plus-65 on the inside. You just have on a T-shirt and your body armour. We used to get burns on the hand – you're actually injured.

But I'm so happy. Everybody's really good. I really have pride in my regiment, the utmost pride. Obviously the whole thing is a worry to my wife, well 'cos me being on tour is a worry; her husband got blown up and was being shot at. In Afghanistan I was driving a Spartan [armoured reconnaissance vehicle]. We were hit by a land mine and the deck blew off, and the instrument panel was totally destroyed. Engine block totally destroyed. All I got was this scratch and the Commander was OK. Everyone was generally OK.

Captain David Basson, Welsh Guards

Adjutant of the Welsh Guards who was Operations Officer for the Prince of Wales's Company in Iraq, September 2004 to March 2005

On Iraq

Our job was to look after the city of Basra. Of course, many others operated within it but we were the ones who needed to patrol it. One General was trying to describe the difference between the Regiments and I think that he said if he needed to undertake a daring assault he would use the Parachute Regiment; if he needed to fight in jungles he would use the Gurkhas and if he wanted to defend something to the death, he would use the Guards.

This was a sort of environment that needed real discipline in order to survive. It was all about guys when they were absolutely on their chin straps, still taking their turn in the sangars, an exposed breastwork in the middle of a city, as you can imagine, completely overlooked by roads such as RPG (Rocket-Propelled Grenade) Alley. As a Guardsman, once or twice a week you would probably be on guard and that's a 24-hour commitment and you are going from sangar to sangar in the baking heat.

The second you sit down and say, 'I can't be bothered, I'm going to take 10 minutes off', that's when something happens. The guys were remarkable. It was real Guards traditional discipline that you need to survive in a place like that and if we couldn't have trusted our Guardsmen and had that sort of discipline we wouldn't have been as safe as we were.

On His Role As Adjutant

In partnership with the Regimental Sergeant Major, my job is to make sure that the Battalion is running correctly on a day-to-day basis, that people are kept on their toes and not needing to be checked up on. Cutting corners leads to loss of life and I like to think that as a Guards Battalion we don't cut corners and we do things by the book. By checking that you have taken the time to maintain your drill boots to the correct standard of studs underneath, translates absolutely exactly 100 per cent to the cleanliness of your SA80 Rifle and to the fact that you had made sure that your cartridge link is laid out correctly in the ammunition case and that it is going to fire correctly.

Lance Corporal of Horse Jonathan Woodgate, The Blues and Royals

Driver On Operation TELIC 1 During A Friendly Fire Incident

We lived off the wagons [Scimitar armoured vehicles] for so long, it just became the norm. It was proper recce stuff. In Afghanistan it was similar. The patrols we'd do from Camp would last a couple of weeks. In Operation TELIC 1, we were scouting out against other tanks: following tank tracks, stuff like that; tried to find berms [mound or wall of sand/earth] so we could go turret up and engage tank on tank. We heard over the radio that there were A-10s [US tank-busting aircraft] in the area. The first thing I knew when we actually got hit, was the wagon just stopped dead, and these two sparks came round, flying over my shoulders. I wasn't quite sure what had happened, so I checked over my shoulder; the whole thing full of smoke and then flames, you know, it just lit up. I thought at first that we had been ambushed. We were in that part where the Iraqi 6th Army Brigade was in so I thought it would be them that smashed us in. Then I just tried to get out; the driver's hatch jammed; so I had to struggle about with that for quite a while. I was pretty shocked, as I was only 19 years old.

It became pretty evident, what was going on. The A-10s came on their second swoop. They were pretty low. The whole end of the back of the vehicle was ripped open, and the turret had been blown off; if you stood in front of it you could see out of the back of it.

Left: Lieutenant Armstrong Fleming of the Scots Guards above Basra.

came to demand investment but always accompanied by conditions and therefore were sent away empty handed. Eventually, patience ran out and I said that I was coming in anyway, either to fight or to reconstruct – which option they took was up to them.

The re-entry to Majar al-Kabir took the form of my Multiple of three Snatch Land Rovers delivering the funding for a range of projects in the town, preceded by an Anti-Tank Platoon Multiple who bore the brunt of a minority who chose to demonstrate against our presence. However, stretching from the outskirts of the town back to Camp Abu Naji 20km away was a column including 4 Challengers, 48 Warriors, 2 Mortar-carrying Fighting Vehicle, 432 armoured personnel carriers and 3 helicopters overhead. This suggested any serious attempt to take us on would be met by overwhelming force. The money was delivered, the status of the District Council enhanced and the town ceased to be a no-go area as we patrolled it extensively in the coming days and months. Our reconstruction projects delivered benefits that militia and tribal fighting

had previously prevented and our training of the Iraqi Security Forces allowed them to take on the mantle.

Like every battle group in Iraq, we had a large number of small arms engagements with insurgents, were hit by numerous roadside bombs, targeted by mortars and 107mm rockets fired at the camp and ambushed with grenades and homemade devices. That is par for the course in Iraq and the Guardsmen's professionalism, determination and good humour saw us through. Although the expeditionary campaign infrastructure that we lived in was remarkably good, the constant patrolling against a substantial threat, the incessant indirect fire disrupting the routine, the sometimes exasperating task of training the Iraqi Security Forces and dealing with local, District and Provincial political and administrative leaders, took its toll. Despite the negative impression given in the media, the British Army (and Household Division in particular) can take considerable pride in what we have achieved there. The elections in 2005 and then again in 2006 passed off remarkably peacefully and replaced the appointed government with one the Iraqis voted for themselves. Thousands have been recruited and trained into the Iraqi Police and Army and reconstruction projects, along with free trade, has meant that the economy in a very poor part of Iraq has improved.

What the eventual legacy is only time will tell, but what is certain is that the Household Division has played a full part in the campaign, doing exactly what was asked by our political masters and to the highest possible standards. A perfect example of Excellence in Action.

Left: Top cover maintains a watchful eye on patrol in Matsan.

Major James Gaselee, The Life Guards

James Gaselee led a squadron of the Household Cavalry Regiment to Iraq in 2003. The Squadron was responsible for mentoring the Border Police along the whole Iranian and Kuwait land borders in the British Sector. He kept a blog, which he emailed to friends and family.

The First 50 days

The Iraqi policemen are keen but stuck in Fort Zinderneuf without electricity, air-conditioning or beds their enthusiasm does wane. It is therefore quite difficult to get them to do their jobs properly. They are also a little worried by the smugglers who are better armed than they are.

The gentleman who runs the Border Police in this province is a wonderful character called Colonel Hussein. He is about 5ft tall, always immaculate and speaks relatively good English. I went to see him a couple of days ago and we went on a tour of his patch. At each Fort, the guard turned out and presented arms. This drill might not quite have cut the mustard on the forecourt of Buckingham Palace but I have seen plenty worse. At the final location, the duty NCO appeared, complete with red sash and pace stick.

Life in Iraq

We have now properly settled into our work and routine which invariably means that it will all change shortly. Myself, and some of the Squadron are living in the rather grandly named Shatt Al Arab Hotel, reputedly the best hotel in Basra. Well, it was until the Royal Fusiliers fought their way through it in the war. The bullet holes can still be seen, although the chandeliers are still intact. It is now home and I cannot complain; I have my own room with en-suite facilities although the bidet and shower do not work and you cannot touch the water because it comes from the Shatt Al Arab itself.

The threat in Basra has gone up in the evenings. Figures emerge from the hotel clad in a towel, helmet and body armour and make their way gingerly over to the shower block. Only in the Army can this be considered remotely normal behaviour. It is odd what things one misses: proper plates and cutlery spring to mind currently.

Above: View over the vast expanse of water that is the marshes.

Above right: Sunrise in the desert.

Right: 3 Troop on the move through the Maysan countryside.

Above: 1 Tp in the grounds of the Shatt Al Arab Hotel.

Below: Squadron Corporal Major Stephenson, Major General Rollo (late The Blues and Royals), Major Gaselee.

Everything in this country is of a varying shade of khaki. The buildings, the dirt, the water, the people, all khaki; even the palm trees and plants have a brown tinge to them, it is quite extraordinary. It is therefore lovely to dive into Country Life Magazine and, for a few moments imagine lying under a tree in Windsor Great Park, or playing tag with the children in the garden.

Cavalry Sunday

On Cavalry Sunday we held a memorial service for two Household Cavalrymen who were killed during the war last year. We managed to find the spot where it happened, indeed it is marked by the remains of their vehicle's tank track. The service was very simple but poignant for us all and we even managed to belt out Jerusalem rather badly. I wish I could report that the site where they died was particularly beautiful or spectacular, but I can't. It is in the middle of a large flat piece of scrubby desert intersected by waterways with large oil wells looming in the distance belching out huge palls of black smog. A depressing spot which I hope has now been enlivened by a plaque that the Squadron has made and placed there. This has a sign in Arabic, in the hope of preventing it being pinched, saying that this is a memorial to British soldiers who gave their lives for the liberation of Iraq.

Sadr Uprising

This brings us to the latest violence, which according to the BBC nearly caused the British Army to retreat with their tails between their legs to Kuwait. As you can imagine this is not quite true, although our families were not to know that at home. There were a number of incidents in Basra and large numbers of Sadr supporters did appear on the streets but soon disappeared when the Army appeared. Even more encouraging, large numbers of police stayed at work rather than running away which up until now has been their usual modus operandi in these situations.

There was also no general Shia uprising, indeed one of my troops went to support an infantry company clear a bridge of a number of Sadr militia. As soon as our vehicles were spotted these brave martyrs went into the nearest building to get the women and children out in order to form human shields. Needless to say they disappeared as soon as the infantry advanced.

The Soldiers

There is nothing better than commanding Household Cavalrymen, especially on operations. The soldiers in the Squadron come from every background and area; there is one gentleman trooper who reads John Simpson's book on Iraq while the rest of the troop read dodgy magazines; a Zimbabwean whose ambition is to foment an anarchist revolution anywhere. My driver is half Iranian and from Sunderland. As you can see we are a real mixed bag but the one thing that unites them is their sense of humour; they can see the funny side of anything, no matter what.

THE GUARDS ON PARADE

Above: The Queen's Life Guard, formed from soldiers of The Blues and Royals, leaves Horse Guards to return to Hyde Park Barracks, a duty that occurs every day of the year.

HORSE GUARDS, WHITEHALL

John Martin Robinson

The Horse Guards comes near the top of the list of an Englishmen's favourite London buildings. It is a dignified 18th-century set piece in a street equalled only by the High Street at Oxford for picturesque urban composition. The other façade deploys friendly, country-house architecture and is the ideal foil to the Humphry Repton landscape in St James's Park.

Add to this the rare atmosphere, the smell of horses, the glittering steel cuirasses of The Blues and Royals and The Life Guards, and the military ritual, and it all adds up to a scene of perfection. This is one of those special places where architecture still serves its original function. As a military headquarters, guarded gateway and a ceremonial stable, it is the only one of its type to survive in any European capital.

Now for the first time it is possible to visit some of the ground floor interior. Part of the brick-vaulted stables in the north wing has been restored by the architect Barnaby Wheeler (of Hampshire Country Council architects) and converted to two galleries for the new museum of the Household Cavalry, moved here from Combermere Barracks, Windsor. These splendid 18th-century spaces, which were originally the stables for the building, were divided in the 20th century into a warren of small offices with concrete floors and partition walls.

All modern detritus has now been cleared under the guidance of English Heritage; the 18th-century vaults supported on square stone piers, and even some of the original cobbled floors have been revealed and restored. Through a glass screen it is possible to see the stables still in use with 20 black Irish horses, their individual painted name boards over each stall, and the distinctive Household Cavalry drill for cleaning and feeding.

Two sections of the former stables are devoted to displaying the collection of the Household Cavalry, including uniforms, presentation swords, embroidered saddlecloths, silver by Fabergé and paintings by Alfred Munnings. Gallery One explains the present ceremonial and operational role of The Life Guards and The Blues and Royals, while Gallery Two explores the origins and history of the regiments of the Household Cavalry. The former museum at Combermere Barracks, Windsor, is to become a new archive and interpretation centre. The new museum represents an unrivalled opportunity to explore and understand a building and its activities at the heart of English life.

The Horse Guards is closely bound to the history of the English (British from 1707) standing army. At the Restoration of Charles II, a regiment of Foot Guards and two troops of Horse Guards were established for the King's protection at Whitehall Palace. It was for the accommodation of these Guards, both foot and mounted, that the building which preceded the present one was erected in 1663, overlooking the Tilt Yard of Whitehall Palace (now Horse Guards Parade) which the Tudors and Stuarts had used for ceremonial jousts and other pageants.

The 17th-century building, like its successor, had stabling for 62 horses on the ground floor with officers' rooms above, and a central gateway from St James's Park to Whitehall Palace in the form of a pavilion with a prominent clock-turret. It was erected by the Office of Works and has been attributed to Sir Christopher Wren, but there is no evidence for that. The bricklayer was Maurice Emmett (Senior), one of a family of Wren School craftsmen, and he or his son may have been the designer, too; as was the case, for example, with the still extant College of Arms in the City designed by Maurice Emmett (Junior) in 1671.

Whoever was the designer, the old Horse Guards was not very well built and the timbers proved too weak to support the weight of the clock tower which slowly collapsed and so had to be propped up in an unsightly manner. In 1745, the two Colonels of the Life Guards, Lords Delawarr and Cadogan, complained to the Secretary of War that the place was 'in a very rotten and decayed condition … is now become so dangerous that it is not safe for the Coaches of his Majesty … to pass under the Gateway, and the Men and Horses doing duty there are in perpetual danger of losing their lives by the falling down of the Buildings.'

The Board of Works concurred, and in July 1745 the Treasury gave an order to prepare plans for rebuilding. The Board comprised four architects – Henry Finch, Thomas Ripley, William Kent and Westby Gill – and the new design was entrusted to William Kent, the most able of them all. His preliminary design is in the Victoria & Albert Museum, and shows a staccato composition, with octagonal cupolas, inspired by Holkham Hall in Norfolk. Execution of the scheme was delayed by the Jacobite Rising of 1745–6, and the concurrent War of the Austrian Succession; and the Treasury only approved building work after the Peace of Aix-la-Chapelle in 1749.

Kent himself had died the previous year, but his executors sold a complete, numbered set of finished drawings (now lost) to the Office of Works in November 1749, and these were presumably for the scheme as executed. The building has always been attributed to Kent, and John

Above: Horse Guards parade, the scene of centuries of ceremony by the Household Cavalry and Foot Guards.

Vardy inscribed 'Wm. Kent invt.' below the view of the west front which he published in 1752 (See *Survey of London*, Vol. XVI).

Though Royal Whitehall had largely been burnt to the ground 60 years previously, the new building still took the form of a ceremonial gateway to the vanished palace, with guards' accommodation in the south wing, and guards' stables in the north. The square centre block was intended as a new War Office, with rooms for the Secretary at War, the Judge Advocate-General, and the Commissioners of Chelsea Hospital. It served as the headquarters of the British Army up to the Crimean War; since when it has been the office of the Major General Commanding the Household Division and London District.

In view of its character as a 'Publick Building', the Board of Works planned to build it in 'a very substantial Manner and the whole faced in Portland stone'. They appointed John Vardy and William Robinson as joint clerks of works to supervise the construction, and estimated the cost at £31,748.

As so often with British public contracts, the actual cost was more than double, eventually notching up £65,000. Various modifications to Kent's design were made during the work, including the rustication of the elevations, and the revised form of the central clock turret as a tall domed cupola more like the old one than Kent's proposed lower octagon.

These modifications all seem to have been made by the Board itself in committee; they devoted 181 meetings to the building between 1750 and 1759. Isaac Ware made the necessary drawings, being paid £100 a year for acting as 'draughtsman'. (See the *History of the Kings' Works*, Vol. V).

The excellence of the detail, such as the Ionic Order of the Venetian windows, owes much therefore to the solicitude of the Board of Works, while the overall composition and silhouette shows Kent's particular scenic design flair. The central pavilion was built first, the foundations being laid in 1750 and the clock turret constructed in 1753. The old clock, after overhaul by the clock-maker John Seddon, was reinstalled. It had the reputation of being the most accurate in Westminster.

The sharp-eyed may notice that a portion of the dial-face behind the gilt numeral 2 is painted black, commemorating the hour at which Charles I was executed outside the Banqueting House on the other side of Whitehall in 1649. For those who love such antiquarian arcana, the

Garrison Sergeant Major Mott, Welsh Guards

Responsible For All London Parades

My official title is Garrison Sergeant Major of London District. I am the Warrant Officer that deals with ceremonial tasks that involve all tri service elements, Royal Navy, Army and Royal Air Force when it comes to any of the state occasions held here in London. It is such an honour to be the Garrison Sergeant Major because of all the great history behind the Household Division. In my 26 years in the British Army I have met some absolutely fantastic soldiers and the camaraderie that I have learnt enables me to feel more than just pride in the profession that I have got but also in the post and the appointment that I hold.

Drill is important to me because, as I have learnt as a young recruit and then Guardsman, it instils first and foremost the self discipline which is the most important aspect of the drill side, with its ceremonial implications, and also of the operational side. Consequently I am a very strong believer in drill and it allows a man to take personal pride not only in his appearance but in his attitude towards others. When the chips are down in an operational situation, that drill background that he has been nurtured and trained for, that self discipline allows him to react where the body's natural reaction is to close down. He listens, hears a word of command, hears an order and rather than being a shock process he can act to it immediately in the same way he would if he was on the square.

If someone was to say to me that there was no place in this society for anything ceremonial I would argue quite strongly that that is rubbish. It is an incorrect statement. You have to look at her Majesty's Golden Jubilee to see the presence just here in London of the general public and I think sadly we don't get to see that view as often as needs to be seen. We get to see all the bad things and hear about all the bad things that are happening and we know they are happening but we never get to hear the good things, the individual that is outstanding, or the group of men, the group of individuals, the group of women that have stood up and been counted and I think the ceremonial aspects allow us to show our grandeur, our splendid attitude towards the pomp and ceremony, our loyalty to each other and our camaraderie.

GSM Mott's interview is taken from a DVD produced and directed by the Curator of The Guards Museum, Andrew Wallis, and is used with permission and grateful thanks. Copies of the DVD are available from The Guards Museum, Wellington Barracks, Birdcage Walk, SW1E 6HQ

central archway of the Horse Guards bestrides the old parish boundary, so that the south wing is in St Margaret's Westminster, and the north wing in St Martin-in-the-Fields. The parish-bounds can be seen marked above the arch itself, and also in the middle of the entablature of the doorcase in the Major General's office on the piano nobile. One can stand on its axis with a foot in different parishes.

The main part of the interior survives little altered. Two sets of stone cantilevered stairs lead up from either side of the archway, and give access to a central octagonal tribune, lit from small lunettes in the clock turret. To the east is the Wellington Room, originally intended as a chapel and now a conference room. The adjoining offices have painted timber panelling with box cornices, and Kentian chimneypieces.

To the west is the Major General's room with a magnificent view of St James's Park, and an ornamental plaster panelled ceiling, inspired by Inigo Jones's at the Banqueting House. The walls were restored to their original grey and green colour scheme by Costains ten years ago. The contents include full-length portraits of George III and Queen Charlotte, busts of The Dukes of Marlborough, York and Wellington; while the elegant Heppelwaite/Sheraton style oval desk of about 1785–90 is that used by York, Wellington himself and Lord Hill as successive Commanders-in-Chief from 1795 to 1852.

This is a room in which the historical continuity of England can be strongly felt, as is true of the whole building. There is even a well-preserved cockfight pit in the basement. It is the horses that steal the show, however, in their grand vaulted Kentian stables (inspired by those at Houghton Hall, Norfolk) on the ground floor, and in the two stone, pedimented sentry boxes facing Whitehall, still defending a long-vanished royal palace.

Extracted from Country Life magazine

CEREMONIAL DUTIES

The ceremonial side of life in the Household Division is divided into two categories: State Ceremonial and Public Duties.

State Ceremonial events are the great, national parades that take place every year. These include State Visits when the monarch welcomes a fellow head of state. In 2007 there were two State Visits. One was in March by the President of the Republic of Ghana and the other in October/November by King Abdullah of Saudi Arabia.

Other important parades include The Queen's Birthday Parade and its two rehearsals; on the Saturday before The Queen's Birthday Parade is the Colonel's Review. This takes exactly the same format but instead of The Queen, her place is taken by one of the Colonels of the Foot Guards Regiments. This could be Prince Philip, Prince Charles or The Duke of Kent. On the Saturday before that is the Major General's Review. Such is the preparation required for the rehearsals, and the necessity of not disrupting an already congested traffic system, that the men of the Household Cavalry get up at 2.30 am in order to be out on the streets for an 'early morning rehearsal'.

The Major General also separately inspects all the Regiments of the Household Division (and The King's Troop, Royal Horse Artillery) before the full ceremonial season gets under way in the summer. The Major General's inspection is one of the few occasions that the Household Cavalry Mounted Regiment will canter past in line abreast. It is not a public parade but makes an impressive spectacle in Hyde Park.

The Household Cavalry Mounted Regiment is permanently based at Hyde Park Barracks (known informally and simply within the Regiment as Knightsbridge), although the soldiers and officers are posted between this Regiment and the Armoured Reconnaissance Regiment in Windsor. Only the Riding Staff, Farriers, Tailors and Saddlers have longer-term postings. Under the leadership of the Riding Master, the Riding Staff are responsible for the standard of riding and ceremonial drill within the regiment. The Foot Guards are based at Wellington Barracks, Victoria Barracks, Windsor and Woolwich Barracks.

Other events include Beating Retreat, the State Opening of Parliament and the Cenotaph parade. Smaller occasions include a presence at the Lord Mayor's Show; and the Garter Ceremony at Windsor Castle, the only occassion when the Household Cavalry Mounted Regiment parades on its feet.

Public Duties are those that require a permanent presence by members of the Household Division. These include The Queen's Life Guard at Horse Guards, the Queen's Guard at Buckingham Palace and St James's Palace and the Ceremony of the Keys at the Tower of London as well as the Quadrangle mounts at Windsor Castle.

There are occasional one off regimental parades such as the Standards Parade held by the Household Cavalry once every ten years. In 2007 the Household Cavalry Pageant held on Horse Guards was an event to help raise money for the new museum at Horse Guards. Held in the presence of The Queen, it was the first time that the Regiment had conducted a Rank Past 'in line of regiment' for many years.

Ceremony of the Keys, Tower of London

This ceremony has taken place in some form or other since the 14th century. Just before 10 pm, the Chief Warder, dressed in Tudor period uniform, meets the Escort of the Key, made up of four men of the Guard detachment, which is found from one of the Foot Guards battalions. Together, they secure the main gates of the Tower. Upon their return to the Bloody Tower archway, the party is halted by the sentry and challenged to identify themselves:

Left: Troopers of The Blues and Royals wait to mount up at their barracks in Knightsbridge.

Above: Four men of the Guard detachment accompany the Chief Warder to secure the main gates of the Tower of London.

Right: Her Majesty The Queen returns to the inner quadrangle at Buckingham Palace following the State Opening of Parliament in 2006.

Sentry: 'Halt, who comes there?'
Chief Warder: 'The Keys.'
Sentry: 'Whose Keys?'
Chief Warder: 'Queen Elizabeth's Keys.'
Sentry: 'Pass Queen Elizabeth's Keys. All's well.'

Following this, the party makes its way into the fortress, where the Guard presents arms, and the Chief Warder raises his hat, proclaiming:

Chief Warder: 'God preserve Queen Elizabeth.'
Guard and the Escort: 'Amen!'

The Chief Warder then takes the keys in for safekeeping, while the Last Post is sounded.

It takes quite a bit to interrupt a ceremony where Guards are participating but during the Second World War some incendiary bombs fell on the old Victorian guardroom during an air raid, just as the Chief Yeoman Warder and the Escort were coming through the Bloody Tower archway. The shock and the noise of the bombs blew over the Escort and the Chief Yeoman Warder, but they stood up, dusted themselves down, and carried on.

The Tower holds a letter from the Officer of the Guard apologising to The King that the ceremony was late and a reply from The King, which says that the Officer is not to be punished.

Queen's Guard

The Queen's Guard is the name given to the contingent responsible for guarding Buckingham Palace and St James's Palace including Clarence House. The Guard is made up of a company of Guardsmen, which is split in two, providing a detachment for Buckingham Palace and a detachment for St James's Palace.

Because the Sovereign's main residence is still St James's, the Captain of the Guard (the Guard commander) is based there, as are the Regiment's Colours. When the Sovereign is in residence, The Queen's Guard numbers 3 officers and 32 other ranks, with four sentries each posted at Buckingham Palace (on the forecourt) and St James's Palace (two sentries are posted in the Stable Yard Road from Pall Mall and two in Cleveland Row). This reduces to 3 officers and 29 other ranks, with two sentries each when the Sovereign is not in residence.

Guardsman Ben Stone, Grenadier Guards

On Nijmegen Company

The main focus area is ceremonial duties. I did one Trooping of the Colour, and I did Palace Guard (Buckingham Palace), Tower of London and Windsor Castle. We'd have rehearsals in the morning on the day of the mount at about 8 am and normally have rehearsals for 45 minutes just to clear up where everyone is going and I think we mounted at 10 or 10.30 am. You do your boots and belt the night before. It sometimes takes two or three hours. I think I prefer wearing a tunic to the greatcoat in winter. The greatcoat is hard to march in, very restrictive. I used to wash my bearskin once a week with shampoo and then comb it. You can soak it and rinse it out.

The first time I went on Guard, it was a difficult time, because you are afraid to move, but once you get into it, you can march up and down, you can patrol and change arms. In the summer months it is definitely hard work standing there in the sun for two hours but you get used to it. The Tower of London and St James's Palace were not as bad as, say, Buckingham Palace which is quite boring. There you can't speak to anyone. I mean on St James's Palace you go on the street, where you have people coming up to you and it passes the time.

Incremental Companies

There are three incremental companies permanently based in London. They are F Company Scots Guards, Nijmegen Company Grenadier Guards, and Number 7 Company Coldstream Guards.

Under the Options for Change Review of the Army in 1993 the three Guards regiments that had two battalions were allowed to place their second battalion into 'suspended animation' as a company. These companies are able to retain the regimental colour and the Queen's colour and technically, at least, they can re-inflate, at a moment's notice, back to battalion strength. All three are based permanently in London and if all three of the public duties battalions are on operations, the incremental companies can fill the breach.

The workload depends on who is available to carry out public duties, but the three incremental companies could not sustain a permanent public duty role alone without further assistance. That is why other regiments and formations are then invited to participate in public duties. However, there is a rule that there is 'always a bearskin on the forecourt' meaning that either the Guard coming on or the Guard coming off is provided by the Foot Guards.

In the case of the Scots Guards, all recruits from Catterick go straight to F Company after passing out and remain with the company for nine months or so. Major James Kelly, officer commanding F Company, calls it 'our finishing school'. The Guardsmen are able to learn all about being with a company before joining the main battalion. They will have obtained basic trades that will make them immediately useful. In an age when it is highly likely that a Guardsman will be joining his battalion on operations, this final step is useful preparation.

When a soldier leaves the incremental company not only will he have participated in the Trooping of the Colour but he will have taken his driving test and know the basics of fighting in a Warrior. There are also the Mandatory Annual Training Tests, which include fitness, and Nuclear, Biological, and Chemical warfare. In the case of the Scots Guards the 'satisfied soldier', as Major Kelly refers to them, will be posted back to augment regimental recruiting teams for a week or so at Edinburgh Castle.

The Queen's Guard is not purely ceremonial. It provides sentries during the day and night, and during the latter hours they patrol the grounds of the Palace. Until 1959, the sentries at Buckingham Palace were stationed outside the railings. This was stopped following an incident involving a female tourist and a Coldstream Guardsman. Due to the continued pestering of tourists and sightseers, the Guardsman kicked the tourist on the ankle as he marched. The tourist made a complaint to the police and, despite sympathy, the sentry was confined to barracks for ten days. Not long after, the sentries were moved inside the fence. However, the Household Cavalry are still exposed at Horse Guards to the whims, demands and idiosyncrasies of passing tourists.

Postings

At any one time, up to three infantry battalions are usually committed to Public Duties; two of these are Guards battalions (one based at Wellington Barracks, next to Buckingham Palace and one at Victoria Barracks in Windsor), while the third is a line infantry unit (based at Cavalry Barracks, Hounslow).

In addition, there are three Incremental Companies based at Woolwich and Wellington Barracks. All of them come under the command and administrative authority of London District. As Public Duties units, they not only take part in ceremonial, but are also committed to providing military aid to the civil authorities when it is requested.

Changing of The Queen's Guard

The Changing of the Guard takes place in the forecourt of Buckingham Palace. The St James's Palace detachment of The Queen's Guard, led usually by the Corps of Drums, and bearing the Colour (if The Queen is in residence, then this will be The Queen' Colour; if she is not, then it

Lieutenant Tom Radcliffe, Coldstream Guards

On Trooping The Colour

I was on The Queen's Birthday Parade (Trooping the Colour) in June. Extremely hard work but I'm glad that I did it. Generally the harder and more miserable things are at the time, the more fondly you look back on them. Going around in slow time, it's a big thing. The band is right next door to you and you can feel the air vibrating in your lungs. Although going on Guard is exciting when you first do it, the duty becomes less adrenalin-fuelled as time goes on and it's good to get a chance to go away.

Below: The Queen standing next to The Duke of Edinburgh is eager to watch the beginning of the ride and march past by the members of the Household Division who have returned her to Buckingham Palace after the State Opening of Parliament. Her daughter, The Princess Royal, Colonel The Blues and Royals, and Goldstick-in-Waiting, stands at the bottom of the steps.

is the Regimental Colour), marches along the Mall to Buckingham Palace, where the Buckingham Palace detachment has formed up to await their arrival.

These two detachments are the Old Guard. Meanwhile the New Guard is forming up and awaiting inspection by the Adjutant on the parade square at Wellington Barracks. The Band, having been inspected by the Adjutant, forms a circle to play music while the New Guard is inspected. The Guard provides a full military Band consisting of no fewer than 35 Musicians (usually, though not always, from one of the Guards regiments) accompanied by their Director of Music.

When the New Guard is formed up, led by the Band, it marches across into the forecourt of Buckingham Palace. Once there, the New Guard advances towards the Old Guard in slow time and halts. The Old Guard presents arms, followed by the New Guard presenting arms. The Captains of the Guards march towards each other for the handing over of the Palace keys. The new reliefs are marched to the guardrooms of Buckingham Palace and St James's Palace where new sentries are posted.

Queen's Life Guard

This is the senior Royal Guard. Every day a detachment of either The Life Guards or The Blues and Royals (they take it in turns) rides down to Horse Guards from Hyde Park Barracks to replace the Guard coming off. It is usually a 24-hour Guard, apart from exceptional circumstances, and the New Guard arrives at Horse Guards as the clock strikes 11 am (the Major General commanding the Household Division has the best view from his office to judge their punctuality). During the day there is a Mounted Trooper in each of the two boxes facing on to Whitehall and two dismounted Troopers. Only those with an ivory pass are allowed to pass through Horse Guards in a vehicle. If a member of the Royal family is passing through, the Guard is expected to turn out and give a Royal salute. Failure to do this may result in a less harsh punishment than that meted out by Queen Victoria when she established the 'Four O'Clock Inspection'. As a young officer this book's general editor had a near-miss after looking in the

Trooper Adam Semakula, The Life Guards

I hadn't had any physical contact with a horse whatsoever before I joined The Life Guards. Training at riding school was just gruesome, because all you had to think about was cleaning, cleaning, cleaning. And you would get inspected thoroughly every other day. Once I passed out, I was put into Two Troop, The Life Guards. The routine for a Trooper who isn't on Queens Life Guard starts at half-five in the morning in the stables: you muck out horses and make sure there have been no injuries during the night. That takes about half an hour, so by six o'clock we start on grooming, getting ready and prepped for watering order.

The Orderly Officer will take the whole Troop out, for a watering order around London for an hour/hour-and-a-half. So at seven o'clock pretty much the whole Regiment would leave Hyde Park Barracks for an hour-and-a-half watering order.

We take a different route each time. Sometimes a Troop Leader will ask the Corporal of Horse to pick the route, or he will decide he wants to talk to a certain Trooper. He'll say: 'Yes, let's go this route, Sir'.

I like the Kensington route, where you go up Kensington High Street and Holland Park, or the West End route a lot, because I'm from around there.

If you happen to be on Queen's Life Guard that day, you'll have started your day the day before. So from 12 o'clock the day before you'll have started cleaning your State kit and cleaning your black kit – that's the horse's tack.

I always started with the black kit which was pretty much just taking all the sweat off it first, letting it get dry, then getting polish on it. While that was settling in for half-an-hour or so: I'd start on the brasswork, the State bit. Give that a thorough cleaning, put it through various different stages of cleaning including the headstall. Then I put all the kit together in a line. You know it's all there; and pretty much go through the whole thing as a oner using a tin lid, and do that as many times as I could. Racing against the clock to do it as quickly as possible, but also as many times as possible; then get a nylon – ladies tights – and smoothly run it over getting a good shine on the kit. Once the shine was there, then I could concentrate on the attention to detail: the edges, every officer looks for different things. You'll know who's inspecting you the day before, 'cos you'll read the orders – or you'll ask guys who work up the mess. So you'll know what that particular officer's looking for. You'll never leave the cleaning rooms until you know your kit is the best, up to the best you can get it.

When I first started I was one of the slow guys. I'd do more talking than cleaning, so I was in the cleaning rooms up until 2 o'clock in the morning, and still had other pieces of kit to clean.

The best turned out gets the best reliefs. The more guards I did, and with the 3-bars on my back, it got easier – I improved, bit by bit I improved, getting picked up for less points: and only in my last six months of Knightsbridge I started getting: "Wow! You're immaculate!" So it took me a year and a half to get to that point.

I did two Trooping the Colours, two Garter Services, two State Opening of Parliament, and several State visits. They are all exciting.

To me doing the regalia on the State Opening of Parliament, escorting the Crown Jewels was my biggest highlight. We did an advance ride to Buckingham Palace, picked up the Crown Jewels and escorted them to the Houses of Parliament.

The same standards apply on operations in Iraq as at Knightsbridge: Knightsbridge helps in terms of pride.

Guard book and noting that 'DoE green van' would be passing through Horse Guards at noon. He felt that the Department of Environment did not warrant a guard turnout until a more experienced Corporal of Horse pointed out that the person we were expecting was the Duke of Edinburgh.

Four O'Clock Inspection

This has been carried out at Horse Guards by the Orderly Officer of the Household Cavalry Mounted Regiment ever since Queen Victoria came through and the Guard failed to turn out. She decreed that they would have to be inspected every day at four o'clock for 100 years. Though the century is now up, the tradition continues and if there is not an officer on guard (in other words, if The Queen is not in London), then the orderly officer rides down on his own from Hyde Park Barracks in Frock Coat order, to carry out this duty.

Changing of the Windsor Castle Guard

The ceremony for changing the Windsor Guard is broadly the same as that which takes place at Buckingham Palace. At 10.40 am, the New Guard marches from Victoria Barracks, through Windsor and turns onto Castle Hill into the quadrangle of the castle itself, where the Old Guard has formed. Once there, while the Band plays and the Ensigns patrol with the Colours, the Captain of the Old Guard hands the keys to the Captain of the New Guard. The new sentries are posted, and any special orders given, before the Old Guard is marched back to barracks, and the New Guard takes over.

The Sovereign's Birthday Parade (Trooping The Colour)

This has marked the official birthday of the Sovereign since George II in 1748, and has occurred annually since 1820 (except in bad weather, periods of mourning and other exceptional circumstances). Edward VII moved Trooping the Colour to its June date, because of the vagaries of British weather.

Excellence in Action

Right: The Commander in Chief reviews her troops during *The Queen's Birthday Parade.*

Below: A trooper of The Blues and Royals uses a mounting block to mount up at Hyde Park Barracks.

Below middle: Grenadier Guardsmen.

Above middle: The Major General shares a joke with a Guardsman during his official inspection, 2006.

Above: The Princess Royal hands out Shamrocks to the Irish Guards on St Patrick's Day.

Opposite bottom left: Corps of Drums.

Opposite bottom right: The Silver Stick in Waiting, Lieutenant Colonel Commanding the Household Cavalry, Colonel Patrick Tabor in ceremonial uniform on parade.

List of Regiments Trooping the Colour

Only one Colour can be trooped down the ranks each year, and the Foot Guards take it in turns.

2007: Number 7 (Incremental) Company, Coldstream Guards, carrying Colour of 2nd Battalion, Coldstream Guards.

2006: 1st Battalion, Welsh Guards.

2005: 1st Battalion, Irish Guards.

2004: 1st Battalion, Grenadier Guards.

2003: 1st Battalion, Grenadier Guards.

2002: 1st Battalion, Scots Guards.

2001: Nijmegen Company, Grenadier Guards, carrying the Colour of 2nd Battalion, Grenadier Guards.

2000: Number 7 (Incremental) Company, Coldstream Guards, carrying the Colour of 2nd Battalion, Coldstream Guards.

Trooping the Colour allows the Household Division to pay a personal tribute to the Sovereign with great pomp and pageantry. The Queen has attended Trooping the Colour in every year of her reign except when prevented by a rail strike in 1955.

It is a great honour for a young officer to be selected to carry the Colour, as historically only the most courageous Ensigns were assigned to do so in battle. Nowadays the honour is normally given to Second Lieutenants who are good at drill and ceremonial. In 2007, Second Lieutenant F. Mills, Coldstream Guards was the Ensign.

The numbers who participate in the Trooping the Colour has reduced in recent years. The contraction in size of the Household Division at the same time as extraordinary operational commitments has made the

Opposite: Her Majesty The Queen on the dais at The Queen's Birthday Parade on Horse Guards.

parade even more challenging. For example, the Welsh Guards, who trooped their Colour in 2006, had just returned from Iraq and redeployed to Bosnia later in the year. In 2007 the Coldstream Guards Incremental Company was Trooping its Colour but the Field Officer was provided by the Welsh Guards. The format of the ceremony has remained the same over the centuries following routines of old battle formations.

After the Ceremony

Each year when The Queen returns to Buckingham Palace, two detachments of the new Queen's Guard enter the forecourt, forming up opposite the old Queen's Guard. Standing with the Duke of Edinburgh on a saluting base in the central gateway she receives the salute as the remainder of the Foot Guards and then the Household Cavalry file past to their regimental marches, played by the Massed and Mounted Bands respectively.

Marking The Queen's 80th birthday in 2006

Trooping the Colour on 17 June 2006 was marked by several special events to mark The Queen's 80th birthday.

The largest ever flypast for The Queen's official birthday featured 49 planes led by the Battle of Britain Memorial Flight, culminating with the Red Arrows. It was followed by a *feu de joie* ('fire of joy') from the Guards on the forecourt interspersed with bars from *God Save The Queen*. Although there have been other *feux de joie* during The Queen's reign, this was the first one fired in her presence. The Guards then 'grounded arms', removed their headdress and gave three cheers for The Queen.

Glossary for Trooping the Colour

Guards Numbers 1–6
Six Guards of the Foot Guards are lined up in an L-shaped formation along two sides of Horse Guards Parade. Each 'Guard' consists of 70 non-commissioned officers and Guardsmen, and 3 officers (Captain, Subaltern, Ensign).

Escort for The Colour: Denotes Number One Guard, whose Colour is being Trooped. Later in the ceremony, it becomes Escort to the Colour.

Colour Party: The Colour Sergeant and two other Guardsmen of Number 1 Guard who are holding the Colour at the start of the ceremony.

Sovereign's Escort: The Household Cavalry who escort The Queen to Horse Guards Parade.

Saluting Base: Where The Queen and Duke of Edinburgh stand to take the salute.

Neutral March: March music that is not associated with any particular regiment. It is used at the beginning and end of each March Past in the ceremony.

Regimental March: Each regiment has its own signature Quick and Slow March.

Massed Bands: Amalgamation of all five Foot Guards regimental bands.

Corps of Drums: Denotes a military band of fifes, drums and sometimes also bugles.

Mounted Bands of the Household Cavalry: The combined musicians of the two Household Cavalry regiments, mounted on horses, wearing state dress, and led by two drum horses.

Royal Salute: Includes the playing of the National Anthem, *God Save The Queen*.

Spinwheel: A complicated manoeuvre by the Massed Bands to turn 90 degrees anti-clockwise prior to the Trooping of the Colour.

INSIDE THE GUARDS

THE GUARDS PARACHUTE PLATOON

Formed in 2001, the Guards Parachute Platoon is the descendant of the Guards Parachute Company which was disbanded in 1975 when G company of the SAS was formed. Soldiers are recruited from all the battalions of the Foot Guards. Because the Household Cavalry already has a significant Parachute element it does not provide soldiers for this platoon. It is based in Colchester as part of B company in 3 Para and is also regularly used independently as a support Para platoon in exercises involving Guards battalions. In 2003 they went to Africa as part of Exercise Grand Prix with the Grenadier Guards.

The Parachute Company welcomes this addition to their strength. They know that the platoon will be made up of particularly motivated soldiers who will have passed P Company and are looking to broaden their range. The Commanding Officer of 3 Para also enjoys the fact that this platoon is an extra contingent on his strength.

The platoon was most recently on operations in Afghanistan in 2006 where they were involved in regular engagements against the Taliban. The platoon had 13 Grenadier guardsmen, 1 Welsh Guardsman, 7 Coldstream Guardsmen (including Platoon Commander Captain Guy Lock), 3 Scots Guardsmen and 3 Irish Guardsmen. They join on two-year secondments. In one operation they had to recover two Household Cavalry vehicles that had been destroyed. The overall commander in that area, Colonel Charlie Knaggs, was an Irish Guardsman. A true example of Household Division co-operation on operations.

Captain Guy Lock was wounded in Afghanistan when a grenade that had been lobbed into a building was either kicked out or bounced off the Taliban insurgent hiding in the door way. He is now making a good recovery and, after acting as a temporary equerry to The Queen, took up a staff job in the Ministry of Defence.

Captain Guy Lock, Coldstream Guards

I finally managed to complete my six training jumps and fly out and join 3 Para in Afghanistan in May 2006.

The nature of warfare in Afghanistan couldn't be more different from Iraq, and the year spent on Salisbury Plain in 2004 proved invaluable in the dismounted attacks that we conducted during that summer. The Platoon spent two months in Kandahar, working with the Canadian Forces and in Musá Qal'eh with the Pathfinders. We also found ourselves in the Sangin District Centre for the majority of July, fighting off attacks as it became a melting pot for insurgent activity over that period. This was followed up with clearing operations into Now Zad and Musá Qal'eh and a final battle group attack into Sangin in late September, in order to clear it fully of insurgents. During this attack, I was wounded and CASEVACd out of theatre to Selly Oak where I was operated on in order to repair damaged and severed nerves in my arm. I then rehabilitated at Headley Court, near Leatherhead, the Defence Rehabilitation Centre in the period up until Christmas.

Major Adam Lawrence, The Life Guards

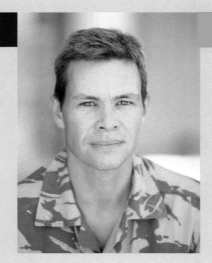

On Forward Air Controllers

We were lucky that we deployed to Iraq with two Forward Air Controllers, which is about right for the Household Cavalry Squadron I was commanding. It is only generally Army Air Corps, Gunners, Formation Recce and Special Forces who are allowed to train them. Within theatre, other than the Special Forces and one or two of the Gunners, our FACs were the only ones available and therefore were very much a Brigade asset. They belong to the Squadron but we willingly give them up to the Brigade. It reflects incredibly well on the Squadron as a whole. People at Brigade see individuals knocking around with just two stripes, but confident and professional. And the soldiers themselves love it. They are very competitive amongst themselves. They have these logbook competitions as to who controls the most aircraft. Anything that is on operations goes in red, whereas anything that is in training is in black, so they have strange get togethers where they compare how much red they have in their books.

Captain Matt Nicoll, The Life Guards

On Surveillance/Reconaissance Troop

This has developed to fill a niche within the Household Cavalry Regiment and to expand the Regiment's and Corps' mobility. There's an ever-increasing amount of infantry work that is done within the Household Cavalry. In my two operational tours, most of my operational experience has been away from vehicles.

SR troop is trying to fill in a gap that formation reconnaissance can't quite cover in vehicles. As a regiment carrying out formation reconnaissance, we're the eyes and ears of the battle group, miles in front of our own battle obtaining intelligence. SR troop has assets such as Man Portable Radar and we are trained to dismount and put in an observation post.

With 24 men SR troop is double the size of a normal troop. At the moments it's still evolving. It started two years ago and since then we've worked with Spartans. We're now looking at going into an even lighter role using Land Rover. It makes us flexible.

Lance Corporal Edward Bateman, The Blues and Royals

On being a sniper

Before I joined the army I was a Gamekeeper for nearly six years at Ripley Castle, North Yorkshire. I'm competent with rifles and confident as well.

To become a sniper involves a nine-week course at Pirbright. You have to learn and master seven skills. Shooting, obviously; you spend three weeks on the range, and most people pass that once you've worked out all your wind, distances and got all your data for your rifle. Stalking; cover and concealment; judging distances; map and navigation. You've got to bring all these things together.

In Iraq I went down to the PJCC in Basra with the Irish Guards' snipers. We were using the L96, which is the current sniper rifle. The police station was getting attacked every day so we had snipers on the roof all the time. We had bullets pinging off the sangar every now and then; RPG attacks and very, very accurate mortars.

We observed where all the fire was coming from. Also, in the evening, the enemy rockets were aimed at the COB and that sort of area, as well. So we gave a pre-warning to their pre-warning system that there were rockets in the air.

Family Loyalty

The close connection to their Sovereign, the Colonel-in-Chief, is the first focus of a Guardsman's loyalty. Guardsmen are not alone in valuing this loyalty, and they bear a second loyalty, to their regiment. Loyalty to the regiment is manifest in different ways: loyalty to people, to ways of doing things, and to traditions – an inherited ethos. British regiments have a corporate or family spirit, and like a family they look after the individual: the serviceman, servicewoman or family member in good times, and when the troops are away on operations. Regimental Associations, which comprise the regiment past and present, provide welfare support and funds to look after those who have served in a regiment, and sometimes their family members, from enlistment to grave, a service that reinforces the loyalty and family feeling.

Loyalty to regiments is also reflected in recruiting. Many members of the Household Division are from families who have contributed soldiers in the past. There are Guardsmen whose fathers and grandfathers served in Household Division Regiments: some well-polished ciphers and capstars are now into their third generation of service. There have been Warrant Officer fathers and sons. A Quartermaster and his son both paraded on the same Major General's inspection together not long ago, and Sergeants' Mess celebrations have been known when sons have outranked fathers.

Loyalty to regiments is no different in the Officers' Mess. Comparing the memorial names on the West wall of the Guards Chapel, all of whom served before 1944, and the lists of Officers serving in Household Division Regiments now, is instructive. The conflicts in the first half of the 20th century meant that many, both Officers and Guardsmen whose fathers had fought in the Great War in the Foot Guards or Household Cavalry followed them into the same regiments during the Second World War. However, many in subsequent generations also followed suit after 1945. In the past decade, the Household Division has had Officers serving who are the direct descendants of those who fought in Household Cavalry or Foot Guards Regiments in the wars and campaigns of the 20th century, or in South Africa, or in the Egyptian and Sudan

Above: 6 February 1996. The Roberts Family is inspected by their mother on mounting Queen's Guard. At the end of his time in command Lieutenant Colonel Sebastian Roberts (right) mounted Queen's Guard as Captain, with his brother Major Cassian Roberts (left) as the Subaltern, and his younger brother, Fabian (centre) as the ensign.

campaigns of the 1880s, or in the Crimea or under Wellington in the Peninsula, and even in the American War of Independence.

Family connections do not help the aspiring Household Division Officer pass the Army Officer Selection Board that sets the standard for Army Officers, or Sandhurst which trains them all, regardless of background or regiment. An understanding of life in the Army, and an inherited ethos, however, may help the sons of Guardsmen when they join the Army. People will judge you, however, on what you produce and the way you produce it, now. They will be delighted when you do something well, and consider you a chip off the old block but the important thing is that you, like all the others and your illustrious forbear, do it well. Several current Guards Generals have had fathers and uncles, and even brothers and sons serving in the Household Division.

Having Officers whose ancestors have served in the past may help maintain traditional standards, and give an exceptional depth to applying those values intelligently in new and unfamiliar, and often frightening circumstances. Regiments firmly point out, however, that in recent years as many Officers without family connections have joined as with them, and brothers have occasionally elected to serve in different Household Division Regiments in order to avoid being overshadowed by their siblings.

Loyalty to a regiment, and to an inherited ethos, may have its perils on occasion. For example, the subaltern of a Guard on one Queen's Birthday Parade lost his name for having the point of his sword too far back, during a rehearsal. The sword had been made in the 1860s with a slightly curved blade designed to pierce greatcoats of Crimean proportions; it had almost certainly been drawn in anger near Khartoum in 1885; carried on a 19th century Queen's Birthday Parade; and sharpened for war in 1914. This did not convince the Garrison Sergeant Major, but the loss of name was not repeated.

A second Officer (whose name appears in this book) joined another Regiment following his Father and Grandfather, both of whom became Generals. Unfortunately both Father and Grandfather had also been wounded, each losing an eye, an arm and a leg. The Officer of current generation was relieved to escape this fate.

Colonel Hugh Boscawen, Coldstream Guards

Scots Guards fathers and sons on the occasion of the Third Guards Club's final visit to Münster, 2007: L–R: Lieutenant Hamish Barne (3yrs) with his father, Major Nick Barne CVO (10 yrs); Lieutenant Colonel William Swinton MBE (22yrs) Commanding Officer; Major Peter Balfour CBE (12yrs) with his son Captain Hew Balfour (5 yrs) and grandson Captain Peter Balfour (3yrs).

SPORT AND ADVENTURE TRAINING

Guards Cricket Club

The first issue of the *Household Brigade Magazine* in 1862 described a match played at Lord's cricket ground between the Household Brigade and the Peripatetics. Household Brigade fixtures at that time included I Zingari, Eton, Harrow and the Quidnuncs. The first three still feature on the current fixture list, which now also includes MCC, Free Foresters, some school old boy XIs and longstanding military matches against The Rifles and the Highland Brigade.

Early matches were played at Prince's Ground, Chelsea, before moving to nearby Burton's Court in 1887, which, apart from 1914–26 and 1939–46, has been the Club's home ground ever since.

The distinction of the origin of 'Brigade Colours' can be directly attributed to the Household Brigade Cricket Club. Shortly after the Crimean War, in 1856, it was thought that the Club should have some distinctive colours. Three officers approached a leading firm of ribbon manufacturers, and obtained various samples of ribbons. Among them was the one selected – a ribbon of three equal stripes of blue, scarlet and blue. A tie of the same colour soon followed, which was subsequently referred to as the Brigade tie, worn by all ranks.

The object of the Guards Cricket Club is to encourage cricket for all ranks of the Household Division, past and present. In 1969, with the change of title to the Household Division, the Club became the Guards Cricket Club. In recent seasons over 80 players have turned out for the Club, and this has been no mean achievement considering military commitments and the changes in civilian working practices.

For 30 years until 1982 the Club undertook an annual long weekend tour to Jersey in July, which occasionally included a match in Guernsey. These tours were notable for high-scoring matches and spectacular hospitality, thanks to the kindness and generosity of those locals with Household Division connections. It was in Jersey that Colonel H.M.C. Havergal was given out 'handled the ball', an event which has occurred neither before nor since in the history of the Club. In 1965 history was re-created when a special fixture was arranged in Brussels between the Club and the Brussels British Sports Club to celebrate the 150th anniversary of the Battle of Waterloo. The result was a tie. The occasion was repeated in 1990 with two matches played resulting in one win for each side.

One must not forget those officials who have added to the enjoyment of cricket whether at Burton's Court or elsewhere, not all of whom have had Household Division connections. E. Montague was groundsman and umpire from 1900 to 1930 while E.A. Carter arrived in 1924 and was groundsman for 45 years, before turning to the scorebook. The report on the 1947 season, the first at Burton's Court following the Second World War, stated that 'many of the bowlers have complained that the wicket is too good'! He was known to give the batsman the benefit of the doubt in the event of a tight decision. He died in January 1987. His funeral was timed for 11.30 am, the traditional start time for matches at Burton's Court. Those who attended represented arguably as strong a Guards XI as has ever taken the field. Carter's Tree stands as his permanent memorial at the Royal Hospital end of the ground.

The Guards Cricket Club has, since its inception, occupied a special place in the Household Division's way of life. Thanks to the active support over the years of so many, it has always risen to the challenges of the day. At no time have they been more pressing than in this 21st century, for both the military and civilian worlds alike. In spite of these, long may the Club continue to flourish, and provide enjoyment for future generations of Guardsmen.

Above: The Guards Cricket Club, 2007.

Major Edmund Wilson, Irish Guards

Above: The Scots Guards ski team with the Commanding Officer and Adjutant.

On Skiing

I ran the Battalion ski team for five years which involved going to a training camp with all the other infantry ski teams for five weeks including a week of racing. I would normally take six or eight people depending on what our budget was at the time. I used to take a mixture of about a third accomplished skiers, a third intermediate skiers and a third complete novices. It used to work best if we had a total of two officers. It was nice to have a Lance-Sergeant, or certainly a Lance-Corporal, and then the rest Guardsmen.

We stayed in self-catering apartments. It's useful for the Guardsmen to get used to cooking for themselves. There were three key aims. One was to get a young officer organising a large training session with quite a significant budget of about £15,000. Second, the aim was to do well in the racing – but probably the most important one was to give soldiers a completely new experience. Not just the skiing, but operating away from the normal hierarchy of the Battalion: away from the Sergeant shouting at him the whole time: in a very relaxed, close-knit environment. It was great. They loved it. Absolutely brilliant.

Golf

Golf has been played in the Household Division since 1919 and adopted the name the Guards Golfing Society in 1969. There is a membership of around 200. All officers past and present in the Household Division, of any handicap, are entitled to join.

The Household Division Championship (Spring Meeting) is open to all ranks. It is a straightforward strokeplay event with prizes awarded in both the scratch and handicap categories. The autumn meeting is held at Royal St Georges and has provided a stern test for many years for those willing to take on an Open Championship course.

The Colonel-in-Chiefs Cup (for all ranks) is the Society's only matchplay event and began back in 1933. The Cup was presented by King George V who stipulated that the Cup should be competed for annually between Regimental Golf Teams. His two sons, The Prince of Wales and The Duke of York both played for their Regiments (Welsh and Scots Guards respectively) in the 1934 event. Until 1988 all matches were singles matchplay, and then the format was changed to foursomes whereby more players were able to compete in a unique competition to represent their Regiment.

There have been many memorable moments over the years. The Coldstream won both trophies in 1999 the only recorded instance of this happening. The Household Cavalry having never won it before the 1990s, won it four years in a row, 1994–7.

Guards Adventure Training Wing

The Guards Adventure Training Wing was originally formed in the early 1970s by Capt (Later Col) Johnny Forbes (Scots Guards) as the Guards Outward Bound School. He liked to play the bagpipes and was even known to have played them while crossing Crib Goch, a knife edge ridge

Household Division Yacht

Officers of the Household Division have been sailing for pleasure since Charles II and his brother James took to the water in Royal yachts after the Restoration. More recently, since the end of the Second World War, more soldiers have had the opportunity to get afloat. The 'Windfall' [war prize] yachts, Nazi leader Hermann Göring's fleet of racing vessels, built for the 1936 Berlin Olympics, 56ft long, were requisitioned by the British and sailed back to the United Kingdom from Kiel after May 1945.

One such yacht, *Reiher*, was allocated to the Household Brigade Yacht Club; she was renamed *Gladeye* and was later used primarily to get officers and Guardsmen of the Household Division afloat. This special yacht was sailed to success in many an ocean race, including the Fastnet Race in 1951. She was sold to Lloyd's of London in the early 1970s and a 44ft Moody replaced her. Following her, an Oyster Heritage 37 was purchased in 1994. They have been in the safe hands of generations of boatswains, Sergeant Ankers, Welsh Guards, in the original *Gladeye* and Sergeant Court, Grenadier Guards, in the other three yachts, to name but two of them, and skippers eager to extend their experience. *Gladeye* through the years, in her four guises, has provided the ideal vessel to introduce our soldiers to offshore sailing. The Oyster won the Governor's Cup in 1999; a race from Cape Town to St Helena. She was replaced in 2003 with the current *Gladeye*, a Swan 391. Guardsmen and Troopers have enjoyed sailing in both UK and Mediterranean waters in recent years.

The origin of the name *Gladeye* derives from the Guards Divisional 'Eye' tactical recognition sign first introduced in 1915 and reintroduced in 1942. Original inspiration must surely have come from the 1914 musical *The Glad Eye* and the song *Give her the glad eye now!*

The definition of the term 'glad eye' is: 'To look at someone seductively' and Guardsmen, whether on leave during the Great War or home from operations in Iraq and Afghanistan are no strangers to adjusting their focus when a woman walks into the room. Guardsmen through the generations may change their taste in music (there are no more music hall songs to sing) and *Gladeye*

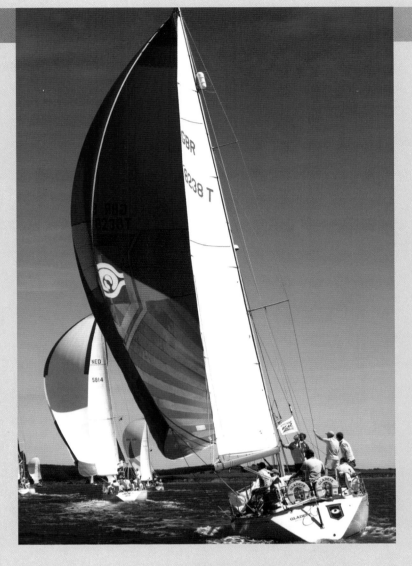

through the years has changed four times but her *raison d'être* remains; to challenge Guardsmen and Troopers by introducing them to an often hostile and unforgiving environment thus engendering teamwork, self-reliance and confidence. Whichever *Gladeye* Guardsmen of any rank have sailed in, they will never forget the experience – for good, or seasick.

Lieutenant Colonel Toby Gray, Coldstream Guards

on the Snowdon Horseshoe, and was clearly eminently qualified to run an organisation designed to encourage leadership and originality.

At that time the Outward Bound School was based at the Guards Depot in Pirbright and was run out of a small store by the post office. From here they would travel to Salisbury Plain, North Wales, Dartmoor and Cornwall to carry out Adventure Training. In the early 1980s the Guards Adventure Training Wing was moved to a small camp on Dartmoor, now demolished, but shortly after, the Wing moved to Fremington Training Camp and was based there until October 2006.

One of the most significant Officers in charge was Major Tony Bradborn, who joined the Wing in the early 1980s and made it what it is today. In his time he ran the Brigade Squad Courses, which took Trainee Guards Officers before they went to Sandhurst and put them through their

paces using Adventurous Training and other Command Task style activities. The soldiers weren't forgotten either with Guards Depot Recruits spending a week or two of their Training at Fremington, doing Adventurous Training and sampling such delights as the Rope Swing and the Chain Jump.

In 1993 GATW started anew as a wing of the Household Division, offering adventure training to all Household Division Regiments. Since November 2006 the Guards Adventure Training Wing has been part of the new Army Level 2 Adventurous Training Centre at Capel Curig Training Camp in the Snowdonia National Park. The stated mission is to carry on supplying quality adventurous training to the Household Division and the wider army. It is now also responsible for providing decompression training for troops returning from Afghanistan and Iraq.

From top left, clockwise: Lance Corporal Davies, selected to box for Wales; Welsh Guards front row; Welsh Guards in Bosnia; James Kelly, Scots Guards, as he begins his descent on the Cresta Run; Members of the Household Cavalry relaxing with their horses at Holkham Beach, Norfolk.

Left: Lieutenant Murray-Threipland, Scots Guards, taking part in the Swan European Regatta.

Below: Captain James Allan qualifying for the Army ski team;

Bottom: Members of the Iron Guardsman Challenge cycle through the Bosnian countryside.

Below: The Prince of Wales, Colonel of the Welsh Guards, and The Duchess of Cornwall in Bosnia on St David's Day 2007 prepare to signal the start of the Challenge for an intrepid group of Welsh Guardsmen.

Iron Guardsman Challenge, 2007

This was a novel way of returning from Bosnia dreamt up by Lieutenant James Westropp, assisted by Lieutenant Tom Spencer-Jones. An example of original, physically demanding adventure training on a regimental scale, it involved cycling back to the French coast, kayaking across the Channel and running the equivalent of three marathons from Dover to Wellington Barracks. They had done two weeks training, including a week in Wales to prepare.

The Commanding Officer, Lieutenant Colonel Richard Stanford, gathered them together before set off and wished them the best of luck. 'It's probably not something that you enjoy at the time but when you look back you feel good that you have done it', said team member Sergeant Ed Mills. He had a bike constructed locally, especially for the challenge. 'They're brilliant at doing things like that round here'. A young officer confirmed that many of the Bosnian interpreters seemed to have degrees in mechanical engineering but there just weren't the jobs for them to use their degrees.

Sergeant Steven Hughes, Coldstream Guards

Life In The Guards

My present job is Platoon Sergeant having joined aged 20 in 1992. I went to join the Royal Marines aged 15 but there was a waiting list for a year and there was also a Coldstream Guards recruiting sergeant. He persuaded me. It sounded smart. I now own a house in my native Devon with my girlfriend.

Career highlights have included four six-month tours of Northern Ireland. I served in Canada at the British Army Training Unit for two years as a Guardsman on the safety staff and winter maintenance. I do a lot of adventure training having been a Joint Service Mountain Expedition Leader and Rock Climbing Instructor.

Lieutenant Tom Radcliffe, Coldstream Guards

I was brought up in London and Shropshire. My father is in the Territorial Army. I did a gap year, before graduating with a Geography degree from Cambridge University, with the Coldstream Guards as a Short Service Limited Commission. I visited a lot of regiments when I was at school.

Generally speaking it ended up going to the mess and getting drunk. James Rous said to me when I was 17, 'Do you want to come and see the Regiment on exercise in Wales?'. The Guardsmen were brilliant. I could carry a rifle and put up a poncho. Although it was quite intimidating I had a really good time. The thing that will keep me in, after joining permanently in 2006, is the camaraderie you have with fellow officers and guys out on the ground.

Doing Guards at the palaces is very demanding work. The guys work tremendously hard. Also people forget that we have people up all night in webbing ready to run out and arrest hang gliders. Just because we're back from Iraq, it's not down time. We're trying to catch up with courses and our soldiers' compassionate leave.

On Foreign Postings

I went to Nigeria in November 2006 for three weeks to help train the Nigerian Army. There were three young officers, two sergeants and one company sergeant major in our party. Those kind of things give you much more depth to your skills base. Going to foreign countries, dealing with foreign troops is a pretty important experience. In Iraq I became the quasi logistics/intelligence officer. I was hopelessly out of my depth to start with but soon got used to it.

Sergeant Major Dave Groom, Grenadier Guards

On Being Regimental Sergeant Major At The Honourable Artillery Company, A Tied Grenadier Post

The Honourable Artillery Company (HAC) is the oldest regiment in the British Army. It was founded in 1537 under Charter of Henry VIII and they are very proud of this.

It is a Territorial Army (TA) unit and tied to 1st Artillery Brigade. The HAC do surveillance and target acquisition. The role has changed slightly now. This is a very specialised TA Regiment and is very different from any other in the country. Its home is Armoury House, a fantastic ancient building right in the middle of the City of London on City Road, surrounded by office blocks and towers. You can see the Gherkin. The HAC troopers do ceremonial. They are the only TA troops in London District who do ceremonial duties. They do guards of honour for state visits and they fire gun salutes down at the Tower of London on about 11 occasions a year. So they have a Regimental Sergeant Major which they have had since the First World War, who is always a Grenadier. They tend to be businessmen, they mostly work in the City. So you have a trooper whose average age is 28–29, who comes here on Wednesdays and weekends and plays soldier and during the week he may be working on a million pound deal.

I had soldiers who lived in Portugal who came in on Wednesday nights to do training. My drill sergeant was a Queen's Counsel. They absolutely cherish their ties with the Grenadier Guards. We all went to dinner, all of the officers and Sergeant Majors were invited over just before we were deployed to Afghanistan so they put on a little dinner for us to wish us good luck and cheerio and all that which was very, very good.

We do maintain these ties and as a Sergeant Major, that is one of the jobs that I take very seriously. It is nice to have that extended family sort of feeling.

Staff Corporal Henry Newton, The Life Guards

On Training

When I went through training I was at the Guards Depot and then I went as an instructor in army training to Pirbright. The Household Cavalry now train at Pirbright and the Foot Guards have gone to Catterick.

When I first joined the army, I went to the Guards Depot, it was the Blue Red Blue, and I always wanted to return as an instructor. You see that as the pinnacle. So I returned with the Guards, and it was everything that I thought it would be. You are working with top class instructors at the top of their game across the Household Division

I was a Section Commander. Every single one of them is ultra-professional, and I wanted to be No 1. You can imagine the sound of the Guards Depot: marching soldiers and plenty of PT instructors. I gained a lot from working with the Household Division. Obviously it put me in good stead for the rest of my career when I finished with the Guards Company.

Second Lieutenant Andy Joyce, Coldstream Guards

First Impressions As A New Officer (speaking in November 2006)

I have been in six weeks and come from Great Marlow (Buckinghamshire). My father is an Army Padre. My degree from Coventry University is in International Disaster Engineering and Management. One thing that's always struck me is how friendly this regiment is. The officers are on first name terms although I still call the adjutant 'adjutant' by mistake and he gets rather cross. I love the hands-on element, interacting with the soldiers themselves and getting to know their lives.

In 2007 we are Trooping the Colour and soon after that we're going to Afghanistan. It's a year which sums up this regiment. It puts into context beautifully the seamless transition from one to another. It's the little things you notice. We have an eclectic mix from the North East and from Devon and Cornwall but our soldiers show the character of a Coldstreamer through swagger and style.

Captain Karl Dawson, Welsh Guards

Regimental Careers Management Officer To The Irish Guards

This is quite a new role. I work alongside the Adjutant and take a lot of pressure off him regarding individual careers. I meet up with my commanding officer on matters relating to careers. I contribute to CLM, Command, Leadership and Management, the new education system, and also I deal with the retention side of life. Retaining young men is key and being an ex-ranker I have managed some success in that area.

I monitor that and I make sure that every individual does CLM. He is then eligible for promotion. Young Guardsmen need to do it, they have to do their literacy and numeracy assessment before they can move on. It's important to promote that with regards to retention and letting individuals know that when you do leave the Army, you've got something in your pocket that you can offer.

Enhanced learning credit is £3,000 at the moment. As of next year it will be £6,000. That's £2,000 each year, over three years, that you can draw to go and spend on education. It's their money and they can use it and it's great. But they don't know about these things. And that's the advantage of me being where I am. I also look at their confidential reports and advise what is best practice about the way they are written and then inviting the subordinates in and telling them exactly what it means, what they need to do, areas to improve on. If their aspirations are to reach the dizzy ranks of Warrant Officer, well I'm there to advise them on best practice on how they're going to achieve that. A lot of these young lads think they've got themselves into a rut and they seem to think that they're stuck in it. They think they've lost their chance and that's it. Well, you can turn round and say to them 'well actually, no – if you do this and do that it will put you back on track'.

Equality And Diversity

If someone has got a complaint I am the impartial person who sits there and explains to them what their rights are. The advantage of coming to see me is that I am outside their chain and I can offer sound advice.

My loyalty is very much to the Regiment first. But I will give them sound advice and what it is that they can do and what it is they should be doing about it. But the Battalion does benefit from that.

It all links into retention, acting as a father figure and putting them back on track.

Sergeant David Rodgers, Pipe Major, Irish Guards

I was in the pipes myself, in the band 17 years. When not playing the pipes we were the Assault Pioneer Platoon. We did a lot of exercises for combat engineering, and we would go and assist the Royal Engineers. We had the Assault Pioneer Courses, and also did the Piping Courses up in Edinburgh.

I learned to play the pipes as a very young boy back home in Northern Ireland. I specifically joined to play the pipes. It has its own career path, and you stayed with the pipes. You can leave it and go off to various other career paths if you choose to. And some people have done that. I had a break for three years when I was doing recruitment in Northern Ireland. That was my only time away from the pipes.

Our military role is as a machine gun platoon, and also as a rifle platoon. Whilst we are serving out here in Iraq we are a rifle platoon within a rifle company, taking part in ground patrols, convoy taskings and any ops that come up. We're part of the Badgers Group Squadron, which is attached to us from the Royal Tank Regiment.

Years ago in the army everybody had their own instruments; and we used to play the Irish Pipes: but then, in the early 1970s, they decided to change it all to the Great Highland Bagpipe, the Scottish Bagpipe. And that is what we play now. Obviously we still play our traditional Irish music on the same instrument.

Back in the UK the Pipes and Drums is used a lot for functions in the officers' and sergeants' mess at weekends, and engagements outside of the Regiment such as beating the retreat. We've done a lot of Army Benevolent Fund work; we took part in the Edinburgh Military Tattoo in 2005 and 2006; and just before we deployed out here in Iraq, the pipes and the corps of drums both went to Virginia, for the Virginia Military Tattoo in Norfolk, Virginia. We were out there for a week, and then come back to the UK for a week before we deployed to theatre.

We also come on to Troop the Colour. The pipers always form in the Mass Bands' Household Division. We play different Irish airs and jigs and reels.

Father Nick Gosnell, Padre to the Irish Guards

One of the advantages of being a Padre to the Irish Guards is the uniqueness of the environment in terms of family. Quite often as Padres we are posted to a Unit, which doesn't have the cohesive nature of a Household Division Unit. Often it's disparate, especially at the edges and there are lots of attached people. And what with amalgamations and one thing and another being owned – and you are very well owned and looked after by the Irish Guards – as you can imagine, is a great advantage. They take you under their wing and do everything for you.

We also have the advantage as a chaplaincy of having a weekly Church Parade, every Tuesday morning, which we continue out here in Iraq. I never have to stop at the gate and introduce myself.

I've managed to get my office as far away from the Battalion Headquarters as possible so the Guardsmen don't mind coming to see me for a coffee and a chat, which is great.

Welfare problems or opportunities are referred to the Families Officer and career opportunities or problems are referred to the Career Management Officer. My job is more of a facilitator, both inside and outside the chain of command. For instance, a Guardsman might come to me and indicate that he was having a problem getting to see someone he needed to see or being interviewed about something he needed to be interviewed about, in which case I can grease the wheels as it were. In the same way, I might bump into the Commanding Officer and ask him that he needs to come and have a cup of coffee because there are one or two things I need to discuss with him. So it's an advantage with not having a specific and particular role, apart from the overall pastoral and spiritual care of the Battalion. But not having an executive role within the set up allows me the freedom to be involved in everything but not responsible for anything in terms of having to write the letters or reports.

The idea of chatting this morning in the O Group about Ramadan of course is that it is coming up soon and there are particular reasons for being excited or concerned about that month with everything that may or may not go on. Normally in the O group, the only thing I talk about are pertinent things to do with whatever is going on or they ask me to do a Saint of the Day, out of which I try to give a little thought of the day in terms of their lives which only lasts for about a minute and a half.

But particularly in the environment in which we are at the moment in Basra, where we engage with the local population because they come in to us and because we go out to them, then we need to be conscious of what people might be doing or wearing and why they might be about at night rather than about during the day and vice versa. So all these things are helpful.

I suppose in military terms it's all about situational awareness. The more you have your finger on the pulse of who the people are that you are dealing with the better. Our particular role as the Security Sector Reform battle group is to engage with as many of the local population, but particularly the security forces, in order to train the Iraqi Army, and facilitate the training of

the Iraqi Police. And we've just trained the Palace Protection Force which have gone into Basra Palace, with a view to them being the main Guard Force when our forces pull out, in addition to the Iraqi Army that are there.

So we are mostly involved with mentoring, monitoring and training the new Iraqi Army in order to hand back to the people that part of their lives which has been taken off them for the past four years, so they can look after their own country and govern themselves, hopefully in peace and security.

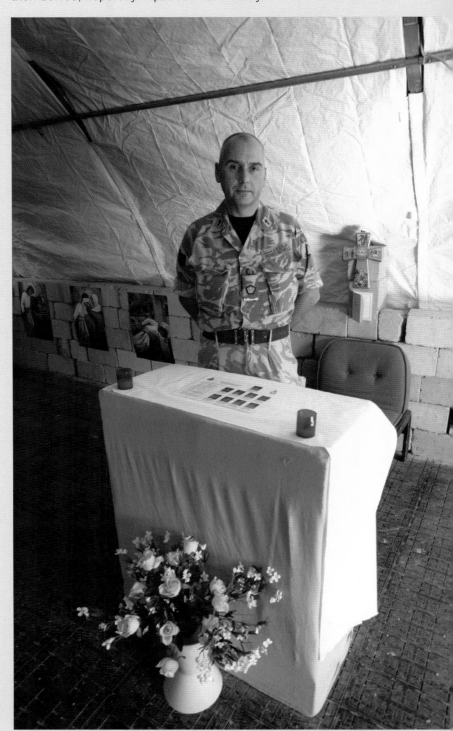

THE BANDS

The Household Cavalry Mounted Bands and Dismounted Bands of the Guards Division

The Life Guards

At the public entry of King Charles II into London on 29 May 1660, he was escorted by three Troops of The Life Guards each preceded by its own Kettledrummer and four Trumpeters. This proud occasion began the history of the Band that you hear today.

The use of kettledrums and trumpets was, at this period, confined to the Army and the nobility and, even in the King's troops, The Life Guards alone had the privilege of using kettledrums. The Musicians held warrants of appointment from the King and were paid at the rate of five shillings per day. In 1678 they wore uniforms of velvet, silver laced, their instruments having richly embroidered and trimmed banners, the whole cost defrayed by the King. This is the origin of the State Dress worn to this day by the Band and Trumpeters.

The Blues and Royals

The Royal Horse Guards (The Blues) had Drummers and Trumpeters from the outset, as did the 1st, or Royal Regiment of Dragoons which was also raised in 1661 for service in Tangier, hence the original title, the Tangier Horse. By 1702 the Tangier Horse had changed to a dragoon

regiment and had a band consisting of eight Drummers and eight Hautbois. Soon after, in 1710, Kettledrummers were added and in 1766 the Drummers were converted to Trumpeters. The Royal Horse Guards' (The Blues) Trumpeters and Drummers had also evolved and in 1805 King George III personally presented a pair of solid silver kettledrums, as testimony to their 'Honourable and Military conduct on all occasions'. These kettledrums continue to be used today, and can be seen carried by the Drum Horse and played by the mounted Drummer on The Queen's Birthday Parade on Horse Guards.

Today both 35-strong bands of the Household Cavalry play mounted on horseback, and all members of the Band must undertake the five-month Household Cavalry equestrian course. Both Bands travel extensively in this country and overseas providing State Trumpeters,

Top: The Kettle Drums were given to the Royal Horse Guards by George III.

Left: Members of the Scots Guards band prepare to perform at Royal Ascot.

Left: Household Division bands perform at Royal Ascot each year.

Below: The Life Guards band leads the New Guard through Windsor to the castle.

Marching and Concert bands, Salon Orchestra and numerous small ensembles. The Orchestra performs at Investitures at Buckingham Palace, the ceremony of the Garter and State Banquets. The Band wears Gold State coats and blue velvet jockey caps when they perform at major ceremonial events at which senior members of the Royal Family are present. Members of the Band have seen active service in both Gulf conflicts in their operational role in support of medical units.

The Band Of The Grenadier Guards

From its formation, Drums and Fifes alone provided the Regiment's music but in 1685 Charles II signed a Royal Warrant authorising the maintenance of 12 Hautbois (the forerunner of the oboe) and the foundations of the oldest surviving infantry Band in the British Army were laid. Mr George Handel, the Master of the King's Music, was an early admirer and presented the March from *Scipio* to the Regiment in 1726. Until 1844 the Band numbered 12 to 19 Musicians rising to 38 four years later. By 1979 the total was 60 and the present establishment is 49.

The Band Of The Coldstream Guards

From the earliest days the Regiment had Drummers and a 'Band of Music' from 1742. This was in fact eight civilian musicians who were hired by the month by officers of the Regiment to provide music for the

Changing of the Guard. When, in 1785, the Musicians were asked to perform at an aquatic excursion to Greenwich, they declined on the grounds that the performance was 'incompatible with their several respectable and private engagements'.

This was too much for the officers who asked the Duke of York, the new Colonel of the Regiment, for a regular attested Band. He agreed and from Hanover in Germany sent 12 Musicians under the direction of Music Major C.F. Eley. The instrumentation consisted of two oboes, four clarinets, two bassoons, two horns, one trumpet and a Serpent. The date of the Band's formation was 16 May 1785. The establishment today is 48 plus the Director of Music.

It was on Sunday, 18 June 1944 that the greatest tragedy in the history of the Band occurred. The Band was playing in the Guards Chapel, Wellington Barracks when a German V-1 flying bomb or 'doodlebug' struck it. Over 120 people were killed including the Director of Music, Major Windram, and five Musicians. Despite this disaster the band continued to function and followed the Allied Forces to Europe after D-Day.

Since 1945, the Band has performed world wide, including tours to North America, Japan and Australasia and achieved international acclaim when it played the American National Anthem in the forecourt of Buckingham Palace following the 11 September 2001 disaster of the terrorist attacks on America.

The Band Of The Scots Guards

The precise origins of the Band of the Scots Guards are lost, although by 1684 there was a drum-major and four 'hautbouys'. By about 1749 there were eight Musicians. During the early part of the 19th century the Band

Above: The Scots Guards band.

grew in strength and by 1838 could boast some 32 performers. In 1888, there was an establishment of 44. Nowadays the Band's strength is 49.

In 1990 the Scots Guards were the only complete Foot Guards Band to be deployed on active service during the First Gulf War. The Musicians' work there involved them in many different aspects of hospital duties attached to the various departments of Number 33 General Hospital based in Al Jubayl, Saudi Arabia. The Band earned much praise from Guardsmen, the Medical Corps, nurses and patients alike.

The Band Of The Irish Guards

The Regimental Band was formed around the same time as the founding of the Regiment in 1900 and initially consisted of 35 Musicians under a Bandmaster, Captain Charles Hassell, and it quickly gained a reputation for excellence.

In 1905 the Band was invited to make its first tour of Canada, during which the people of Toronto presented an ornate silver cup that remains a cherished possession of the Band. Since then, the Band has continued to tour extensively, and during a visit to Japan it was accorded the unique honour of being the first band ever to play in the Imperial Palace in the presence of the Empress and Crown Princesses.

The Band's main duty is, of course, to play for state ceremonial occasions and Public Duties but it has made many broadcasts and recordings over the years, as well as television appearances (most notably for The Queen's 80th Birthday Celebration in Windsor) and in films including *The Ipcress File* and *Oh! What a Lovely War*.

Three Musicians served in the First Gulf War of 1990/1 and in June 1999 the Band was deployed to Kosovo as part of a NATO peacekeeping force.

The Band Of The Welsh Guards

The Band of the Welsh Guards was formed in 1915, and consisted of 44 musicians and a Warrant Officer. Their instruments were presented by the City of Cardiff and on St David's Day 1916 they played at their first King's Guard Mounting and their first concert at the London Opera House. Both occasions were great successes.

Above: The Irish Guards band visits Paris and the Arc de Triomphe, June 1989.

The Band has toured extensively: in recent years it has visited Europe, Egypt, and North America.

Links in Wales are maintained by regular appearances there, often with many of the male voice choirs. Close ties with schools and colleges are developed through instrumental clinics and music workshops. Concerts are regularly given in aid of various service charities.

Spreading Music And Goodwill In Today's World

To get an idea of how busy the Bands are and how they act as ambassadors for the Household Division and the country as a whole, just look at the programme of the Scots Guards over the last ten years.

The Band's travels have taken it to the US, Canada, Kenya, Germany, Italy, France, Spain, Malta and Cyprus as well as coast to coast in the United Kingdom. In June 1997 the Band was heavily involved in the handover ceremonies of Hong Kong to China. The Band also undertook a very successful tour of North America from January to March 1998 and in 2000 performed a concert tour of Australia before going on to New Zealand to take part in the Edinburgh Military Tattoo 2000 in Wellington. The Band also visited Australia in October 2000 to take part in the Brisbane Festival 2000 International Military Tattoo. In 2002 the Band performed a major role in The Queen Mother's funeral procession, The Queen's Golden Jubilee and the Edinburgh Military Tattoo. During

2003 the band performed at the Wimbledon Tennis Championships and then in December took part in the British Military Music Show in Halle Münsterland, Germany. In July 2004 they travelled to Italy for the Modena International Tattoo. In September it was off to the South of

Above: A trombonist warming up before the arrival of Prince Charles in Bosnia on St David's Day.

France near Nice for the Festival de Musique of Beaulieu-sur-Mer and finally that year they visited South Korea for the Wonju Tattoo and then stayed in Seoul for a few days afterwards, performing for the British Embassy. At the start of 2005 they visited Sydney, Australia, to perform in the Edinburgh Tattoo and then in September the Band travelled to the South of France to perform once again, at Beaulieu-sur-Mer.

In 2005 they performed at the British Military Music Show in Halle Münsterland, Germany, along with a visit to the Battalion afterwards. During the summer of 2006 the Band was involved in the Edinburgh Military Tattoo and this was shortly followed by performing at RMA Sandhurst in the outdoor event 'Music On Fire'.

Above: 'Music On Fire' at RMA Sandhurst.

Right: A member of The Blues and Royals band enjoys a break at Royal Ascot.

Corps of Drums and Pipes

All members of the Drums are 'duty' soldiers and not part of the Regimental Band. All members of the Drums will go with their respective battalions on operations and will be expected to be both musicians and soldiers; some are trained additionally as medics or form the Assault Pioneer platoon.

A Corps of Drums is made up of side drummers, a base drummer and flautists/buglers – led by a Drum Major; the Pipes and Drums has about 12 pipers(including a Pipe Major), side drummers, 2 tenor drums and a base drummer.

Pipers are often required to play at funerals, dinners and weddings, while the band can take part in Highland Games as well as ceremonial duties in London.

Currently the Scots Guards have integrated their Corps of Drums into the rifle companies, so they only have a single entity, the Pipes and Drums, while the Irish Guards still have both.

Above: Members of the Corps of Drums of the Welsh Guards bonding with fellow NATO troops from Norway in Bosnia, 2007.

Special Forces

The Household Division have proved indispensable to Special Forces over the years. From the outset, Scots Guardsman David Stirling's fledgling Special Air Service (SAS) Regiment relied almost exclusively on volunteers from the Guards' Commando and many of the well-known regimental figures were Guardsmen – both officers and men. The next significant influx was on the disbandment of the Guards Parachute Company in 1975 when most of the organisation volunteered and passed into the Special Forces. These days the Household Division still provides soldiers and officers for the SAS, and they continue to flourish.

To what can the Household Division's success in Special Forces be ascribed? That mix of self-discipline, integrity, reliability, élan, innovation allied with an entrepreneurial spirit and a buccaneering unconventionality.

Above: David Stirling and his desert raiders in North Africa, taken shortly before his capture in 1943.

The London Regiment

Today, The London Regiment is the TA battalion aligned to the Household Division, the first such affiliation in history. Since 1992 soldiers and officers have served as individuals and formed groups in Northern Ireland, Kosovo, Macedonia, the Falkland Islands, Bosnia, Iraq and Afghanistan.

In 2004 Cambrai Company was the first TA sub-unit to deploy to Iraq on Op TELIC immediately followed by Messines Company on Op TELIC 5. Both companies provided Force Protection to MND South East in Basra.

In early 2007, Somme Company deployed on Op HERRICK 6 as Force Protection Company to 12 Mechanised Brigade. This was the first time a platoon of Regular Infantry soldiers, in this case from the 1st Bn Grenadier Guards, had come under TA command since the Second World War.

The London Regiment proudly bears the title given to the Territorial infantry of London in 1908. All the present day component parts of the Regiment trace their origins back to London volunteer units and this fact remains an important element of their unity. Whilst there are five different cap-badges within the Regiment and Companies, each is charged with the protection of its heritage and identity. However, allegiance to The London Regiment is a powerful motivating and cohesive factor in the structure of the Regiment.

LIFE BEYOND SOLDIERING

What Guards officers and soldiers go on to do is a testament to the experiences and skills that they have gathered during their time with the Household Division. This is a selection of mostly recent serving soldiers who have gone on to perform great feats or achievements in civilian life and the Household Division family follows their careers with interest and pride.

There is no typical career to which those retiring turn. For example, of 1st Battalion Grenadier Guards' 18 officers photographed together in 1960, only three served a full career in the Army. They reached the ranks of (full) General, Major General and Colonel. And so what happened to the rest? Two became stockbrokers, and the remainder comprised a judge, a university administrator in Australia, the director of a charity, a member of the Royal Household, a farmer, an overseas British Council official, a well-known photographer, the manager of a chain of book shops, the Household Division Public Relations officer, the representative of De La Rue banknote manufacturers in India, representative of Cathay Pacific airline in the Far East and the Treasurer to Household Division Funds.

Marcus Barnett, Garden Designer
Scots Guards

He left the Scots Guards after six years in 1997 having served as the Duke of Kent's equerry for two and half years. Since leaving he has become one of the country's top garden designers winning a Royal Horticultural Society gold medal at the Chelsea Flower Show in 2005 and 2006.

James Blunt, Pop Singer
The Life Guards

James Blount (he dropped the 'o' on the advice of his record label to make it easier for people to pronounce) left The Life Guards in 2005 having served in Kosovo and been a highly acclaimed regimental skier. He was the first solo artist to have a Number One single (*You're Beautiful*) and Number One album, *Back to Bedlam,* in the pop charts at the same time since Michael Jackson in 1983. One of his songs on the album, *No Bravery*, is based on his experiences in Kosovo; on the album sleeve he is called Captain James Blunt and The Life Guards cap badge is displayed.

Jackie Charlton, Footballer
The Blues and Royals

The Former England player who was a member of the 1966 World Cup winning team was also a successful manager of the Republic of Ireland team.

Mark Coreth, Sculptor
The Blues and Royals

As a young officer in The Blues and Royals Mark Coreth commanded a troop during the Falklands War in 1982. On his return to England he was commissioned to make a silver sculpture of his regiment's drum horse 'Belisarius' for the Warrant Officers' Mess and later a second cast in bronze became the Household Cavalry wedding present to The Duke and Duchess of York. Fired by his passion for wildlife first awakened during his idyllic childhood in the Kenyan Highlands he has since completed many wildlife commissions including a life-size elephant that was recently sent to a client in Australia. A second cast has subsequently been ordered from a client in Europe.

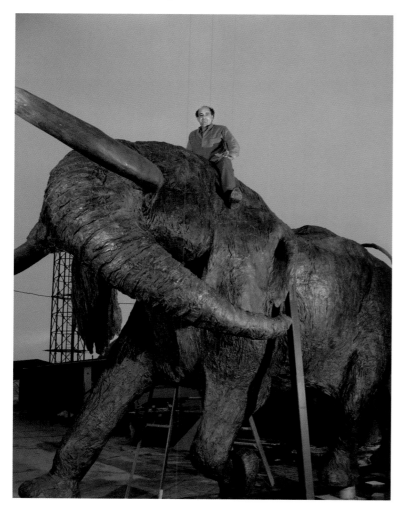

Iain Duncan Smith, Politician
Scots Guards

A Member of Parliament since 1992, Duncan Smith was leader of the Conservative Party from 12 September 2001 to 6 November 2003. He has served as shadow Secretary of State for Defence. In December 2005 he was appointed Chairman of the Social Justice Policy Group of the Conservative Party by David Cameron.

Charlie Mayfield, Chairman of the John Lewis Partnership
Scots Guards

A former equerry to The Duke of Kent, the Scots Guards officer was awarded the Sword of Honour at Sandhurst and left the army in 1997. He became chairman of John Lewis in 2007, before his 40th birthday.

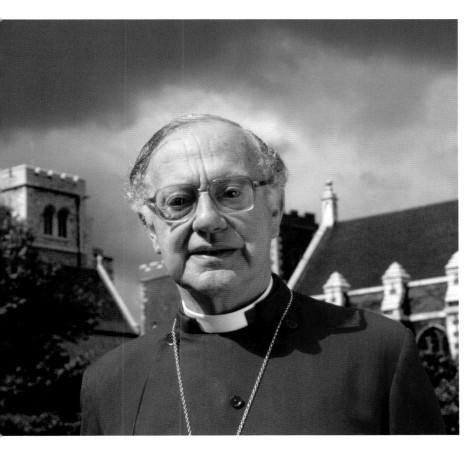

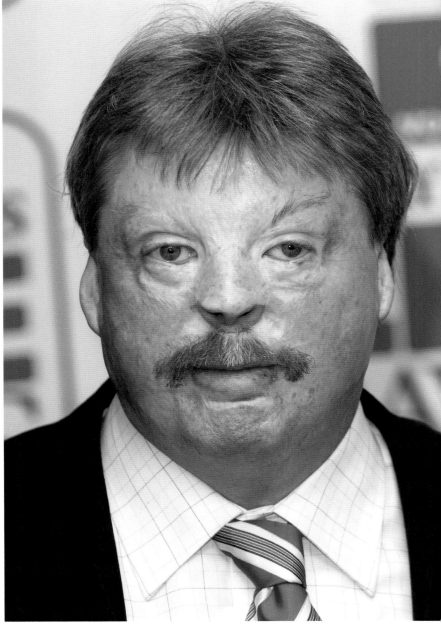

The Right Rev. Robert Runcie, Archbishop of Canterbury
Scots Guards

He served in 3rd (Tank) Battalion Scots Guards during the Second World War in North-West Europe as a tank commander and was awarded the Military Cross for two feats of bravery. In March 1945 he rescued one of his men from a crippled tank under heavy enemy fire, and the next day he took his own Churchill tank into an exceptionally exposed position in order to knock out three anti-tank guns. In May 1945 he was among the first British troops to enter Bergen-Belsen concentration camp.

In 1981, Runcie officiated at the marriage of the Prince of Wales to Lady Diana Spencer. In a dramatic gesture of goodwill, he knelt in prayer with Pope John Paul II in Canterbury Cathedral during the Pope's visit to Great Britain in 1982. Lord Runcie, as he became, died in 2000.

Terry Waite, Peace Envoy
Grenadier Guards

He served with the Grenadier Guards before attending Church Army College in London in 1958 and studied theology. In 1980 he was made responsible for advising the Archbishop of Canterbury on a wide range of international issues. In January 1987 he was captured in Beirut whilst attempting to secure the release of hostages. He was kept in solitary confinement for four years and kept hostage for almost five years, 1763 days in all.

Simon Weston, Fundraiser
Welsh Guards

He joined the Welsh Guards in 1978 at the age of 16. In 1982 he was with other members of his regiment in the ship, the Royal Fleet Auxiliary *Sir Galahad*, just off the Falkland Islands, when she was set on fire by enemy bombs. Weston survived with terrible burns, following which his face was barely recognisable. Rejecting the extensive plastic surgery that might have helped him return to something like his original appearance, Weston set out to give hope and courage to other sufferers.

He has since worked for his charity, Weston Spirit, which has made him a public figure. In 1992 he was appointed to the Order of the British Empire. After recovering from his initial injuries, Weston became a well-known personality on radio and television, especially within Wales, and used to present his own radio show on BBC Radio Wales.

TRAINING FOR EXCELLENCE

THE ROYAL MILITARY ACADEMY SANDHURST

Major Stephen Segrave, Irish Guards

'You forget the name of the Commandant but you never forget the name of your Colour Sergeant,' goes the saying. The Colour Sergeant, who with a Captain platoon commander is responsible for the day-to-day training of officer cadets, makes a lasting impression on generations of potential officers. Most of the Colour Sergeants at the Royal Military Academy Sandhurst come from the Foot Guards. There is an inextricable link between the Guards, Sandhurst and officer training.

Above: Cadets at Sandhurst during the Log Run.

RMA Sandhurst in its current form is relatively young. Traditionally, officers destined for the Cavalry and the Infantry received little or no formal training until they joined their regiment having first purchased a commission. An attempt to correct this began when the site at Sandhurst (near Camberley, Surrey) was built in 1812. Gunners, Engineers and Signals officers continued to be trained at the Royal Military Academy, Woolwich, until 1947 when it combined with the Royal Military College to become the RMA Sandhurst. The experiences of the Boer War led to an increase in officer training and a further building was developed within Sandhurst's grounds which came to be known as New College. Old College is the original building.

The methods of training officers have taken many forms over the years. Successfully passing the three-day Army Officer Selection Board (formerly the Regular Commissions Board) at Westbury, Wiltshire, is a prerequisite for all British cadets. They then spend a three-term year at Sandhurst. The junior term provides the foundation for subsequent training; the second term provides the skills required to be an officer and the third and final term develops the more complex side of officership. Adventurous training and expeditions take place in the two periods of leave between terms.

The Guards hold a number of prestigious appointments within the Academy. For over 100 years the Academy Adjutant has been a Guardsman. Major Frederick 'Boy' Browning, later Lieutenant General Sir Frederick Browning, is credited as being the first Adjutant to begin the tradition of riding up the steps of Old College at the Sovereign's Parade in 1927. History relates that he was either escaping an impending shower or wanted to remonstrate with the cadets who had just been commissioned when he decided to take his grey charger up the nine sets of steps and into the Grand Entrance of Old College. The Adjutant of New College is always a Guardsman and rides on the Sovereign's Parade along with the Academy Adjutant.

Perhaps the most important Household Division appointment in the Academy is that of the Academy Sergeant Major. As the senior serving soldier in the British Army, his opinion is sought out by Kings, Field Marshals and Generals. His duties are numerous and outside the Academy routine they include sitting on committees such as the Trustees of the Army Benevolent Fund, The Army Dress Committee and the Army Medals Committee. Old and New Colleges both have Guardsmen as their

Corporal of Horse Goodwin, The Blues and Royals

Regimental Signals Instructor

The Bowman radio system was introduced into the Army to bring us up to date with the other leading nations. The problem with Clansman was that it was analogue, and it was insecure; it took a long time to transmit a quick message securely, by having to encode everything before you could send it.

Bowman allows us to have a digitised picture on the space around you, so that on the screen you can actually observe where your call signs are, where the enemy call signs are and get your orders sent over the air digitally: the days where you used to have to traipse half way round the world to get to Orders groups, and then come back at four o'clock in the morning and shoot off are now technically over. There's no reason why you can't have a complete set of orders straight over the net. We still use the old voice procedure. Everyone has approval now. So you still have your brigade net, battle group net, regimental command nets and squadron command nets; and then within the Squadron nets everyone talks now. The old rules of minimal battle group nets, and brigade nets still apply.

Warrant Officer Class 2 Chant, Grenadier Guards

On Sandhurst

I was a Colour Sergeant and then a Company Sergeant Major at Sandhurst. You need a Guardsman or a quality Household Division soldier there to impress on a young officer, male or female, straight away to do it the right way – whether that is happening in the field, teaching tactics or on the drill square. For a Foot Guardsman instructor it is also part of our schooling. It puts us in with other quality Colour Sergeants, Warrant Officers and Platoon Commanders. And there is nothing better than giving your experiences to a young, creative, charming, enthusiastic graduate or non-graduate. It is very fulfilling. There is no prouder moment than seeing them march up those steps to earn their commission. And now I have seen these young gentlemen and women in Afghanistan producing the goods and think 'I was a part of it'. The ultimate and pinnacle job is to be the Sergeant Major at the best military academy in the world. Any soldier would want that.

As Regimental Quartermaster Sergeant

There are always two in any regiment in the British Army. There is the technical side and the maintenance side. I look after the running of the Barracks, the refurbishment, contractors, the skips, cleaners, all that sort of stuff, and I have ammunition, accommodation and clothing on my account.

Company Sergeant Major MacPhee, Scots Guards

Regimental Fitness Regime

The Commanding Officer and the physical training instructor devise a battalion training programme that is handed out to the Company Sergeant Majors on a monthly basis which tells you what lessons may be conducted on a daily basis. The physical training instructor will determine the natural progression of building people up. So you're not just going to come on day one and try and do an eight-mile forced march. It's all progressively building up until the annual Combat Fitness Test.

The other one is the personal fitness assessment where you do two minutes worth of press-ups, two minutes worth of sit-ups and then you do a mile and a half run. As Company Sergeant Major it's important that you not only liaise with physical training staff and work out when and how we're going to do these different tests in order to keep within the time bracket of the yearly training tests we need, but you're also looking into making sure individuals who have maybe slipped through the net because they're on courses, on leave, or whatever, do get picked up. Also, any individuals who are maybe not achieving the standards are given remedial training in which to improve themselves and their fitness, and then given an opportunity to retake the test at a later stage or at a time when the physical training instructor assesses that they will be able to pass that test.

It's definitely part of my job to remind new young soldiers that they are Guardsmen and particularly Scots Guardsmen. You want to instil the spirit of the Battalion and the Company into the individual. In physical training, you all wear your own company tops. So it gives the boys that sense of identity, we know who's who and it's a sense of belonging as well. In my case we are C Company. On the daily detail I'll publish a Battle Honour so the boys know on this given day the Regiment was awarded Battle Honours for specific actions or campaigns.

Sergeant Major John McCallum, Scots Guards

Regimental Sergeant Major

To become Regimental Sergeant Major is a dream come true for anybody that starts at the bottom. All you see is this big badge when you're a boy, and aspire to get there. Apart from the Garrison Sergeant Major London District and the Academy Sergeant Major at Sandhurst the large Coat of Arms is only worn by Guards Regimental Sergeant Majors. The big challenges for a Regimental Sergeant Major today are maintaining the discipline and maintaining the standard of the Battalion. I think you've got to keep that as your priority. The young lads understand the firm ethos of the Household Division. That's one thing that other regiments don't have and are jealous of.

You only need to look at the young lads that are winning medals now and the things they are doing under fire. Without a shadow of a doubt, we've got some of the hardest-working boys in the Army at the moment and some of the bravest. You know, you could ask these boys to put their lives on the line. Did it happen 20–25 years ago? Yes it did. It happened when we went to the Falklands, same detail. I remember joining and they said 'Depot is never as hard as when I was there' and it happens today 'Depot is never as hard'. But whatever that young lad's coming through, and whatever his home background, it's as hard for him as it was for me.

Gone are the days when you're behind your desk, you go wild, throw a few things about your office. That doesn't work these days. You've got to get the guy in, understand him. But then you've still got to be hard and bite them when it's required. He needs to understand if he's done wrong, and then that will be reflected when he goes in on the charge. The Non-Commissioned Officers have a thing called AGAI 67 now which has brought the powers back to the Junior Non-Commissioned Officers. So the Non-Commissioned Officers can now put a Guardsman on a charge before everything

has gone through to the Sergeant Major. Now these minor offences are getting dealt with at a lower level. It's working for us. It's taking a lot of the dealings away from the Commanding Officer.

Regimental Sergeant Majors and currently seven out of ten Company Sergeant Majors are in the Foot Guards.

Of greater impact to the cadets under training is the role of the platoon Colour Sergeant. There is no quota system for how many Colour Sergeants a regiment can send to Sandhurst. They are selected on merit after a gruelling four-week assessment course. Traditionally, about a third of the 60 Colour Sergeants at the Academy are Guardsmen. This says as much about the quality of the senior Non-Commissioned Officers as it does about the importance that the Division places on sending good men to instruct there. Although many of the subjects are similar to those taught to recruits, the Sandhurst Colour Sergeant is faced with a different pupil compared to his colleague in the Guards Company at Catterick. Most of the cadets in the 30-strong platoon will be 23-year-old university graduates who, by and large, are highly intelligent, fit and enthusiastic to learn as much as they can.

The Sovereign's Parade takes place three times a year, where up to 240 officer cadets are commissioned in front of an audience of 4,000 proud friends and family as well as representatives of regiments and corps, Commonwealth high commissions and other embassies. The success of this high-profile parade is down to the professionalism of the staff, particularly the Guardsmen among them. The Household Division at Sandhurst was once described by an ex-Commandant as 'the golden thread running through the Academy without which things would begin to fall apart and would certainly not be of such good quality'.

GUARDS TRAINING COMPANY, CATTERICK, NORTH YORKSHIRE

All five Foot Guards Regiments train their soldiers at the Infantry Training Centre in Catterick in the Guards Training Company. The Guards Company is part of 2nd Infantry Training Battalion which includes Parachute Company, P Company, Gurkha Company and Anzio Company (short courses and Territorial Army).

Trainee Guardsmen undertake the 28-week Combat Infantryman's Course (Foot Guards) abbreviated as CIC (Gds). The course takes the Trainee Guardsmen from his first day in the Army to the Pass Out Parade when he is ready to join his Battalion on operations or Public Duties (there is no longer a phase 1 and phase 2 for infantrymen).

The CIC (Gds) is two weeks longer than the CIC (Line). This allows for 90 drill periods to be woven into the course to train the Trainee Guardsmen for the Public Duties role – known as Military Task 2.5 (MT 2.5).

The CIC (Gds) has a number of milestones:

Weeks 1–6: confined to barracks (ie no booking out) and the basics taught in the field and in barracks. This culminates in the Adjutant's Drill Inspection after which, if completed successfully, the Trainee Guardsman receives his first weekend leave.

Week 6 to mid course: continue learning weapon handling, drill, physical training, navigation, First Aid, defence against Chemical, Biological,

Above: Recruits from all the Foot Guards regiments on their passing out parade at Catterick

Radiological and Nuclear weapons, and field skills on Introduction Exercises (teaching exercises). At the end of this period the Trainee Guardsman will have passed the Annual Personal Weapons Test (APWT) and be considered proficient in the use of the SA80 rifle and also undergone some tactical exercises. Midway through the course there is a two-week block leave.

Mid course to Week 24: Further tactical exercises and in-barracks training. There are two main hurdles – the Company Commander's Drill inspection in which all aspects of ceremonial drill are tested. The second

Guardsman Jack Payne, Irish Guards

On Basic Training, Catterick

I spent 48 weeks at The Army Foundation College in Harrogate before going to Catterick which is recruit training for all infantry. The Foot Guards are in a separate camp as are the Paras. The most challenging part was physical training, which involved running, assault courses, circuit training in the gym, log runs plus the standard infantry tests like the Combat Fitness Test. We also trained with the Light Support Weapon, the Light Machine Gun, grenades and bayonet training.

There's a lot of psychological training involved in the bayonet training. You get in teams of two. The one with the bayonet has to run along, attacking the targets and the person behind has to shout encouragement. It's all about aggression. It's a good experience. The final exercise in Scotland was also rewarding. The instructors were the Section and Platoon Commanders and we acted as second in command of the 10-man sections. We had

to do the sentry roster and generally supervise the section, making sure everyone was doing their admin in the morning and getting a hot meal.

During a contact [fire fight] you assess the section's ammunition, the strength of the section, and casualties. Obviously you take charge of your half of the section. So it's quite a lot of responsibility, especially if you're just a junior Guardsman, but its all part of the experience because you need to know how to do it when you get to the Battalion. You need to have that confidence.

Drill was okay. We did two weeks more than the rest of the infantry. I quite enjoyed it to be honest. The worst part about the drill is probably when they are so picky about the uniform. But that is like second nature by the time you get to the end of the course, doing your kit, making it immaculate. The other divisions of recruits at Catterick are mix and match but the Household Division are all Guards so there is a strong sense of identity.

hurdle is the March and Shoot Competition which includes the Basic Combat Fitness Test which is eight miles over undulating terrain, carrying 45lb plus personal weapon to be completed within two hours. This is followed by a mile and a quarter timed run as a 10-man section and then a falling plates competition on the ranges.

Weeks 25 and 26: the final exercise is followed by Live Firing Tactical Training (LFTT). The former tests all field skills taught throughout the course. It takes place either on Garelochhead (Scotland) or Otterburn (Northumberland) army field training areas and is run over six days. LFTT follows this where the Trainee Guardsmen undertake fire-team and section live-firing attacks. The week culminates with a live-firing platoon attack

Weeks 27 and 28: this fortnight is largely taken up with preparation for the Pass Out Parade but includes driver theory training, instruction on Joint Personal Administration (JPA) and, of course, admin. The Pass Out Parade is on the last Friday of the course and friends and family are invited to attend. The parade format is similar to that of The Queen's Birthday Parade.

The course was lengthened from 26 weeks to 28 weeks for all courses forming up after 1 April 2007. This allows for increased instruction on weapon systems, driver theory training and JPA training. At any one time the Company has in the region of 340 Trainee Guardsmen in seven platoons, all at various stages of training. There is a permanent staff of approximately 60. Guardsmen are always trained by Guardsmen. As with most infantry companies, Company Headquarters consists of: the Company Commander (a Major), Company Second in Command (a Late Entry Captain), Company Sergeant Major (senior Warrant Officer Class 2) and Company Quartermaster Sergeant.

Major Edmund Wilson, Irish Guards

Operational Training And Advisory Group

This is a successor to NITAT the old Northern Ireland Training and Advisory Team which then morphed into UNTAT the UN Training and Advisory Team. With the rise of Iraq it became the Operational Training and Advisory Group. And that is responsible for training people for operations wherever they go. So, if you are going to be a UN Military Observer in Sierre Leone or if you're going to Iraq or Afghanistan, you come through a packet at OPTAG.

I was what's called the Formation and Training Advisor and the role there was to advise commanders from mainly brigade level and commanding officers, as to how to plan and structure their training – on the basis of the experience I've built up and also on the basis of what they wanted to achieve.

The majority of the formation level packages for brigades and their constituent battle groups happens wherever that brigade is based. So I spent three months last year in Germany training 20 Brigade; I then moved to Catterick, where most of 19-Brigade was.

The key Household Division elements that I trained were the Coldstream Guards for Afghanistan, in the summer of 2007. Included in that was the Headquarters of the Household Cavalry battle group, and one of their squadrons; and also a Company of the Scots Guards. They are all going to Afghanistan this Autumn. But they all did very different training. For the Coldstream Guards, for example, they would have come through as a whole battalion, with two days of All Ranks briefing, and mandatory skills training for everyone. So they start with a common baseline of knowledge. For example: extraction from Minefields; rules of engagement, things that every single person has to know for an operation. And so that's two days worth of training for everyone in the battle group. Then we took their commanders predominantly, on even more specialised training, in some of the other tactics that are required: the use of specialist types of weapon and search skills.

For example the batten gun that might be used for crowd control situations. Some of the newer types of weapons that we have, such as laser aimers that attach on to the side of weapons. We would train a cohort of the battalion, who could then go back, and cascade the information down. We teach specific search skills. Four people per company would come and be given more in depth training in how to search people, how to search vehicles, how to conduct basic checks of houses; and they would again go back to cascade that down.

I think it's good to have a couple of days to think about some of the other issues such as the political aspect. We get almost daily feed-back from the different theatres of operations. All the instructors involved in producing the training package have gone on at least a 10 day recce before they start. It's good to be able to say 'I was there last week'.

From OPTAG we would have about 40 training the Guards made up of all arms. The dominant being trainers from the teeth arms – the infantry, cavalry and some gunners; and we would have some logisticians as well. Of that 40, probably 20 of them would be from OPTAG itself: with the other 20 being from the brigade which has just finished. So they come back; rather than with two weeks experience, with six months experience.

You do your own special to arms training: so if you're a Warrior battalion, a whole lot of Warrior stuff; which you do yourself. But in terms of dismounted skills and any skills which may be for the Land Rover which is very generic; or a snatch vehicle then they come to Thetford for seven days for a proper confirmatory exercise, where they are put in a theatre-specific environment for that part of the theatre they're going to. And as far as we can do, we replicate the kind of scenarios that they might come across.

On a weekly basis I have 70 soldiers to act as Taliban if I am doing an Afghanistan package; or militia for Iraq; then we would have round about 50 to 60 Nationals, from that country who are resident in Britain. And so I have 50 to 60 Afghans assisting me for each exercise I do. And they can do pattern of life, and we have women there; so we can bring in the aspect of females and the difficulty of searching women. It also creates the language barrier; because some of those 50 or 60 will be employed as interpreters: so we get used to working with each other. Working with interpreters takes practice.

OPTAG training is only as good as the people who are listening to it; and how imaginative you can be in development training. I think the high point of my time there was when I read a Brigade's post-training report which they do once they've been in theatre on operations for six weeks by which time they've seen whether what we've done has been realistic and we develop the next package based on it. There was a quote which came out earlier on this year that there was a soldier who found an IED, a roadside bomb; and the quote was 'Just like it was on OPTAG': and you think, well … I've saved someone's life.

HOUSEHOLD DIVISION AND PARACHUTE REGIMENT CENTRALISED COURSES

James Leask

In the mid 1960s the Major General Commanding the Household Division found that, as a result of ceremonial duty, the basic infantry skills of Junior Non-Commissioned Officers were not at the high standard they needed to be. A training team was established at the Guards Depot, Pirbright to rectify this. The main course they ran was aimed at Lance Corporals and was an early version of the current Section Commanders Battle Course.

The training team also established a sniper school. In conjunction with the training team in Pirbright, a battle camp was set up in Stonebridge, with the Parachute Regiment running a similar camp in Brecon. After a number of successful years, it was decided that all infantry soldiers should train their Lance Corporals in Brecon and the Stonebridge Battle Camp ceased to play such a significant role. The success of the training team was such that the hierarchy were reluctant to lose them. They changed their remit and began preparing soldiers for the various new Brecon infantry courses. Sniping continued to be highly valued and the school became a centre of excellence; as it remains to this day. In the early 1990s, following Options for Change, the Guards Depot ceased to exist. The Parachute Regiment was experiencing the same challenges and in 1992 it was decided that both training teams should merge to enable the excellent service to continue. The real estate was available at Pirbright and in 1996 the centralised training team became known as HDPRCC.

Household Division and Parachute Regiment Centralised Courses is now the envy of the rest of the British Infantry. As a non-established organization or 'Black Economy' unit, HDPRCC is able to draw the best aspects of the modern Army while not being weighed down by bureaucracy. The relationship with the Parachute Regiment means that HDPRCC is responsible for the promotion of a third of the British Infantry. It is a unique institution that has evolved over the past sixty years into its cult status now. It is something that can never be replicated and should never be lost. Every Non-Commissioned Officer and Officer within the five Regiments of Foot Guards will have harrowing tales of thrashings over the sisters or being forced to march up sand banks in newly bulled drill boots. It is however this heritage that makes it such an outstanding location for developing leaders and snipers within the Household Division.

It is impossible to explain succinctly how this organization fits together so neatly. It is simply an immaculate demonstration of team work combined with carefully applied influence. The Officer Commanding is selected by the Major General from the Foot Guards with the Company Sergeant Major being drawn from the Parachute Regiment. The remainder of the manning is extremely fluid and fluctuates. Essentially every Regiment is mandated by a charter to provide two members of the permanent staff. Unusually the Royal Marines provide a Colour Sergeant as the chief instructor of the Sniper Wing on an exchange programme with the Parachute Regiment.

The origin of many of the other resources is perhaps more uncertain. The result of camps closing and an Army shrinking has left HDPRCC with a considerable pool of surplus equipment. Vehicles, temporary staff and ammunition are all provided on a similar basis to the personnel. Weapons are borrowed on a long term basis from the Household Division Bands and the buildings are signed out on a yearly basis from Brunswick Camp Commandant, who happens to have served in the Grenadier Guards for

Lieutenant Folarin Kuku, Grenadier Guards

On The Platoon Commanders' Battle Course At Brecon

I always wanted to join the Army and at Harrow School we were very much pushed towards the Guards because the Sergeants in charge of the Cadet Force were Guards. The Grenadiers came round one day and I had a look and liked what I saw and I got signed up. I was commissioned on 11 August 2006 and almost immediately went on our 'Beat-Up' course down in Pirbright which is run by the Household Division and the Parachute Regiment.

Anyone going on a course from the Household Division or the Parachute Regiment are sent on a combined courses preparation cadre. Everyone is sent down there for a week or so to work on their skills and brush up on fitness and it just gives them a feel for what the course might be like. It gives you a chance to sort

your kit out before spending three months at Brecon (Wales) on the Platoon Commanders' Battle Course.

It is 14 weeks long, including four weeks live-fire tactical training which gives you the qualifications to run firing ranges. It's lots of fun but it's hard work. Platoon Commanders' Division (PCD) is very intensive and the tension is high and everything you do is referred to in an operational sense. We were reading reports sent back from Afghanistan while we were on PCD which impressed on us that what we were training to do is actually very serious and very real.

Three months after I left PCD, all the Grenadiers had gone away on deployment, as well as the Micks, and the Right Flank Company of the Scots Guards was in Afghanistan. The other two companies of Grenadiers were in Iraq.

30 years. The day to day welfare and administrative support is provided by staff within the Army Training Regiment located nearby and the Adjutant is currently a Coldstream Guards officer.

Brunswick Training Camp is not a modern camp designed to meet the expectations of modern society. In fact students pay no accommodation charges on the courses since the huts have changed little since their construction before the Second World War. We would have it no other way. The layers of blue red blue paint, with a touch of maroon, layered year after year provide ample support for rotting woodwork. Seeping from that paint is the blood and sweat of men who have gone before. It instills an enormous sense of pride and breeds motivation and determination. In more recent times the large dormitories act as a gathering place for soldiers returning from all corners of the world and

sharing tales of exploits, which is invaluable in itself. For a Guardsman on Public Duties to be billeted with a member of the Pathfinder Platoon returning from operations in Afghanistan ensures we will continue to compete with the best no matter what the role.

Currently HDPRCC conducts five Junior Non-Commissioned Officer Cadres per year each lasting six weeks. The final week is spent on exercise on Sennybridge Training Area culminating with a Platoon live firing attack along the bun lines of Box 10. The output is approximately three hundred Lance Corporals every year many of whom deploy straight on war fighting operations as Section Commanders. The value and importance of HDPRCC is no more evident than on current operations.

In addition to the JNCO Cadre, HDPRCC runs four nine-week Sniper Courses under the guidance of the Royal Marine Sniper Instructor. The course is now one of only three run in the British Army. It is undoubtedly an outstanding course, which allows the black art of snipering to be passed from generation to generation. Recently students were assessed on their ability to destroy static enemy targets from a hovering helicopter on the west coast of Wales. Critically, the training continues to be relevant and constantly adapted to modern operations. The calendar year culminates with a Sniper concentration, which again allows expertise to be shared amongst the elite Infantry Regiments.

As outlined in the original charter set by the Major General, HDPRCC continues to prepare soldiers for Section Commanders, Platoon Sergeants and Platoon Commanders Battle Courses. In addition, physical training courses are conducted for those aspiring to join the Guards Parachute Platoon and the Special Air Service. Ultimately, as a Non-Established Unit, HDPRCC is flexible and able to concentrate its resources wherever required. In the past ten years individuals have supported training across the Division. The recent inclusion of the London Regiment as part of the Household Division has seen HDPRCC begin to prepare Territorial Army soldiers for operations. Ultimately the organization holds a unique status within the British Army and the hearts of every member of the Household Division. The calibre of the staff ensure it is forward thinking and proactive in its development. It is and will continue to be the custodians of the standards expected of our leaders well into the future.

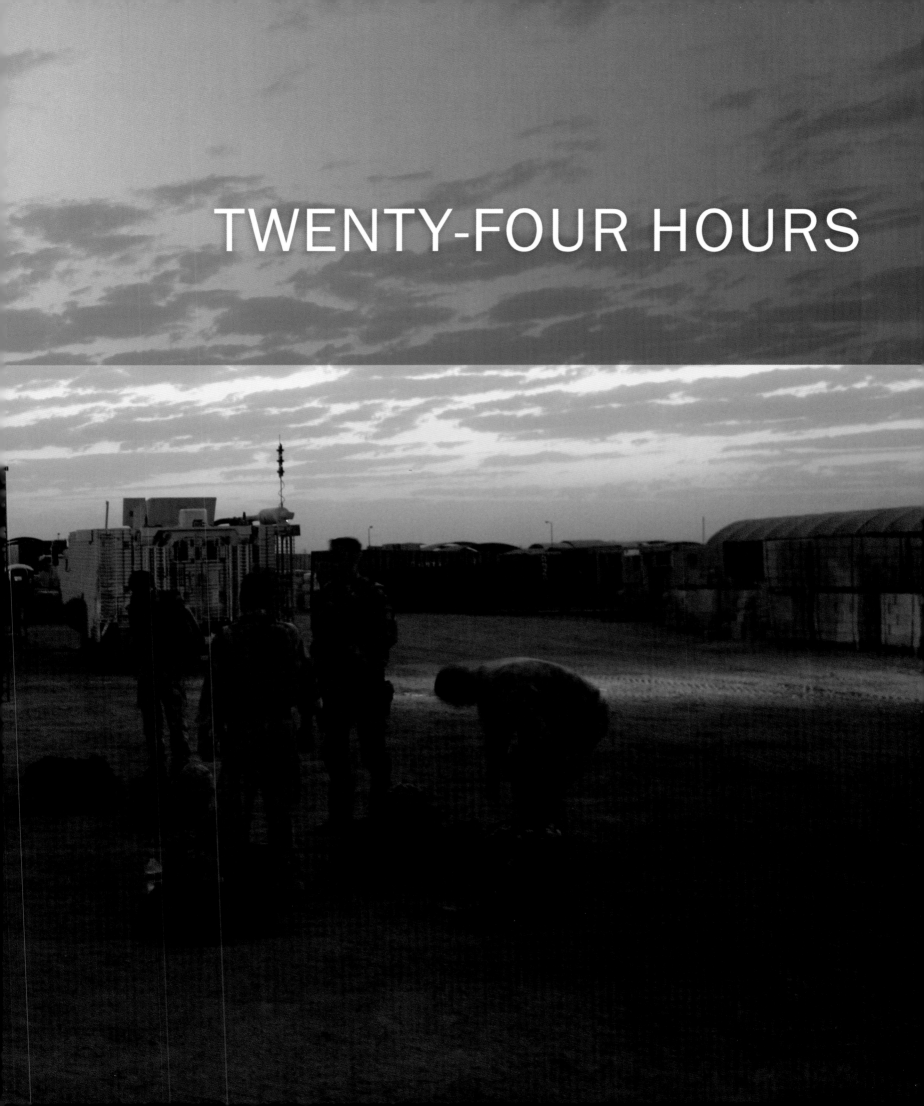

TWENTY-FOUR HOURS

0400 – 0800 hours

Top left: RSM WO1 P. Lally parades Irish Guardsmen for the repatriation of a soldier killed while on operations in Iraq, 2007.

Middle left: The white socks of this Cavalry Black are given a good shampoo at Knightsbridge Barracks before going on The Queen's Life Guard.

Bottom left: Victoria Barracks, Windsor. Members of the Coldstream Guards are put through a final morning rehearsal before they march up to Windsor Castle to mount the Guard.

Above: Dawn in the Iraqi desert. Members of A Squadron of the Household Cavalry Regiment prepare for morning patrol.

Top right: Early morning PT.

Opposite bottom left: The Queen's Life Guard forms up on the square at their barracks in Knightsbridge for inspection before heading to their duties at Horse Guards.

Opposite bottom right: Banja Luka, Bosnia. Eyes right by members of the Welsh Guards as they line up to receive their leeks on St David's Day from The Prince of Wales.

0900 – 1300 hours

Left: A Non-Commissioned Officer of the Coldstream Guards prepares to give a sentry his orders while the remainder of the Guards wait in line at Windsor Castle.

Below: The Welsh Guards lay up their Colours at Bangor Cathedral. The Colours are renewed every ten years and the old ones are installed in a church, cathedral or other building which has connections with the regiment.

Below right: A Corporal of Horse of The Life Guards ensures that two troopers who have just dismounted from The Queen's Life Guard at Horse Guards, know what their next duties are.

Below left: Kent. Selected members of the Welsh Guards returned from their tour of Bosnia by bicycle, kayak and feet. Here they are running the final phase through Kent towards London where they ran the equivalent of three marathons to reach Wellington Barracks in central London, raising £34K for charity.

Bottom: Welsh Guards checking positions in Iraq.

Opposite left: South Wales. The Household Cavalry Regiment take part in their annual firing at Castlemartin in South Wales. Here the crew of a Spartan Command Vehicle get into position.

Opposite top right: Prince William Wales on his Troop Leaders' course at Bovington in Dorset. As a cornet in The Blues and Royals he is serving in the regiment of which, one day, he will be Colonel-in-Chief.

Opposite middle right: Members of the Household Cavalry Mounted Regiment preparing their kit.

Opposite bottom right: Basra, Iraq. It is the turn of 'Badger Squadron' to read the lesson at the weekly service and prayers conducted by the Irish Guards. Badger Squadron was attached from the Royal Tank Regiment for the duration of the six-month tour. They became honorary Irish Guards. Badger was also the name given to the Officer Commanding the Squadron.

1400 – 1800 hours

Above: The finishing touches are applied before the Major General's inspection.

Top left: A young Welsh Guards officer irons his shirt outside his accommodation at the Metal Factory in Banja Luka, Bosnia.

Above left: A patrol from Nijmegen Company Grenadier Guards in Jamaica keeping a good eye out for the 'enemy' and crocodiles.

Left: Iraq. A member of the Irish Guards oversees weapon training for an Iraqi army recruit in Shaibah.

Opposite top right: The officer commanding Right Flank, Scots Guards, introduces General Sir Redmond Watt, Commmander-in-Chief Land (and former Commanding Officer of the Welsh Guards), to members of the company during an exercise in Poland.

Opposite bottom: A member of the Band of The Blues and Royals on duty at Royal Ascot.

Opposite far right: Members of the Household Cavalry Mounted Regiment dress up as French cuirassiers as part of the Household Cavalry Pageant, a one-off event, held in front of The Queen on Horse Guards Parade.

1900 – 2300 hours

Top left: Lance Sergeant Coates, Irish Guards, Airport Camp, Basra, Iraq.

Top centre: Shaibah, Iraq. An Irish Guardsman disguised as an insurgent prepares for an 'ambush' on a training exercise.

Above: Lieutenant Ralph Griffin, Commanding Officer Household Cavalry Mounted Regiment, addresses the Warrant Officers and Non-Commissioned Officers in their Mess at Knightsbridge.

Left: Scots Guardsmen endure the final stages of the three peaks challenge.

Top: Members of the 1st Battalion Scots Guards perform at the Edinburgh Military Tattoo, 2006.

Above: Lance Corporal Cardwell, Scots Guards, fishing at Basra Palace.

Top left: Banja Luka. The Band of the Welsh Guards takes on an alternative role as backing musicians for a version of the X Factor performed by members of the Battalion for a St David's Day celebration.

Left: A Life Guards Trooper marches under the arch at Horse Guards as part of his dismounted duties on The Queen's Life Guard.

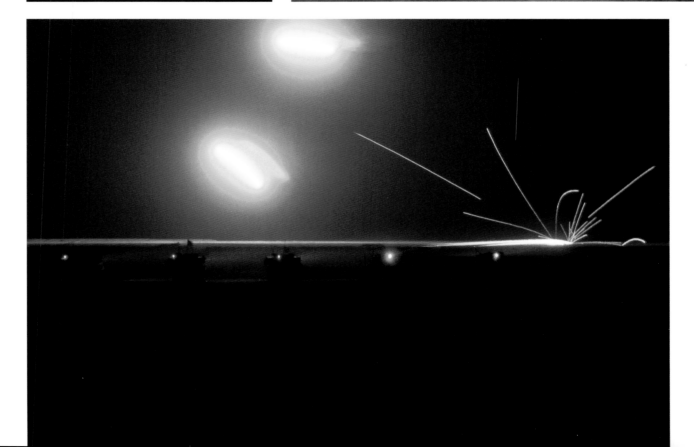

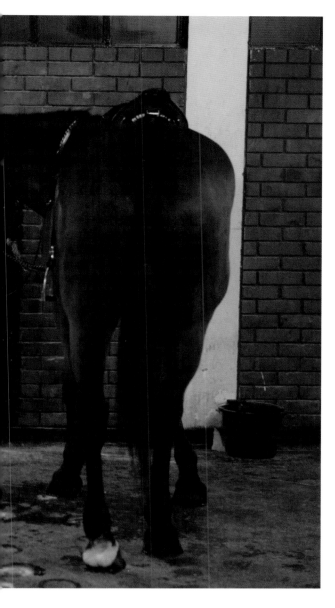

2400 – 0300 hours

Above: Hyde Park Barracks, London. The stable guard takes a pause while waiting for those preparing to go on parade to collect their horses.

Top right: Iraq. A soldier of the Household Cavalry seen through night sights.

Right: Iraq. A Guardsman of the Irish Guards watches a video while relaxing in his fortified bunk at Basra airport.

Opposite top left: Captain R. Shannon, Scots Guards, inside a Warrior.

Opposite bottom: Iraq. Night firing on the ranges by the Household Cavalry.

LIST OF SUBSCRIBERS

This book has been made possible through the generosity of the following subscribers. The regiment, with which each individual is or has been associated, is listed as supplied – with no distinction made between serving and former guardsmen.

The Duke of Abercorn KG	Irish Guards	Lieutenant Colonel Charles M. Bremner	Welsh Guards	Captain James Coleby	Coldstream Guards
Lieutenant George P.H. Aitken	Irish Guards	Niall Brennan	Irish Guards	E.P. Colquhoun	Scots Guards
Captain Dominic J. Alkin	Grenadier Guards	Robert Brockbank		Captain (Retd) E.S. Connolly	The Life Guards
Giles Allan OBE	Irish Guards	Mr J. Brown	Coldstream Guards	Captain E.J. Cooper	Irish Guards
Drummer Peter J. Allen	Grenadier Guards	Colonel Toby Browne	The Blues and Royals	Guardsman Arthur S. Coote	Grenadier Guards
Squadron Corporal Major R.K. Allen	The Life Guards	Lord Bruntisfield	Irish Guards	Captain J.A. Corbet Burcher	
Mr C. Allman-Brown	Irish Guards	Major General R.J. Buckland	Coldstream Guards	Major General Sir Robert Corbett KCVO CB	
Major General The Lord Alvingham		Henry Buckmaster	Irish Guards		Irish Guards
	Coldstream Guards	Lieutenant George J. Bull	Coldstream Guards	D.L.P. Corbin	Scots Guards
Lance Sergeant D.C. Andrews	Grenadier Guards	Captain James Bullock-Webster	Irish Guards	Captain Anthony J. Cordle	Coldstream Guards
Lieutenant Colonel John R. Arthur OBE	Scots Guards	Lieutenant Colonel Robin Bullock-Webster OBE		Major P.H. Cordle	Grenadier Guards
T.J. Atkin Esq.	The Blues and Royals		Irish Guards	Michael Corkery QC	Welsh Guards
Lance Sergeant Norman Bareham	Coldstream Guards	Major (Retd) W. John Burchell	Welsh Guards	William Coulson	Grenadier Guards
In memory of Sergeant Norman Bareham		Sir Adrian Cadbury	Coldstream Guards	Guardsman Donald G. Cowan	Grenadier Guards
	Coldstream Guards	Guardsman Ernest Vain Cademy	Coldstream Guards	Guardsman Leonard J. Cowieson	Scots Guards
Lorne Baring	Scots Guards	Mr Andrew Campbell		Major C.J.G. Cox	Coldstream Guards
Major L.N. Barron	Coldstream Guards		Royal Military Academy Sandhurst	Mr Richard Cox	The Life Guards
Mr Charles Barton		Major Alexander Cartwright	Grenadier Guards	Captain C.E. Crace	Coldstream Guards
Sergeant John Bartram	Grenadier Guards	B.M. de L. Cazenove	Coldstream Guards	Colonel Michael Craster	Grenadier Guards
N.E.A.G.W. Elliot Baxter	Scots Guards	Major Robert Cazenove	Coldstream Guards	M.J. Crawford Esq.	
Lance Corporal B.I. Baylis	Grenadier Guards	Major Thomas F. Charles	Welsh Guards	Mr E.G. Cross MM	Scots Guards
Guardsman Roly Beckett	Coldstream Guards	Guy Feilding Charles-Jones	Welsh Guards	Mr Michael J. Croucher	
Major John F. Bedford	Royal Signals	Guardsman Ian Charters	Grenadier Guards	Lieutenant Colonel Julian E.M. Crowe OBE	
Guardsman M. Bell	Irish Guards	Captain Shane Chichester	Coldstream Guards		Scots Guards
Brigadier Will Berridge MBE	Irish Guards	R.C.B. Chisholm-Broomfield	Grenadier Guards	Guardsman John J. Crowley	Grenadier Guards
Captain C.P.A. Bertie	Scots Guards	Guardsman Church	Irish Guards	Mr Steve Crump	
Anthony W. Bird	Coldstream Guards	Captain Bill Churchill	Irish Guards	Miss Charlotte Cubitt	
Clive I. Blakeway	Coldstream Guards	Captain John Churchill	Irish Guards	Master Edward Cubitt	
Bernard Bloom	Grenadier Guards	Major Frank A.O. Clark	Grenadier Guards	Doctor Geoffrey Cubitt	
Dermot Blundell-Hollinshead-Blundell		Alan James Clark		Master James Cubitt	
	Grenadier Guards	M.W. Clark Esq. CBE DL	Grenadier Guards	Professor Robin Cubitt	
Major Richard Boggis-Rolfe	Coldstream Guards	Lieutenant Colonel W.R. Clarke OBE		Major General William Cubitt CBE	Irish Guards
Alverne Bolitho	Grenadier Guards		Grenadier Guards	Sergeant Noel Cullen	Irish Guards
Colonel Tom Bonas	Welsh Guards	Guardsman Hugh Cleland	Irish Guards	Master George Curling	
Captain Tom Bonham Carter	Irish Guards	Lord Clifford	Coldstream Guards	Derek Charles Curran	Grenadier Guards
Desmond Boyd-Otley	Scots Guards	Mrs Colin Climie		Captain D.J.J. Currie	Coldstream Guards
Captain R.E.J. Boyle DL	Irish Guards	Mr D. Coates	Coldstream Guards	Lance Sergeant V.R. Dales	Coldstream Guards
Major Tony H. Bradborn	Coldstream Guards	Major John Cole DL	Coldstream Guards	Dr D.E. Dalton	

Major Christopher Daly — The Blues and Royals
Lieutenant Colonel Denis Daly — The Blues and Royals
Major Iain E. Dalzel Job — Scots Guards
Major M.P. David MC — Grenadier Guards
George Davidson — Scots Guards
Captain The Hon. E.L.S. Dawson-Damer MVO — Irish Guards
Lieutenant Colonel H.M.P. de Lisle — Grenadier Guards
Major the Viscount De L'Isle MBE — Grenadier Guards
Captain J.E.A. de St John-Pryce — The Blues and Royals
Colin Dean — Chairman International Military Music Society (UK)
Captain T.W.G. Dennis — Grenadier Guards
Alan Dent — Coldstream Guards
The Countess of Derby
The Earl of Derby — Grenadier Guards
M.J.L. Dickson — Coldstream Guards
Major Dominic Dobson — Scots Guards
Captain Oliver Benedict Doherty — Irish Guards
Guardsman Doran — Irish Guards
Major Peter Doyle — Irish Guards
Mrs M.P. Drury — Coldstream Guards
Captain W.J. Duggan — Irish Guards
Colour Sergeant John Keith Duxbury — Scots Guards
Guardsman B. Eastman — Grenadier Guards
Captain Peter B. Edwards — Governor General's Horse Guards
Brigadier James Ellery CBE — The Life Guards
Captain C.E. Elwell — Grenadier Guards
David Emanuel — Scots Guards
Brigadier Douglas Erskine-Crum CBE — Scots Guards
Mr Jeremy C. Evans
Sergeant John A. Evans — Coldstream Guards
Major M.J. Everett TD — Scots Guards
Captain C.T.F. Fagan — Grenadier Guards
Gunner John Fallows — Secretary, New South Wales Guards Club
Henry Farr — The Life Guards
Lance Sergeant T.C. Faubel — Coldstream Guards
Lord Fermoy — The Blues and Royals
Sergeant Colin C. Fiddy — Grenadier Guards
Lance Sergeant Sidney Finnemore — Coldstream Guards
Captain T.J. Fitzgerald — Irish Guards
Lieutenant Colonel Howard C. Flood CD — Grenadier Guards
Mr Ian Flynn
Alexander Forster — Grenadier Guards
Captain J.D.G. Fortescue — Coldstream Guards
Captain Philip Foxwood — Coldstream Guards
Mark Francis — Grenadier Guards
Company Sergeant Major M. Freeman — Coldstream Guards

Captain C.F. Fuglesang — Coldstream Guards
D.W. Fuller — Coldstream Guards
Colin Gardner — Coldstream Guards
Charles Garnett — The Blues and Royals
Major H.C.L. Garnett CBE — Royal Horse Guards (The Blues)
Henry William Mark Garnett — The Blues and Royals
Captain Piers German — The Life Guards
Lieutenant Colonel C.J. Ghika — Irish Guards
Bill Gibbs — Coldstream Guards
Gary Gibbs — Chairman, Friends of the Guards Museum
Major Brian Gilbart-Denham — Irish Guards
Brian Gillow — Irish Guards
Mr A. Goddard — Grenadier Guards
Lance Sergeant Ian Goodman — Grenadier Guards
Captain Mark Goodman — London Scottish, formerly The Blues and Royals
Angus Gordon Lennox — Grenadier Guards
The Governor General's Horse Guards Regiment, Canada
General Sir Michael Gow — Scots Guards
Stuart Gray
Captain Mark Grayson MVO — Irish Guards
Major Patrick Grayson — Irish Guards
Captain James Charles Maunder Greaves — Grenadier Guards
Captain Gavin Green — Coldstream Guards
Captain J. Richard Greenwood DL — Grenadier Guards
Captain Simon Greenwood — Grenadier Guards
Fergus Gregory — Scots Guards
Roly Grimshaw LVO MBE — Irish Guards
Lance Sergeant Ron Groves — Coldstream Guards
Terry Guntrip
Major Nigel Hadden-Paton — The Blues and Royals
C.P. Halford — Coldstream Guards
Martyn S. Hall
Lord Anthony Hamilton — Irish Guards
Colonel J.G. Hamilton-Russell — The Blues and Royals
N.J. Hanbury Esq. — Welsh Guards
Captain P.F. Hanbury — Welsh Guards
Lieutenant Colonel D.M. Hannah MBE — Irish Guards
Hamish Hardy
Colonel William Harvey-Kelly MBE — Irish Guards
Lieutenant Colonel Carew Hatherley — Grenadier Guards
William Hawley — Irish Guards
E.R. Headridge TD MA
Master Robbie Hedges
David Heistercamp — Coldstream Guards
Captain Alan Henderson — Welsh Guards
Lieutenant Colonel N.B. Henderson — Coldstream Guards

David Hewer — Grenadier Guards
Major Tony Heybourn — Scots Guards
Captain Simon Hillard — Welsh Guards
Lieutenant Colonel (DOM) P.E. Hills FLCM, psm — Grenadier Guards
Lieutenant Colonel E.F. Hobbs — Grenadier Guards
Derek Hodgetts — Grenadier Guards
Colour Sergeant Darren Hodgson — Irish Guards
C. Holdsworth Hunt — Coldstream Guards
Yeoman Mick Holland — Grenadier Guards
Michael J. Holt
Captain David Horn — Grenadier Guards
Major Bernard Hornung — Irish Guards
Major James A. Hughes — Scots Guards
Stephen Humphrey
Major Roger W. Humphreys — Grenadier Guards
Michael Hutchings — Grenadier Guards
Malcolm Innes — Scots Guards
Master Archie Jamieson
C.M. Jeanes — Grenadier Guards
Captain Paddy Jeffries — Irish Guards
Captain Niels Jensen — Irish Guards
Major Patrick Johns — Irish Guards
Captain Rupert Johnston — Coldstream Guards
Captain Edward Jones — Irish Guards
Sergeant Glynn H. Jones — Coldstream Guards
K.A. Jones — Grenadier Guards
Garry S. Jupp — Grenadier Guards
Captain Nick Keable — Grenadier Guards
James P. Kearns — Irish Guards
Peter J. Keay — Grenadier Guards
Captain Christopher A.G. Keeling — Grenadier Guards
Major Colin Kennard DSO — Irish Guards
Major J.D. Kennard — Irish Guards
Peter Kenworthy-Browne — Irish Guards
Simon Kenyon-Slaney — Grenadier Guards
Captain Lawrence Kerr MBE — Scots Guards
The Lord Killearn — Scots Guards
Lieutenant Brian Kirkwood — Parachute Regiment
Major Hugh C.D. Laing — Scots Guards
George F. Lane Fox — The Blues and Royals
Christopher Langley — Coldstream Guards
Colonel Christopher Langton OBE — Irish Guards
Captain J.S. Langton — Irish Guards
Guardsman P.G.C. Lawday
Master Merlin Lawrence
Barry Lawton — Coldstream Guards
WOII (Master Tailor) Barry Lawton — Coldstream Guards
Captain Peter Le Marchand — Scots Guards
Hubert Leese
Patrick Leigh — Coldstream Guards

Mr Benedict Leonard

Royal Military Academy Sandhurst
Lieutenant Colonel Gerald Lesinski   Grenadier Guards
T.G. Leslie Esq.   Scots Guards
Captain R.C. Lester-Smith   The Life Guards
Guardsman Brian A. Lethby   Grenadier Guards
Major General P.R. Leuchars CBE   Welsh Guards
Major Gwilym A.G. Lewis   Welsh Guards
Mr R.E. Lewis   Welsh Guards
Captain Mark G. Lissauer   Coldstream Guards
Captain John D. Livesey   Welsh Guards
Colonel J.S. Lloyd MBE   Grenadier Guards
Captain C.B.A. Lloyd-Williams

Royal Army Medical Corps
Esme C.H. Lowe   Coldstream Guards
Josephine (Josie) Lumb
M.C. Lutyens   Coldstream Guards
HRH Grand Duke Jean of Luxembourg KG

Irish Guards
Brian MacDermot   Irish Guards
Lieutenant Colonel D.C. MacDonald Milner

Welsh Guards
Major Charles MacEwan MVO   Irish Guards
Major Michael MacEwan   Irish Guards
Captain Shaun Mackaness   Coldstream Guards
Major General Sir Iain Mackay-Dick KCVO MBE

Scots Guards
Major T.W.J. MacMullen   Irish Guards
Colonel Sir William Mahon Bt   Irish Guards
Major D.J.G. Mahony   The Life Guards
G.A. Mainwaring-Burton   Irish Guards
Colonel A.J.E. Malcolm OBE   Welsh Guards
Guardsman Kieron P. Mallon   Irish Guards
Captain Nathan A. Marsh   Welsh Guards
Major Simon Martin   Coldstream Guards
Lieutenant Colonel Anthony C. McC. Mather CVO OBE

Grenadier Guards
Alastair Mathewson   Scots Guards
Lieutenant William R. Maunder-Taylor   Irish Guards
M.B. Mavroleon   Grenadier Guards
Captain Patrick Mayhew   Irish Guards
Miss Juliet McConnell   National Army Museum
Desmond John McCoy   The Life Guards
Lance Sergeant Alistair McDonald   Scots Guards
Mr John McDowell
Barry McKay   Scots Guards
Major Iain McKay   Scots Guards
Captain Rupert McLean   Coldstream Guards
Lieutenant Colonel Vic McLean   Irish Guards
Captain James McLeod   Scots Guards
John McMeekin   Scots Guards
Steve McMichael   Irish Guards

Brigadier I.H. McNeil OBE   Coldstream Guards
WOII C.M.D. Measey   Coldstream Guards
Lieutenant Colonel E.J.F.V. Melotte MBE   Irish Guards
Ronald G.S. Melvin   Scots Guards
Major A.B. Methven   The Life Guards
Lord Middleton MC   Coldstream Guards
Major Martyn Miles   Welsh Guards
Major R.P.A.V. Miller   Royal Malta Artillery
Sergeant Windy Miller   Grenadier Guards
Guardsman G.B. Mitchell   Grenadier Guards
Captain Jonathan Morris   Scots Guards
Malcolm Morris   Coldstream Guards
Sir Richard Morris KBE   Welsh Guards
Major Mickey Morrissey   Irish Guards
Martin Morton   Irish Guards
Lieutenant Eric D.V. Moxon   Coldstream Guards
Guardsman Glenwood C. Moyle   Grenadier Guards
Guardsman D. Murphy   Grenadier Guards
Sir Philip Naylor-Leyland Bt
Guardsman F. Neal   Grenadier Guards
R.G. Newman   Coldstream Guards
David Norsworthy   Grenadier Guards
Lieutenant Andrew Noyons   Welsh Guards
Mr H.W. Nudds
Sir John Nugent Bt   Irish Guards
Peter Nutting JP DL   Irish Guards
William F. Nutting   Irish Guards
Major John W. Oakes   Irish Guards
T.M.T. O'Connor   Irish Guards
Lance Sergeant J.G. Odell   Coldstream Guards
Lieutenant Colonel S.G. O'Dwyer CVO DL

Irish Guards
Alan Ogden   Grenadier Guards
Lieutenant Colonel Brian O'Gorman   Irish Guards
Hugh Oliver-Bellasis   Welsh Guards
M.E.J. O'Neill   Irish Guards
Richard Onslow
Mark Ormerod   Irish Guards
James Orme-Smith   Irish Guards
Major S.P. Orwin   Scots Guards
Mrs Peter Owen-Edmunds
Lance Sergeant D.G. Oxford   Grenadier Guards
WOII Barrie Padwick   Coldstream Guards
Lieutenant Colonel Sir Julian Paget CVO Bt

Coldstream Guards
Major N.V.S. Paravicini   The Life Guards
Lance Sergeant Ivan Parker   Grenadier Guards
Harry Parshall   Irish Guards
Colonel Andrew Parsons OBE   Scots Guards
Guardsman Jack Payne   Irish Guards
P.G.B. Pedley
Colonel Alan Pemberton   Coldstream Guards

Steve Pengelly   Coldstream Guards
R.A.B. Pickthorn   Coldstream Guards
Ian Piggot   Scots Guards
Captain John Pilley   Coldstream Guards
Captain Richard J.B. Pinfold   Grenadier Guards
Stan Pinnock   Coldstream Guards
Sergeant Joe Pipe   Coldstream Guards
Lieutenant Colonel Hugh Pitman

The Blues and Royals
Brigadier R.A. Plummer   Irish Guards
Major R.J. Plummer   Irish Guards
Peter Pond   Grenadier Guards
Regimental Sergeant Major L. Pownall   Welsh Guards
Guardsman Malcolm A. Print   Coldstream Guards
Andrew Prior   Irish Guards
Charles and Sarah Prior
Major Christopher Pullen   Coldstream Guards
Colonel Hugh Purcell OBE   Irish Guards
Colonel Timothy Purdon OBE   Welsh Guards
Guardsman James A. Purdy   Coldstream Guards
Guardsman Nigel J. Purdy   Coldstream Guards
William Pym Esq.   Irish Guards
Martin Pym MBE   Irish Guards
Lance Sergeant Matt Quick   Scots Guards
Guy Quilter   Irish Guards
Colonel George Ramsay   Scots Guards
Captain The Lord Rathcavan DL   Irish Guards
Robin Reames   Grenadier Guards
Adjutant Leo Regemortels
Captain Iain Reid   Grenadier Guards
James Renwick   Scots Guards
Sergeant Stan Rhymer   Coldstream Guards
Major (Retd) R.G. Rickard
Brigadier J.F. Rickett CBE   Welsh Guards
The Rt Hon. Viscount Ridley KG GCVO TD

Coldstream Guards
B. Ridley   Coldstream Guards
Guardsman Roberts   Irish Guards
Miss Anthea Roberts
Major Cassian Roberts   Irish Guards
Damian Roberts Esq.
Major Fabian Roberts MVO   Irish Guards
Captain Hilarion Roberts   Welsh Guards
Mrs John Roberts
Captain Julian Roberts   Irish Guards
Lucian Roberts Esq.
Nicholas Roberts Esq.
Lieutenant Orlando Roberts   Irish Guards
Major General Sir Sebastian Roberts KCVO OBE

Irish Guards
David Rollo   Grenadier Guards
Lance Sergeant E.J. Rooney   Irish Guards

Guardsman M.H. Rooney — Grenadier Guards
Second Lieutenant Jonathan Ropner — Irish Guards
Captain William Roscoe — Irish Guards
Mr J. Ross — Irish Guards
Lieutenant Colonel Sir Malcolm Ross GCVO OBE — Scots Guards
Company Sergeant Major L.G. Rossiter MBE RVM — Coldstream Guards
John R. Rudd — Royal Horse Guards (The Blues)
Mr J.T. Russell — Coldstream Guards
Captain Roddy Sale — Welsh Guards
Major J.D. Salusbury — Welsh Guards
Patrick Lau Choon Sam
Mrs J. Sayer
Lance Sergeant Scargill — Irish Guards
Lieutenant Colonel M.B. Scott — Scots Guards
Major S.O'N Segrave — Irish Guards
Pipe Major P.H.T. Selwood — Scots Guards
Major D.N.W. Sewell — Grenadier Guards
Major R.M.T. Shannon — Scots Guards
Major John Sharp — Coldstream Guards
The Hon. C.S.C. Sheller AO QC — Scots Guards
Lance Sergeant David Shipsey — Coldstream Guards
Ron Shooter
Major N.C. Shuttleworth — Scots Guards
Guardsman Mick Simmons — Grenadier Guards
Captain A.G.W. Sinclair — Coldstream Guards
Captain Alan Sinclair — Coldstream Guards
Lieutenant Colonel Sir John Smiley Bt — Grenadier Guards
Captain William Smiley — Grenadier Guards
Major Bert Smith MBE — Irish Guards
Lieutenant Colonel Martin Smith — Grenadier Guards
Captain B.H.G. Sparrow MC — Coldstream Guards
Major Andrew P. Speed — Scots Guards
Charles Spencer — Coldstream Guards
Lieutenant Colonel R.J.A. Stanford MBE — Welsh Guards
Sergeant K.G. Starling — Coldstream Guards
Lance Sergeant John Stenton — Coldstream Guards
WOII S. Stevens — Coldstream Guards
Lance Sergeant John Stevenson — Scots Guards
Ken Stimson — Grenadier Guards
James R.H. Stopford — Irish Guards
Kevin Stott

Major General Sir John Swinton — Scots Guards
Colonel Patrick Tabor — The Blues and Royals
P.S. O'C. Tandy — Irish Guards
Guardsman Bryan Taylor — Coldstream Guards
Bryn Taylor — Irish Guards
Captain Sean E. Taylor — Princess of Wales Royal Regiment
Neville W. Taylor RVM — The Life Guards
Mrs Richard Taylor
R.J. Thompson — Grenadier Guards
Lieutenant Colonel D.N. Thornewill — Coldstream Guards
Major Jeremy Thornewill — Coldstream Guards
H. Thornton Ash
Major James H.F. Thurstan — Coldstream Guards
Peter Tidd
Mr J. Tillstone
Major Sacha Tomes — The Blues and Royals
Lieutenant N.D. Torp-Petersen — Grenadier Guards
William E. Townend — Coldstream Guards
Mr S.J.N. Treadgold — Welsh Guards
Colonel Greville Tufnell CVO DL — Grenadier Guards
A.G. Turnbull — Irish Guards
Cameron Turnbull — Scots Guards
Owen Varney — Scots Guards
Nigel Venning — Irish Guards
Major Peter Verney — Irish Guards
Lieutenant Colonel J.M. Vernon — Coldstream Guards
Lord Vestey — Scots Guards
Captain W.G. Anthony Warde-Norbury — Coldstream Guards
Guardsman John Waite — Coldstream Guards
Guardsman R. Wakefield — Grenadier Guards
Julian Waldemar Brown — Grenadier Guards
Sir Victor Walker Bt — Grenadier Guards
Angus Wall MBE — Welsh Guards
Master Alexander Wallace
A.D.M. Wallace-Cook
Robert Wallace-Turner — Grenadier Guards
Captain Peter M. Ward — Scots Guards
Company Sergeant Major K.C. Waters MM — Grenadier Guards
R.J.M. Watkins
Major John Watson

Lance Sergeant A. Weaver — Coldstream Guards
Guardsman Brian Weavers — Grenadier Guards
Major General Sir Evelyn Webb-Carter KCVO OBE — Grenadier Guards
Major S. Weber-Brown — Coldstream Guards
Guardsman Weeks — Irish Guards
Lance Sergeant John Welch — Coldstream Guards
Sir Anthony Weldon Bt — Irish Guards
Lieutenant F.O.B. Wells — Coldstream Guards
Major General Charles West
Guardsman D.G. Westbury — Grenadier Guards
Anthony Wheatley — Irish Guards
Dominic Wheatley — Irish Guards
Richard White Scarlet
Lance Sergeant Robert Whitethread — Scots Guards
D. Whiting — Welsh Guards
Guardsman D. Whyte — Grenadier Guards
Lieutenant Colonel The Lord Wigram MC DL JP — Grenadier Guards
Major The Hon. Andrew Wigram MVO — Grenadier Guards
Major Dan Wilkinson — Irish Guards
Captain Charlie E.V. Williams — Irish Guards
David E. Williams — Welsh Guards
WOII P.O. Williams
Brigadier the Hon. Christopher Willoughby — Coldstream Guards
Mr Sandy Wilmont Sr — Irish Guards
Jacinth Sacheverell Wilmot-Sitwell — Coldstream Guards
Master Alexander Wilson
Major E.K. Wilson — Irish Guards
Major Roderic Wilson — Irish Guards
Squadron Quartermaster Corporal S.R. Wilson — The Life Guards
Captain Ashe Windham CVO — Irish Guards
M. Winn — Welsh Guards
Mr Stephen Wolseley — Irish Guards
Brigadier Christopher Wolverson OBE — Irish Guards
John Woodhouse
V. Wright RVM — Grenadier Guards
WOII K. Wynne — Coldstream Guards
Laurie Young — The Life Guards

INDEX

Acknowledgements

Aside from those listed in the Editor's Note, the publishers would like to thank Juliet McConnell at the National Army Museum for her untiring efforts in combing through the museum archive and helping to ensure that the book was outfitted with a substantial array of historical images. Thanks are also due to Randal Gray, whose knowledge and input at the copyediting stage were of inestimable value.

The Gulf War 1990–1 (p112): The author has drawn on *The 1st Bn Coldstream Guards in the Gulf 1991* published by the 1st Battalion Coldstream Guards; on a letter by Brigadier Iain McNeil dated October 1999; and the Diary of Major H. G. R. Boscawen 1991.

Guards Cricket Club (p157) was written by Major Edward Crofton, Coldstream Guards.

Selected Bibliography

The Regiments

Dallal, Henry, *Pageantry and Performance: The Household Cavalry in a Celebration of Pictures*. Published by the author 2002

Watson, J.N.P., *Through Fifteen Reigns: A Complete History of the Household Cavalry* (Spellmount 1997)

White-Spunner, Barney, *Horse Guards* (Macmillan 2006)

Hanning, Henry, *The British Grenadiers: 350 Years of the First Regiment of Foot Guards 1656–2006* (Pen & Sword 2006)

Lindsay, Oliver, *Once a Grenadier. The Grenadier Guards 1945–1995* (Leo Cooper 1996)

Paget, Julian (Editor), *Second to None. The Coldstream Guards 1650–2000* (Pen & Sword 2000

Naylor, M., *Among Friends: The Scots Guards 1956–1993* (Leo Cooper 1995)

Bullock-Webster, R.; Mahon, W.; Verney, P.; and Weldon, A., *Irish Guards: The First Hundred Years 1900–2000* (Spellmount Publishers 2000)

Additional Publications

Foster, B. and Carman, W.Y., *The Uniforms of the Foot Guards from 1661 to the Present Day* (Pompadour 1995)

Gow, Michael, *Trooping the Colour. A History of the Sovereign's Birthday Parade* (Souvenir Press 1988)

Guards magazine. Journal of the Household Division

Melvin, Ronald (Editor), *The Guards and Caterham. The Soldiers' Story* (Guardroom Publications 2000)

Paget, Julian, *The Story of the Guards* (last published by Michael Joseph 1979)

Turner, G. and Turner, A.W., *Guards & Infantry: The History of British Military Bands* Volume 2 (Spellmount 1996)

Percy, A., *A Bearskin's Crimea: Colonel Henry Percy VC and his Brother Officers* (Leo Cooper 2005)

Watson, J.N.P., *Guardsmen of the Sky. An Account of the Involvement of Household Troops in the Airborne Forces.* (Michael Russell 1997)

Picture Credits

Unless an acknowledgement appears below, the illustrations in this volume have been provided by the Household Division. Every effort has been made to contact the copyright holders of all works reproduced in this book. However, if acknowledgements have been omitted, the publishers ask those concerned to contact Third Millennium Publishing.

Andrews, Julian, 2, 4, 5, 7, 11, 30, 32(top), 33(x4), 34(tx2), 35(t, right), 38–9, 42(x2), 61, 63(leftx3), 64, 65, 66, 72(r), 73, 75(b), 80(x2), 81, 8 (tl, rx2), 84(bottom), 86, 90, 92(x2), 93(b), 111t, br), 117(t), 118, 119, 120(top), 131(b), 132, 136–7, 140, 143(r), 145(r), 146, 147(x3), 148(x3), 149(x3), 151, 152–3, 154(b), 155(x2), 158(b), 160(tr), 161(x2), 162(x2), 163, 164(x2), 165, 166, 167(r), 168(x2), 169(t), 170(b), 171(x3), 172(t), 176–7, 178, 179, 180(x2), 183, 186–7, 188(tl, bl), 189(br), 190(bl, t), 191(tl, middle r), 192(x4), 193(b, r), 194(tr), 195(tl), 197(b); Blenheim Palace, 51; Coates, D., 99(x2); Corbis, 26(t), 54, 67(l), 100(t), 101(b), 102, 105(t)109(b), 111(bl), 173(r), 174(r), 175(x2); Country Life,174(l); Getty Images, 47; Guards Magazine, 104, 105(b), 110(bx2); Heistercamp, D., 98; Lane Fox, Ed, 12/13, 34(bx4), 35(lx3), 43, 4 (top right), 45(t), 142, 167(t), 188(ml, t)189(t, l), 190–1(b), 195(bl), 196(b, l, t), 197(t); Leask, James, 184, 185; Mary Evans Picture Library, 60(b); Museum of London, 15(t); National Army Museum, 14, 15(b), 16(l), 16(r), 17, 18(l), 19(t), 19(b), 20(t), 20(b), 21, 22(t), 22(b), 24(t), 24(b), 25, 28, 29(l)31, 32(b), 40(l), 40(r), 44(l), 45(b), 53, 70; National Museums of Scotland, 62; PA Photos/AP Images, 191(top right); Percy, Algernon, 50(t); Radcliffe, Ashton, 27(t), 112(b), 113, 114; RGJ Museum, Winchester, 18(r); Royal Collection © 2008, Her Majesty Queen Elizabeth II, 52; Short, Danny, 194(br); Wilson, Matthew, 36(x2), 37(x4), 72(top left), 181(x2), 182(x3)